TEST ITEM FILE

SECOND EDITION

Arthur J. Keown
Virginia Polytechnic Institute and State University

J. William Petty
Baylor University

David F. Scott, Jr
University of Central Florida

John D. Martin
The University of Texas at Austin

FOUNDATIONS OF FINANCE
THE LOGIC AND PRACTICE OF FINANCIAL MANAGEMENT

D1310399

Prentice Hall
Upper Saddle River, NJ 07458

Acquisitions Editor: *Paul Donnelly*
Asistant Editor: *Gladys Soto*
Production Editor: *Joseph F. Tomasso*
Manufacturing Buyer: *Arnold Vila*

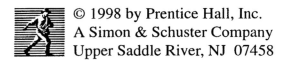
Printed in the United States of America

10 9 8 7 6 5 4 3 2 1

ISBN 0-13-673351-4

Prentice-Hall International (UK) Limited, *London*
Prentice-Hall of Australia Pty. Limited, *Sydney*
Prentice-Hall Canada Inc., *Toronto*
Prentice-Hall Hispanoamericana, S.A., *Mexico*
Prentice-Hall of India Private Limited, *New Delhi*
Prentice-Hall of Japan, Inc., *Tokyo*
Simon & Schuster Asia Pte. Ltd., *Singapore*
Editora Prentice-Hall do Brasil, Ltda., *Rio de Janiero*

Foundations of Finance
Test File

Table of Contents

PREFACE

The objective of this test item file is to provide you, the instructor, with a wide variety of text-based questions and problems to accompany *Foundations of Finance: The Logic and Practice of Financial Management.* As such, together with the Instructor's Manual and the Study Guide, it represents our continued effort to serve the teacher in his or her goal of being effective in the classroom. Toward this end, we believe the three basic criteria for an effective test item file are accuracy, relevance, and completeness. In order to assure its accuracy and relevance, the questions and problems contained in the test item file has been checked and re-checked by a number of outside readers made up of Finance Professors at different universities.

You will also notice that the degree of difficulty of each question is categorized as being a 1, 2, or 3, with a 1 indicating a relatively easy question, a 2 indicating medium difficulty, and a 3 indicating a relatively difficult question. This categorization was done by the authors and, while somewhat arbitrary, is meant to aid the instructor in putting together balanced examinations and tests.

Finally, we, the authors, pledge our support to you, the user, by offering our personal services to resolve any issues which may arise in using this test item file. We solicit you comments, and if you do uncover any errors, please contact one of us. Please feel free to call us.

Art Keown   (540) 231-8647
John Martin (512) 471- 5781
Dave Scott   (407) 823-2632
Bill Petty   (817) 755-2260

Chapter 1: An Introduction to the Foundations of Finance

TRUE/FALSE

1. The goal of the firm should be the maximization of profit.

   Answer: False Difficulty: 1

2. The goal of profit maximization is equivalent to the goal of maximization of share value.

   Answer: False Difficulty: 1

3. One of the problems associated with profit maximization is that it ignores the timing of a project's return.

   Answer: True Difficulty: 1

4. Although maximization of the market value of a firm's common stock is a valid objective of the firm, it is not without its drawbacks since the effects of financial structure decisions are not reflected in this term.

   Answer: False Difficulty: 2

5. For the risk-averse financial manager, the more risky a given course of action, the higher the expected return must be.

   Answer: True Difficulty: 1

6. The financial manager should examine available risk-return trade-offs and make his decision based upon the greatest expected return.

   Answer: False Difficulty: 1

7. The goal of the firm should be to maximize the total market value of the firm's common stock.

   Answer: True Difficulty: 1

8. Only a firm's financial decisions affect its stock prices.

   Answer: False Difficulty: 2

9. Profit maximization is typically set forth as the goal of the firm as seen by its owners.

   Answer: True Difficulty: 2

10. The market price of the firm's stock reflects the value of the firm as seen by its owners.

    Answer: True Difficulty: 2

11. The goal of profit maximization does not stress the efficient use of capital resources.

    Answer: False Difficulty: 2

12. The goal of profit maximization ignores uncertainty.

    Answer: True Difficulty: 1

13. Shareholders react to poor investment or dividend decisions by causing the total value of the firm's stock to fall, and they react to good decisions by bidding the price of the stock up.

    Answer: True Difficulty: 2

14. Only a few financial decisions involve some sort of risk-return tradeoff.

    Answer: False Difficulty: 1

15. The goal of profit maximization ignores the timing of profit.

    Answer: True Difficulty: 1

16. The sole proprietorship can be described as the absence of any legal business structure.

    Answer: True Difficulty: 1

17. In a general partnership all partners have unlimited liability for the actions of any one partner when that partner is conducting business for the firm.

    Answer: True Difficulty: 2

18. The corporation is the best form of organization in terms of raising capital.

    Answer: True Difficulty: 1

19. There is no legal distinction made between the assets of the business and the personal assets of the owners in the limited partnership.

    Answer: False Difficulty: 1

20. The owners of a corporation enjoy unlimited liability.

    Answer: False Difficulty: 2

21. General partners have unrestricted transferability of ownership, while limited partners must have the consent of all partners to transfer their ownership.

    Answer: False Difficulty: 2

22. Ultimate control in a corporation is vested in the board of directors.

    Answer: False Difficulty: 2

23. A net operating loss may be carried back three years and ahead fifteen years and applied against income in those years.

    Answer: True Difficulty: 2

24. A net operating loss may be carried back fifteen years and ahead three years and applied against income in those years.

    Answer: False Difficulty: 2

25. A disadvantage of partnerships is the double taxation faced by the partners.

    Answer: False Difficulty: 1

26. The interest payments on corporate bonds are tax deductible.

    Answer: True Difficulty: 1

27. The Subchapter S Corporation enables the partnership to be taxed as a corporation.

    Answer: False Difficulty: 2

28. Taxes have practically no impact on a corporation's capital structure.

    Answer: False Difficulty: 1

29. There are a significant number of legal requirements to follow when establishing a sole proprietorship.

    Answer: False Difficulty: 1

30. Limited partners may actively manage the business.

    Answer: False Difficulty: 2

31. The life of a corporation is not dependent upon the status of the investors.

    Answer: True Difficulty: 1

32. A sole proprietorship is the most desirable business form in all circumstances.

    Answer: False Difficulty: 1

33. In a sole proprietorship, the owner is personally responsible without limitation for the liabilities incurred.

    Answer: True Difficulty: 2

34. Once a sole proprietor has been in business seven years, he or she must file state and federal forms to remain a sole proprietor.

    Answer: False Difficulty: 2

35. Termination of a sole proprietorship requires a federal filing.

    Answer: False Difficulty: 2

36. In a limited partnership at least one general partner must remain in the association; the privilege of limited liability still applies to this partner.

    Answer: False Difficulty: 2

37. In a general partnership there is a distinction between business and personal assets.

    Answer: False Difficulty: 1

38. Dividends paid to a firm's stockholders, both preferred and common stockholders, are tax deductible to the paying company.

    Answer: False Difficulty: 2

39. In order to maximize shareholder wealth, a firm must consider historical costs as an integral part of their decision-making.

    Answer: False Difficulty: 2

MULTIPLE CHOICE

40. The goal of the firm should be:
    a) maximization of profits
    b) maximization of shareholder wealth
    c) maximization of consumer satisfaction
    d) maximization of sales

    Answer: b Difficulty: 1

41. Consider the following equally likely project outcomes:

	Profit	
	X	Y
Pessimistic prediction	$ 0	$500
Expected outcome	$ 500	$500
Optimistic prediction	$1000	$500

    a) Project Y has less uncertainty than Project X.
    b) Project X has more variability than Project Y.
    c) a and b
    d) Since Projects X and Y have the same expected outcomes of $500, investors will view them as identical in value.

    Answer: c Difficulty: 1

42. Consider the timing of the following certain investment projects profits:

	Profit	
	L	S
Year 1	$ 0	$3,000
Year 2	$3,000	$ 0

    a) Project S is preferred to project L.
    b) Project L is preferred to project S.
    c) Projects S and L both have profits over the two years of $3000 and are therefore equivalent.
    d) A goal of profit maximization would favor S only.

    Answer: a Difficulty: 1

43. Maximization of shareholder wealth as a goal is superior to profit maximization because:
    a) it considers the time value of the money
    b) following the shareholders wealth maximization goal will ensure high stock prices
    c) it considers uncertainty
    d) a and c

    Answer: d Difficulty: 1

5

44. Which of the following best describes the goal of the firm?
    a) the maximization of the total market value of the firm's common stock
    b) profit maximization
    c) risk minimization
    d) none of the above

    Answer: a Difficulty: 1

45. Profit maximization does not adequately describe the goal of the firm because:
    a) profit maximization does not require the consideration of risk
    b) profit maximization ignores the timing of a project's return
    c) maximization of dividend payout ratio is a better description of the goal of the firm
    d) both a and b

    Answer: d Difficulty: 1

46. Which of the following goals of the firm are synonymous (equivalent) to the maximization of shareholder wealth?
    a) profit maximization
    b) risk minimization
    c) maximization of the total market value of the firm's common stock
    d) none of the above

    Answer: c Difficulty: 2

47. Which of the following best describes the goal of the firm?
    a) the maximization of shareholder wealth
    b) the maximization of the total book value of the firm
    c) the maximization of the firm's share price
    d) profit maximization

    Answer: a Difficulty: 1

48. Which of the following statements is true regarding profit maximization?
    a) Profit maximization is the true goal in finance.
    b) Even though simplistic, profit maximization does have some merit for contemporary finance.
    c) Profit maximization adequately deals with uncertainty and time.
    d) Profit maximization is not an adequate goal of the firm.

    Answer: d Difficulty: 1

49. In finance, we assume that investors are generally
    a) neutral to risk
    b) averse to risk
    c) fond of risk
    d) none of the above

    Answer: b Difficulty: 1

50. Consider cash flows for projects X and Y such as:

	Project X	Project Y
Year 1	$3000	0
Year 2	0	$3000

A rational person would prefer receiving cash flows sooner because:
a) the money can be reinvested
b) the money is nice to have around
c) the investor may be tired of a particular investment
d) the investor is indifferent to either proposal.

Answer: a Difficulty: 1

51. Which of the following is not an advantage of the sole proprietorship?
a) limited liability
b) no time limit imposed on its existence
c) no legal requirements for starting the business
d) a and c

Answer: a Difficulty: 1

52. Which of the following is not true for a limited partnership?
a) Limited partners can only manage the business.
b) One general partner must exist who has unlimited liability.
c) Only the name of general partners can appear in the name of the firm.
d) Limited partners may sell their interest in the company.

Answer: a Difficulty: 2

53. The true owners of the corporation are the:
a) holders of debt issues of the firm
b) preferred stockholders
c) board of directors of the firm
d) common stockholders

Answer: d Difficulty: 2

54. In terms of organizational costs, which of the following sequences is correct, moving from lowest to highest cost?
a) general partnership, sole proprietorship, limited partnership, corporation
b) sole proprietorship, general partnership, limited partnership, corporation
c) corporation, limited partnership, general partnership, sole proprietorship
d) sole proprietorship, general partnership, corporation, limited partnership

Answer: b Difficulty: 2

55. Revenues are taxed:
    a) for economic stabilization
    b) to achieve socially desirable goals
    c) to provide revenues for government expenditures
    d) all of the above

    Answer: d Difficulty: 1

56. Ajax, Inc. owns common stock in the Mercury Company. Ajax received $20,000 in dividends in 1993. What amount will it pay in taxes on this amount if it is in the 34 percent tax bracket?
    a) $6,000
    b) $6,800
    c) $10,000
    d) $2,040

    Answer: d Difficulty: 2

57. Which of the following is not a requirement of a Subchapter S Corporation?
    a) All shareholders must be individuals.
    b) The firm must be a domestic corporation.
    c) No more than ten shareholders are allowed at the beginning of the corporation's life.
    d) No more than 20 percent of gross revenues may come from interest, dividends, rents, royalties, and capital gains.

    Answer: c Difficulty: 2

58. A corporation's capital losses can be carried back three years and, if any loss still remains, carried forward:
    a) 1 year
    b) 3 years
    c) 5 years
    d) 7 years

    Answer: c Difficulty: 2

59. Which of the following are tax deductible expenses for a business?
    a) common stock dividends
    b) interest
    c) preferred stock dividends
    d) none of the above

    Answer: b Difficulty: 2

60. Coplon, Inc., an industrial firm, earned $180,000 in dividends in 1993 on their stock holding in the Finco Company. How much of the dividends are excluded from Coplon's taxable income?
    a) $27,000
    b) none
    c) $126,000
    d) $153,000

    Answer: c Difficulty: 3

61. Which of the following categories of owners enjoy limited liability?
    a) general partners in a limited partnership
    b) shareholders (common stock) of a corporation
    c) sole proprietors
    d) both a and b

    Answer: b Difficulty: 2

62. Which of the following categories of owners have unlimited liability?
    a) general partners in a limited partnership
    b) sole proprietors
    c) shareholders of a corporation
    d) both a and b

    Answer: d Difficulty: 1

63. Which of the following are characteristics of a limited partnership?
    a) Limited partners may not participate in the management of a business.
    b) There must be one or more general partners.
    c) General partners have unlimited liability.
    d) all of the above

    Answer: d Difficulty: 2

64. Which of the following forms of organizations have earnings that are taxed twice, once as business income and once as personal income (if the earnings are distributed to the owners)?
    a) corporations
    b) general partnerships
    c) limited partnerships
    d) both a and c

    Answer: a Difficulty: 2

65. Which of the following is a characteristic of a limited partnership?
    a) It allows one or more partners to have limited liability.
    b) It requires one or more of the partners to be a general partner for whom the privilege of limited liability does not apply.
    c) It prohibits the limited partners from participating in the management of the partnership.
    d) all of the above

    Answer: d Difficulty: 2

66. Which of the following categories of owners have limited liability?
    a) general partners
    b) sole proprietors
    c) shareholders of a corporation
    d) both a and b

    Answer: c Difficulty: 1

67. Which of the following forms of business organizations provide limited liability to all its owners?
    a) general partnership
    b) limited partnership
    c) corporation
    d) both a and b

    Answer: c Difficulty: 1

68. The cheapest form of business to organize is generally the:
    a) sole proprietorship
    b) general partnership
    c) limited partnership
    d) corporation

    Answer: a Difficulty: 1

69. Which of the statements below are true?
    a) The sole proprietorship and the general partnership both feature unlimited liability.
    b) It is very complicated (legally) to establish a corporation.
    c) No legal criterion exists for a general partnership.
    d) all of the above are true

    Answer: d Difficulty: 1

70. Which is a way to minimize the discontinuity of business in a general partnership?
    a) There is no way to accomplish this; that is, the partnership dies when the partner dies.
    b) It can be done, but only for cases of withdrawal of a partner, and hence is rarely practiced.
    c) The partnership can be extended through the courts of law.
    d) The partnership can be extended through specifications in the written agreement.

    Answer: d Difficulty: 2

71. Transferability of ownership:
    a) is always desirable
    b) is never desirable
    c) depends on the owners' preferences
    d) has no effect one way or the other

    Answer: c Difficulty: 2

72. Which form of organization is free of initial legal requirements:
    a) sole proprietorship
    b) general partnership
    c) corporation
    d) a and b

    Answer: d Difficulty: 2

73. For these types of organization, no distinction is made between business and personal assets:
    a) sole proprietorships
    b) general partnerships
    c) limited partnerships
    d) all of the above
    e) a and b

    Answer: e Difficulty: 2

74. Which of the following are tax deductible items to a corporation:
    a) interest expenses
    b) marketing expenses
    c) dividends
    d) a and b
    e) a, b, and c

    Answer: d Difficulty: 2

ESSAY

75. The Brown Construction Corporation was formed in 1989 by Harold Brown. Due to the nature of the construction industry, the firm has experienced fluctuating profits since that time. The taxable income for the passive years is given below. Compute the appropriate tax payments and refunds for each year.

1989	($39,000)	1992	$144,000
1990	$ 0	1993	($ 81,000)
1991	$76,200		

Answer:

1989	(39,000)	1992	144,000
1990	0	1993	(81,000)
1991	76,200		

Year 1989 - carry loss forward to 1990 (Actually is carried forward to 1991)

Year 1990 - no taxable income

Year 1991 - tax payment of $5,580

$$\text{taxable income} = \begin{array}{r} \$76,200 \\ -39,000 \\ \hline \$37,200 \end{array}$$

tax payment = (.15)($37,200) = $5,580

Year 1992 - tax payment of $39,410

taxable income = $144,000

tax payment	= (.15)(50,000) =	$ 7,500
	(.25)(25,000) =	6,250
	(.34)(69,000) =	23,460
	(.05)(44,000) =	2,200
Total tax payment		$39,410

Year 1993 - tax refund of $28,660. Carry loss of $81,000 back to 1992. Taxable income in 1992 is then reduced to $63,000. Tax payment based on reduced taxable income is the following:

(.15)(50,000) =	$ 7,500
(.25)(13,000) =	3,250
	$10,750

Tax refund = $39,410 - $10,750 = $28,660

Difficulty: 3

76. The Mason Gift Company had sales of $440,000 in the past year, with operating expenses of $82,500 and cost of goods sold of $137,500. Interest expenses amounted to $32,500, and $8,800 in common stock dividends were received. Common stock, which had been purchased eight months earlier for $22,000, was sold for $27,500. Compute the taxable income of Mason Gifts and its tax liability.

Answer:
Mason Gift Company's Taxable Income

Sales	$440,000
Capital gains	5,500
Dividends (.30 x $8,800)	2,640
Gross Income	$448,140

Less:

Cost of goods sold	$137,500
Operating expenses	82,500
Interest expense	32,500
	$252,500

Taxable Income	$195,640
Total Taxes	$ 59,550

Taxes = (.15)(50,000)+(.25)(25,000)+(.34)(120,640)
+ (.05)(95,640)
= 7,500 + 6,250 + 41,018 + 4,782 = 59,550

Difficulty: 3

77. Pearls, Inc. had sales in 1993 of $2.1 million dollars. The common stockholders received $400,000 in cash dividends and preferred stockholders were paid $200,000. Interest totaling $150,000 was paid on outstanding debts. Operating expenses totaled $300,000, and cost of goods sold was $500,000. Stock that had been purchased for $50,000 in 1987 was sold for $70,000. What is the tax liability of Pearls, Inc.?

Answer:
Pearls Taxable Income

Sales	$2,100,000

Less:
Cost of goods sold $500,000
Operating expenses   300,000

Operating profit	$1,300,000
Other income (Security Sale)	20,000
Earnings before interest & taxes	$1,320,000
Interest expense	150,000
Taxable income	$1,170,000
Total taxes owed	$ 397,800

Taxes on operating earnings =
(.15)(50,000)+(.25)(25,000)+(.34)(1,095,000)+
(.05)(235,000)= 7,500 + 6,250 + 372,300 + 11,750 =
$397,800 or Because taxable income is over $335,001
taxes can be computed 1,170,000 x .34 = $397,800

Difficulty: 3

78. Goodwin Enterprises had a gross profit of $2,500,000 for the year.
Operating expenses and interest expense incurred in that same year were
$595,000 and $362,000, respectively. Goodwin had 200,000 shares of
common stock and 180,000 shares of preferred stock outstanding.
Management declared a $2.50 dividend per share on the common and a $1.50
dividend per share on the preferred. Securities purchased at a cost of
$37,500 in a previous year were resold at a price of $50,500. Compute
the taxable income and the resulting tax liability for Goodwin
Enterprises for the year.

Use the following tax rates:

Income	Tax rate
0-$50,000	15%
50,001-$75,000	25%
75,001-$100,000	34%
$100,001-$335,000	39%
over $335,001	34%

Answer:

Gross profit	$2,500,000
Operating expenses	(595,000)
Interest expense	(362,000)
Income before tax	$1,543,000
Add: Gain on sales	13,000
Taxable Income	$1,556,000

Income		Marginal Tax Rate	Tax Liability
$50,000	X	15%	$7,500
$25,000	X	25%	$6,250
$25,000	X	34%	$8,500
$235,000	X	39%	$91,650
$1,221,000	X	34%	$415,140
$1,556,000			$529,040

Difficulty: 3

Chapter 2: The Financial Markets and Interest Rates

TRUE/FALSE

1. Sales occurring in the secondary markets increase the total stock of financial assets that exist in the economy.

   Answer: False   Difficulty: 1

2. The money market is usually thought of as dealing with long-term debt instruments issued by firms with excellent credit ratings.

   Answer: False   Difficulty: 1

3. Over-the-counter markets include all security markets, with the exception of organized exchanges.

   Answer: True   Difficulty: 1

4. For a firm to have its securities listed on an exchange, it must meet certain requirements. These usually include measures of probability, size, market value, and public ownership.

   Answer: True   Difficulty: 1

5. On a dollar volume basis, more common stock trading occurs over the counter than on organized exchanges.

   Answer: False   Difficulty: 2

6. The syndicate can be thought of as a wholesaler of securities and the dealer organization as a retailer of securities.

   Answer: True   Difficulty: 1

7. A syndicate is a group of investment bankers who purchase an issue of securities from the managing investment banker as an investment for their own clients.

   Answer: False   Difficulty: 1

8. It is common practice among the largest corporations to sell their securities directly to investors.

   Answer: False   Difficulty: 2

9. Total flotation costs expressed as a percent of the gross proceeds of a security issue tend to vary inversely with the size of the issue.

   Answer: True   Difficulty: 2

10. The due diligence meeting is the first in a series of pre-underwriting conferences held between the firm and its investment banker concerning a security issue.

    Answer: False Difficulty: 1

11. Investment bankers are concerned with the turnover of security issues and not the margin associated with any individual issue.

    Answer: True Difficulty: 2

12. The bid price is the price which a broker dealer will pay for a security; the asked price is the price at which he will sell a security.

    Answer: True Difficulty: 1

13. The underwriter's spread is the difference between the gross and net proceeds from a given security issue expressed as a percent of the gross proceeds.

    Answer: True Difficulty: 2

14. In the aggregate, households usually spend more on current consumption than they earn.

    Answer: False Difficulty: 2

15. The Pacific Coast Stock Exchange is an example of an over-the-counter market.

    Answer: False Difficulty: 1

16. The number of shares traded in the over-the-counter markets exceeds the number of shares traded on the NYSE.

    Answer: True Difficulty: 1

17. A red herring does not contain the selling price for the security.

    Answer: True Difficulty: 2

18. State security laws are called red sky laws.

    Answer: False Difficulty: 1

19. Financial markets exist in order to allocate savings in the economy to the demanders of those savings.

    Answer: True Difficulty: 1

20. Financing through common stock is the most popular method for corporations.

    Answer: False Difficulty: 2

21. If a firm has unused debt capacity and the general level of equity prices is depressed, financial executives will favor the issuance of debt securities over the issuance of new common stock.

    Answer: True Difficulty: 2

22. Financial intermediaries all offer their own financial claims, called direct securities, to economic units with excess savings.

    Answer: False Difficulty: 2

23. In a typical year,when new funds are being raised, corporate debt markets outweigh corporate equity markets in terms of dollar volume.

    Answer: True Difficulty: 2

24. It is the function of a financial intermediary to transfer funds from savers to dissavers in the economy.

    Answer: True Difficulty: 1

25. An insurance company is a form of financial intermediary.

    Answer: True Difficulty: 2

26. "Crowding out" refers to the favoring of debt over equity in the financial markets.

    Answer: False Difficulty: 2

27. A "red herring" refers to the preliminary prospectus.

    Answer: True Difficulty: 2

28. Consumer lending is a significant line of business for investment bankers.

    Answer: False Difficulty: 2

29. Common stock is the most relied on financing method used by corporations.

    Answer: False Difficulty: 2

30. Corporate debt markets clearly dominate the corporate equity markets when new funds are being raised.

    Answer: True Difficulty: 2

31. "Crowding-out" means the private borrower is favored over the government in the financial markets.

    Answer: False Difficulty: 2

32. The key distinguishing feature between the money and capital markets is the types of securities traded in each market.

    Answer: False Difficulty: 2

33. Financial markets are institutions and procedures that facilitate transactions in all types of financial claims.

    Answer: True Difficulty: 1

34. There is no difference between real assets and financial assets.

    Answer: False Difficulty: 1

35. In a private placement, the securities are offered and sold to a limited number of investors.

    Answer: True Difficulty: 1

36. The process of shelf registration will reduce the time needed for the firm to take an issue to market.

    Answer: True Difficulty: 1

37. When considering various investments, the investor would receive a desirable rate of return by earning the current inflation rate.

    Answer: False Difficulty: 1

38. The term structure of interest rates usually indicates that longer terms to maturity demand higher returns.

    Answer: True Difficulty: 2

MULTIPLE CHOICE

39. Money market instruments include:
    a) bankers' acceptance
    b) preferred stock
    c) corporate bonds
    d) all of the above

    Answer: a Difficulty: 1

40. Capital market instruments include:
    a) negotiable certificates of deposit
    b) corporate equities
    c) commercial paper
    d) treasury bills

    Answer: b Difficulty: 1

41. Benefits of an organized security exchange include:
    a) helping companies raise new capital
    b) establishing and publicizing fair security prices
    c) providing a continuous market
    d) all of the above

    Answer: d Difficulty: 1

42. Activities of the investment banker include:
    a) assuming the risk of selling a security issue
    b) selling new securities to the ultimate investors
    c) providing advice to firms issuing securities
    d) all of the above

    Answer: d Difficulty: 1

43. The investment banker does not underwrite the securities to be issued in which of the following?
    a) the competitive bid purchase
    b) the negotiated purchase
    c) the syndicated purchase
    d) commission basis

    Answer: d Difficulty: 1

44. Advantages of private placements do not include which of the following:
    a) private placements which allow more financing flexibility
    b) flotation costs which are much lower with a private placement
    c) interest costs which are generally lower
    d) funds which are available more quickly than through a public offering

    Answer: c Difficulty: 2

45. Which of the following relationships is true regarding the costs of issuing the following securities?
    a) common stock > bonds > preferred stock
    b) preferred stock > common stock > bonds
    c) bonds > common stock > preferred stock
    d) common stock > preferred stock > bonds

    Answer: d Difficulty: 2

46. Financial intermediaries:
    a) offer indirect securities
    b) include the national and regional stock exchange
    c) usually are underwriting syndicates
    d) constitute the various secondary markets

    Answer: a Difficulty: 1

47. The SEC requires registration of a public issue in which of the following circumstances?
    a) a railroad bond issue
    b) an issue of commercial paper
    c) a public utility issue
    d) an issue of $5,000,000

    Answer: d Difficulty: 2

48. According to the SEC the correct sequence of events for a security issue is:
    a) red herring, final prospectus, SEC registration
    b) SEC registration, red herring, final prospectus
    c) final prospectus, SEC registration, red herring
    d) red herring, SEC registration, final prospectus

    Answer: b Difficulty: 2

49. Which of the following are not real assets?
    a) preferred stock
    b) inventory
    c) land
    d) b and c

    Answer: a Difficulty: 1

50. The trading of negotiable certificates of deposit takes place on the:
    a) Chicago Board of Trade
    b) New York Stock Exchange
    c) American Stock Exchange
    d) none of the above

    Answer: d Difficulty: 2

51. The telecommunications system that provides a national information linkup among brokers and dealers operating in the over-the-counter market is called:
    a) NCIS
    b) NSQA
    c) NASDAQ
    d) NASQ

    Answer: c Difficulty: 2

52. An example of a primary market transaction is:
    a) a new issue of common stock by AT&T
    b) a sale of some outstanding common stock of AT&T
    c) AT&T repurchasing its own stock from a stockholder
    d) all of the above

    Answer: a Difficulty: 2

53. When crowding occurs:
    a) the government borrower is pushed out of the financial markets in favor of the private borrower
    b) the private borrower is pushed out in the financial markets in favor of the government borrower
    c) the private borrower is pushed out of the financial markets in favor of the non financial business borrowers
    d) the government borrower is pushed out of the financial markets in favor of the nonfinancial business borrowers

    Answer: b Difficulty: 2

54. Savings are generally transferred to the business firms by:
    a) direct transfer of funds
    b) indirect transfer using the investment banker
    c) indirect transfer using the financial intermediary
    d) all of the above

    Answer: d Difficulty: 2

55. The U.S. tax system favors _____ as a means of raising capital.
    a) common stock
    b) preferred stock
    c) debt
    d) I.O.U.s

    Answer: c Difficulty: 2

56. Insurance companies invest in the "long-end"of the securities market.In which of the following instruments would an insurance company be least likely to invest most of its assets:
    a) corporate stocks
    b) corporate bonds
    c) mortgages
    d) commercial paper

    Answer: d Difficulty: 2

57. An advantage of a private placement is:
    a) speed
    b) reduced flotation costs
    c) lower interest rates
    d) a and b
    e) all of the above

    Answer: d Difficulty: 2

58. The demand for funds by the federal government puts upward pressure on interest rates causing private investors to be pushed out of the financial markets. This is called:
    a) the big squeeze
    b) the efficient market hypothesis
    c) the crowding out effect
    d) liquidity preference
    e) government intervention

    Answer: c Difficulty: 2

59. Organized security exchanges provide which of the following benefit(s)?
    a) a continuous market
    b) established and publicized fair security prices
    c) help businesses raise new capital
    d) all of the above

    Answer: d Difficulty: 2

60. In a direct sale the issuing firm sells the security:
    a) directly to the investing public
    b) directly to an investment banker
    c) directly to an underwriting group
    d) directly to a syndicate

    Answer: a Difficulty: 2

61. The investment banker performs three basic functions:
    a) underwriting, distributing, and raising new capital
    b) underwriting, advising, and price-pegging
    c) underwriting, distributing, and advising
    d) underwriting, distributing, and negotiating

    Answer: c Difficulty: 3

62. Which of the following refers to all institutions and procedures that provide for transactions in short-term debt instruments generally issued by borrowers with very high credit ratings?
    a) capital market
    b) commercial banks
    c) money market
    d) stock market

    Answer: c Difficulty: 3

63. Which of the following is NOT a benefit provided by the existence of organized security exchanges?
    a) providing a continuous market
    b) establishing and publicizing fair security prices
    c) standardization of asset pricing models
    d) helping business raise new capital

    Answer: c Difficulty: 3

64. Which of the following best describes "the due diligence meeting" in the negotiated purchase sequence?
    a) the meeting at the beginning of the process to select the investment banker
    b) a "last chance" gathering to get everything in order before taking the offering to the public
    c) the first of a series of preunderwriting conferences that will be held between the firm and the investment banker
    d) none of the above

    Answer: b Difficulty: 3

65. Which of the following best describes the relationship between indirect securities and direct securities?
    a) Indirect securities and direct securities are the same thing.
    b) Financial intermediaries sell indirect securities and direct securities.
    c) Financial intermediaries sell direct securities and use the proceeds to buy indirect securities.
    d) Financial intermediaries sell indirect securities and use the proceeds to buy direct securities.

    Answer: d Difficulty: 3

66. The opportunity cost is defined as:
    a) the rate of return based on historical costs
    b) the rate of return available in the financial markets
    c) the cost associated with the acquistion of investments
    d) the future value of the purchase price

    Answer: b Difficulty: 2

67. The risk premium would be greater for an investment in an oil and gas exploration in unproven fields than an investment in preferred stock because:
    a) oil and gas exploration investments have a greater variability in possible returns
    b) the preferred stock is more liquid
    c) the inflation rate would vary more with oil and gas exploration investments
    d) both a and b are true

    Answer: d Difficulty: 3

ESSAY

68. Given the anticipated rate of inflation (i) of 6.3% and the real rate of interest (R) of 4.7%, find the nominal rate of interest (r).

    Answer:
    $r = R + i + iR$
    $r = .047 + 0.063 + (.063)(.047)$
    $r = .11 + .00296$
    $r = 11.3\%$
    Difficulty: 2

69. If provided the nominal rate of interest (r) of 14.2% and the anticipated rate of inflation (i) of 5.5%, what is the real rate of interest (R)?

    Answer:
    $r \qquad\qquad = R + i + iR$
    $.142 \qquad\quad = R + .055 + (.055)(R)$
    $.142 - .055 = 1.055R + .055 - .055$
    $.087 \qquad\quad = 1.055R$
    $R \qquad\qquad = 8.2\%$
    Difficulty: 2

70. Given the anticipated rate of inflation (i) of 6.13% and the real rate of interest (R) of 7.56%, what is the true inflation premium?

Answer:
We know the inflation premium
to equal $\quad$ i + iR
or $\quad = \quad$ .0613 + (.0613)(.0756)
$\quad = \quad$ 6.59%

Difficulty: 2

Chapter 3: Financial Statements and Evaluating Performance

TRUE/FALSE

1. An income statement reports a firm's profit relative to its total investment in plant and equipment.

   Answer: False Difficulty: 1

2. A balance sheet is a statement of the financial position of the firm on a given date, including its asset holdings, liabilities, and equity.

   Answer: True Difficulty: 1

3. The profit and loss (income) statement is compiled on a cash basis.

   Answer: False Difficulty: 1

4. When the present financial ratios of a firm are compared with similar ratios for another firm in the same industry it is called trend analysis.

   Answer: False Difficulty: 1

5. Both Dun and Bradstreet and Robert Morris Associates publish industry average ratios.

   Answer: True Difficulty: 1

6. The current ratio and the acid test ratio both measure financial leverage.

   Answer: False Difficulty: 1

7. Ratios that examine profit relative to investment are useful in evaluating the overall effectiveness of the firm's management.

   Answer: True Difficulty: 1

8. Financial ratios that are higher than industry averages may indicate problems which are as detrimental to the firm as ratios that are too low.

   Answer: True Difficulty: 1

9. The income statement describes the financial position of a firm on a given date.

   Answer: False Difficulty: 1

10. Under current accounting rules, plant and equipment appear on a company's balance sheet at replacement value.

    Answer: False Difficulty: 1

11. Another name for the acid test ratio is the current ratio.

    Answer: False Difficulty: 1

12. Financial ratios comprise the principal tool of financial analysis, since they can be used to answer a variety of questions regarding a firm's financial condition.

    Answer: True Difficulty: 1

13. Financial ratios can answer questions regarding the firm's liquidity, solvency, and profitability.

    Answer: True Difficulty: 1

14. On an accrual basis income statement, revenues and expenses always match the firm's cash flow.

    Answer: False Difficulty: 2

15. The statement of cash flow explains the changes that took place in the firm's cash balance over the period of interest.

    Answer: True Difficulty: 1

16. A balance sheet reflects the current market value of a firm's assets and liabilities.

    Answer: False Difficulty: 1

17. Ratios are used to standardize financial information.

    Answer: True Difficulty: 1

18. There is no such thing as a liquidity ratio being too high.

    Answer: False Difficulty: 2

19. The lower the average collection period ratio, the more efficient the firm is in managing its investments in accounts receivables.

    Answer: True Difficulty: 2

20. One weakness of the times interest earned ratio is that it includes only the annual interest expense as a finance expense that must be paid.

Answer: True Difficulty: 2

21. Trend analysis is the comparison of the firm's financial ratios for one time period with similar ratios from previous periods.

Answer: True Difficulty: 2

MULTIPLE CHOICE

22. If you were given current assets and current liabilities, what ratio could you compute?
    a) accounts receivable turnover ratio
    b) net profit margin
    c) current ratio
    d) current debt margin

Answer: c Difficulty: 1

23. The quick ratio of a firm would be unaffected by which of the following?
    a) land held for investment is sold for cash
    b) equipment is purchased, financed by a long-term debt issue
    c) inventories are sold for cash
    d) inventories are sold on a credit basis

Answer: b Difficulty: 2

24. Given an accounts receivable turnover of 8 and annual credit sales of $362,000, the average collection period (360-day year) is:
    a) 90 days
    b) 45 days
    c) 75 days
    d) 60 days

Answer: b Difficulty: 2

25. What financial statement explains the changes that took place in the firm's cash balance over a period?
    a) statement of cash flow
    b) balance sheet
    c) income statement
    d) none of the above

Answer: a Difficulty: 1

Table 3-1

Jones Company
Financial Information

	March 1996	March 1997
Net earnings	$1,500	$3,000
Accounts receivable	750	750
Accumulated depreciation	1,125	1,500
Common stock	4,500	5,250
Capital surplus	7,500	8,250
Retained earnings	1,500	2,250
Accounts payable	750	750

26. Based on the information in Table 3-1, calculate the funds provided by operations for 1997:
    a) $3,750
    b) $3,375
    c) $3,000
    d) $2,250

    Answer: b Difficulty: 2

27. Based on the information in Table 3-1, calculate the dividends paid in 1997:
    a) $3,750
    b) $3,000
    c) $750
    d) $2,250

    Answer: d Difficulty: 2

28. The question "Did the common stockholders receive an adequate return on their investment?" is answered through the use of:
    a) liquidity ratios
    b) profitability ratio
    c) coverage ratios
    d) leverage ratios

    Answer: b Difficulty: 1

Table 3-2

Smith Company
Balance Sheet

Assets:

Cash and marketable securities	$ 300,000
Accounts receivable	2,215,000
Inventories	1,837,500
Prepaid expenses	24,000
Total current assets	$3,286,500
Fixed assets	2,700,000
Less: accumulated depreciation	1,087,500
Net fixed assets	$1,612,500
Total assets	$4,899,000

Liabilities:

Accounts payable	$ 240,000
Notes payable	825,000
Accrued taxes	42,000
Total current liabilities	$1,107,000
Long-term debt	975,000
Owner's equity	2,817,000
Total liabilities and owner's equity	$4,899,000

Net sales (all credit)	$6,375,000
Less: Cost of goods sold	4,312,500
Selling and administrative expense	1,387,500
Depreciation expense	135,000
Interest expense	127,000
Earnings before taxes	$ 412,500
Income taxes	225,000
Net income	$ 187,500

Common stock dividends	$97,500
Change in retained earnings	$90,000

29. Based on the information in Table 3-2, the current ratio is:
    a) 2.97
    b) 1.46
    c) 2.11
    d) 2.23

    Answer: a   Difficulty: 2

30. Based on the information in Table 3-2, the average collection period is:
    a) 71 days
    b) 84 days
    c) 64 days
    d) 94 days

    Answer: a   Difficulty: 2

31. Based on the information in Table 3-2, the debt ratio is:
    a) 0.70
    b) 0.20
    c) 0.74
    d) 0.42

    Answer: d Difficulty: 2

32. Based on the information in Table 3-2, the inventory turnover ratio is:
    a) .29 times
    b) 2.35 times
    c) .43 times
    d) 3.47 times

    Answer: a Difficulty: 2

Table 3-3

Young Corporation

Balance Sheet		Income Statement	
Assets:			
Cash	$ 150,000	Sales (all credit)	$6,000,000
Accounts receivable	450,000	Cost of goods sold	3,000,000
Inventory	600,000	Operating expenses	750,000
Net fixed assets	1,800,000	Interest expense	750,000
		Income taxes	750,000
Liabilities and owner's equity:		Net income	750,000
Accounts payable	$ 150,000		
Notes payable	150,000		
Long-term debt	1,200,000		
Owner's Equity	1,500,000		

33. Based on the information in Table 3-3, the average collection period is:
    a) 36.0 days
    b) 9.0 days
    c) 13.2 days
    d) 27.0 days

    Answer: d Difficulty: 2

34. Based on information in Table 3-3, the return on total assets is:
    a) 10%
    b) 12%
    c) 25%
    d) 24%

    Answer: c Difficulty: 2

35. Based on the information in Table 3-3, the total asset turnover is:
    a) 2.0 times
    b) 3.0 times
    c) 1.8 times
    d) 5.0 times

    Answer: a Difficulty: 2

36. Based on the information in Table 3-3, the debt ratio is:
    a) 0.8
    b) 0.1
    c) 0.4
    d) 0.5

    Answer: d Difficulty: 2

37. Which of the following financial ratios is the best measure of the operating effectiveness of a firm's management?
    a) current ratio
    b) net profit margin
    c) quick ratio
    d) return on investment

    Answer: d Difficulty: 2

38. If a company's average collection period is higher than the industry average, then the company may be:
    a) enforcing credit conditions upon its customers which are too stringent
    b) allowing its customers too much time to pay their bills
    c) too tough in collecting its accounts
    d) a and c

    Answer: b Difficulty: 2

Table 3-4

Bird Industries Inc.
Balance Sheet

	1996	1997
Cash	$ 1,000	$?
Accounts receivable	5,000	6,000
Inventories	6,500	6,000
Land	10,000	12,000
Other fixed assets	8,000	9,000
Accumulated depreciation	(1,000)	(1,600)
Total Assets	$29,500	$?
Accounts payable	$ 3,200	$ 6,800
Bonds	4,000	4,000
Common stock	17,000	16,000
Retained earnings	5,300	5,000
Liabilities & Equity	$29,500	?

Bird Industries Inc.
Income Statement

Sales	$84,000
Cost of goods sold	66,400
Gross profit	$17,600
Operating expenses	(13,000)
Depreciation	(600)
EBIT	$ 4,000
Interest expense	(500)
EBT	$ 3,500
Taxes	(1,500)
Net Income	$ 2,000

39. Based on the information contained in Table 3-4, what was the total
amount of Bird Industries' common stock dividend for 1997?
a) $800
b) $2,300
c) $2,000
d) cannot be determined with available information

Answer: b Difficulty: 2

Table 3-5

Snark Enterprises Inc.
Balance Sheet

	1996	1997
Cash	$ 1,000	$?
Accounts receivable	8,000	9,000
Inventories	4,000	7,000
Land	10,000	10,000
Other fixed assets	5,000	5,500
Accumulated depreciation	(1,600)	(2,000)
Total Assets	$29,500	$?
Accounts payable	$ 4,200	$ 7,000
Bonds	4,000	4,000
Common stock	15,000	16,000
Retained earnings	3,200	3,800
Total Assets	$26,400	?

Snark Enterprises Inc.
Income Statement

Sales	$44,900
Cost of goods sold	(22,000)
Gross profit	$12,900
Operating expenses	(10,000)
Depreciation	(400)
NOI	$ 2,500
Interest expense	(500)
EBT	$ 2,000
Taxes	(1,000)
Net Income	$ 1,000

40. Based on the information contained in Table 3-5, what was the total amount of Snark Enterprise's common stock dividend for 1997?
    a) $0
    b) $400
    c) $600
    d) cannot be determined with available information

    Answer: b Difficulty: 2

41. Based on the information contained in Table 3-5, what is Snark Enterprise's cash balance as of December 31, 1997?
    a) $1,100
    b) $900
    c) $1,300
    d) none of the above

    Answer: c Difficulty: 2

42. Based on the information contained in Table 3-5, what is Snark Enterprises' quick ratio for December 31, 1997?
    a) 1.47
    b) 2.47
    c) 2.29
    d) .45

    Answer: a Difficulty: 2

43. Why is the quick ratio a more refined liquidity measure than the current ratio?
    a) It measures how "quickly" cash and other liquid assets flow through the company.
    b) Inventories are generally the least liquid of the firm's current assets.
    c) Inventories are generally among the most liquid of the firm's current assets.
    d) Cash is the most liquid current asset.

    Answer: b Difficulty: 2

44. Smith Corporation has current assets of $11,400, inventories of $4,000, and a current ratio of 2.6. What is Smith's acid test ratio?
    a) 1.69
    b) .54
    c) .74
    d) 1.35

    Answer: a Difficulty: 3

45. Kingsbury Associate's current assets are as follows:

    Cash $3,000
    Accounts Receivable $4,500
    Inventories $8,000

    If Kingsbury has a current ratio of 3.2, what is its quick ratio?
    a) 2.07
    b) 1.55
    c) .48
    d) none of the above

    Answer: b Difficulty: 3

46. Which of the following ratios indicate how rapidly the firm's credit accounts are being collected?
    a) debt ratio
    b) average collection period
    c) accounts receivable turnover ratio
    d) both b and c

    Answer: d Difficulty: 2

47. Smart and Smiley Incorporated have an average collection period of 74 days. What is the accounts receivable turnover ratio for Smart and Smiley?
    a) 4.86
    b) 2.47
    c) 2.66
    d) none of the above

    Answer: a Difficulty: 3

48. Billing's Pit Corporation has an accounts receivable turnover ratio of 3.4. What is Billing's Pit Corporation's average collection period?
    a) 106 days
    b) 102 days
    c) 73 days
    d) none of the above

    Answer: a Difficulty: 3

49. Snype Inc. has an accounts receivable turnover ratio of 7.3. Stork Company has an accounts receivable turnover ratio of 5. Which of the following statements are correct?
    a) Snype's average collection period is less than Stork's.
    b) Stork's average collection period is less than Snype's.
    c) Snype has a lower accounts receivable account on average than does Stork Company.
    d) Stork Company has (on average) a lower account's receivable account than does Snype.

    Answer: a Difficulty: 3

50. Brighton Industries has an average collection period of 72 days. If Brighton's accounts receivable balance is $100,000, what is Brighton's average daily credit sales?
    a) $20,000
    b) $500,000
    c) $6,945
    d) $1,389

    Answer: d Difficulty: 3

51. Ortny Industries has an accounts receivable turnover ratio of 4.3. If Ortny has an accounts receivable balance of $90,000, what is Ortny's average daily credit sales?
    a) $387,000
    b) $1,548
    c) $1,075
    d) none of the above

    Answer: c Difficulty: 3

52. Snort and Smiley Incorporated has a debt ratio of .42, noncurrent liabilities of $20,000 and total assets of $70,000. What is Snort and Smiley's level of current liabilities?
    a) $8,400
    b) $9,400
    c) $12,348
    d) $10,600

    Answer: b Difficulty: 3

53. Spinnit Limited has a debt ratio of .57 current liabilities of $14,000, and total assets of $70,000. What is the level of Spinnit Limited's total liabilities?
    a) $25,900
    b) $24,600
    c) $39,900
    d) $53,900

    Answer: c Difficulty: 3

54. Lorna Dome Inc. has an annual interest expense of $30,000 and pays income tax equal to 40 percent of Earnings (EBT). Lorna Dome's times-interest-earned ratio is 4.2. What is Lorna Dome's net income?
    a) $96,000
    b) $57,000
    c) $126,000
    d) $57,600

    Answer: d Difficulty: 3

55. Sharky's Loan Co. has an annual interest expense of $30,000. If Sharky's times-interest-earned ratio is 2.9, what is Sharky's Earnings Before Taxes (EBT)?
    a) $87,000
    b) $57,000
    c) $117,000
    d) $60,000

    Answer: b Difficulty: 3

Table 3-6

In 1997, Snout and Smith Inc. had a gross profit of $27,000 on sales of $110,000. S&S's operating expenses for 1997 were $13,000, and its net profit margin was .0585. Snout and Smith had no interest expense in 1997.

56. Using the information in Table 3-6, what was S & S's gross profit margin for 1997?
    a) .127
    b) .325
    c) .245
    d) .364

    Answer: c Difficulty: 2

57. Using the information in Table 3-6, what was S & S's operating profit margin for 1997?
    a) .245
    b) .118
    c) .127
    d) .157

    Answer: c Difficulty: 2

58. Using the information in Table 3-6, what was S & S's tax rate in 1997?
    a) .54
    b) .46
    c) .50
    d) none of the above

    Answer: a Difficulty: 2

Table 3-7

Cow Chow Inc.
Balance Sheet

	1996	1997
Cash	$ 2,000	$?
Accounts receivable	6,000	6,500
Inventories	4,500	4,000
Land	10,000	10,000
Other fixed assets	8,000	9,900
Accumulated depreciation	(2,000)	(2,500)
Total Assets	$28,500	$?
Accounts payable	$ 5,500	$ 6,000
Bonds	12,000	12,000
Common stock	7,000	7,000
Retained earnings	4,000	5,000
Liabilities & Equity	$28,500	?

Cow Chow Inc.
Income Statement

Sales	$98,000
Cost of goods sold	72,500
Gross profit	$25,500
Operating expenses	13,000
Depreciation	500
EBIT	$12,000
Interest expense	1,000
EBT	$11,000
Taxes	5,000
Net Income	$ 6,000

59. Based on the information contained in Table 3-7, what was the total amount of Cow Chow Inc.'s common stock dividend for 1997?
a) $6,000
b) $5,000
c) $1,000
d) none of the above

Answer: b Difficulty: 2

60. Based on the information contained in Table 3-7, what is Cow Chow Inc.'s "Sources of Funds" as would be found on a Statement of Sources and Uses of Funds for year end 1997?
    a) $7,000
    b) $1,500
    c) $2,500
    d) $7,500

    Answer: a Difficulty: 2

61. Based on the information contained in Table 3-7, what was Cow Chow's quick ratio at year end 1997?
    a) 2.10
    b) 1.43
    c) 1.08
    d) none of the above

    Answer: b Difficulty: 2

62. Based on the information contained in Table 3-7, what was Cow Chow's returns on common equity for year end 1997?
    a) 50%
    b) 85.7%
    c) 71.4%
    d) 41.7%

    Answer: b Difficulty: 2

63. Based on the information contained in Table 3-7, what was Cow Chow's gross profit margin for year end 1997?
    a) .260
    b) .122
    c) .061
    d) .112

    Answer: a Difficulty: 2

64. The firm obtains cash from which of the following:
    a) from operations
    b) by the sale of assets
    c) by borrowing
    d) all of the above

    Answer: d Difficulty: 2

65. The Cash Flow provides an accounting for resources:
    a) at a point in time
    b) during a specific period
    c) always during a set 5-year interval (for trend analysis)
    d) none of the above

    Answer: b Difficulty: 1

66. Examples of uses of cash are:
    a) giving cash dividends to stockholders
    b) repaying a loan
    c) purchasing machinery
    d) all of the above

    Answer: d Difficulty: 1

67. An example of liquidity ratio is:
    a) quick ratio
    b) debt ratio
    c) times-interest-earned
    d) return on assets

    Answer: a Difficulty: 1

68. A Cash Flow Statement can be used to answer a variety of questions. Which of the following would this statement not be likely to answer?
    a) Why was money borrowed?
    b) Where did profits go?
    c) What is the current level of inventory?
    d) How was the retirement of debt accomplished?

    Answer: c Difficulty: 1

69. Which of the following represents an attempt to measure the net results of the firm's operations over a given time period?
    a) balance sheet
    b) Cash Flow statement
    c) income statement
    d) Source and Use of Funds statement

    Answer: c Difficulty: 1

70. Firm X has current assets of $8,000,000, current liabilities of $4,200,000, inventory of $1,000,000, and sales of $12,000,000. What is the acid test ratio?
    a) 1.9
    b) 1.67
    c) 0.67
    d) 1.4

    Answer: b Difficulty: 2

71. An inventory turnover ratio of 5.2 compared to an industry average of 4.1 indicates that:
    a) The firm has higher sales than the industry average.
    b) The firm is investing less in inventory per dollar of sales than the industry average.
    c) The firm is investing heavily in their inventories.
    d) The firm is investing heavily in their inventories, causing their average to be higher than the industry's.

    Answer: b Difficulty: 2

72. A firm that wants to know if it has enough cash to meet its bills would be most likely to use which kind of ratio?
    a) liquidity
    b) leverage
    c) efficiency
    d) profitability

    Answer: a Difficulty: 1

ESSAY

Table 3-8

Financial Data for Dooley Sportswear December 31, 1997:

Inventory	$ 206,250
Long-term debt	300,000
Interest expense	5,000
Accumulated depreciation	442,500
Cash	180,000
Net sales (all credit)	1,500,000
Common stock	800,000
Accounts receivable	225,000
Operating expenses	525,000
Notes payable-current	187,500
Cost of goods sold	937,500
Plant and equipment	1,312,500
Accounts payable	168,750
Marketable securities	95,000
Prepaid insurance	80,000
Accrued wages	65,000
Retained earnings-current-year?	yes

73. From the information presented in Table 3-8, calculate the following
financial ratios for the Dooley Sportswear Company.

current ratio	operating profit margin
acid test ratio	net profit margin
average collection period	total asset turnover
inventory turnover	times-interest-earned
gross profit margin	

Answer:

Current ratio=

$$\frac{\$180,000 + \$95,000 + \$225,000 + \$206,250 + \$80,000}{\$168,750 + \$187,500 + \$65,000} =$$

$$\frac{\$786,250}{\$421,250} = 1.87$$

Acid Test Ratio =

$$\frac{\$180,000 + \$95,000 + \$225,000 + \$80,000}{\$168,750 + \$187,500 + \$65,000} =$$

$$\frac{\$580,000}{\$421,250} = 1.38$$

Average collection period= $\$225,000/(\$1,500,000/360\ \text{days})= 54\ \text{days}$

Inventory turnover = $\$937,500/\$206,250 = 4.55$

Gross profit margin = $\$562,500/\$1,500,000 = 0.375$

Operating profit margin = $\$37,500/\$1,500,000 = 0.025$

Net profit margin = $\$26,750/\$1,500,000 = 0.0178$

Total asset turnover = $\$1,500,000/\$1,656,250 = 0.906$

Times-interest-earned = $\$37,500/\$5,000 = 7.5\ \text{times}$
Difficulty: 2

Table 3-9

Hokie Corporation Comparative Balance Sheet
For the Years Ending March 31, 1996 and 1997
(Millions of Dollars)

Assets	1996	1997
Current assets:		
Cash	$ 2	$ 10
Accounts receivable	16	10
Inventory	22	26
Total current assets	$ 40	$ 46
Gross fixed assets:	$120	$124
Less accumulated depreciation	60	64
Net fixed assets	60	60
Total assets	$100	$106

Liabilities and owners' equity:	1996	1997
Current liabilities:		
Accounts payable	$ 16	$ 18
Notes payable	10	10
Total current liabilities	$ 26	$ 28
Long-term debt	20	18
Owners' equity:		
Common stock	40	40
Retained earnings	14	20
Total liabilities and owners' equity	$100	$106

Hokie had net income of $26 million for 1997 and paid total cash dividends of $20 million to their common stockholders.

74. Construct a cash flow statement from the information given in Table 3-9.

Answer:

Hokie Corporation
Statement of sources and uses of funds
for the year ending March 31, 1997
(millions of dollars)

Cash balance (April 1, 1996) $ 2
Sources of funds:
Funds provided by operations
    Net income $26
      Depreciation   4   30
   Decrease in accounts receivable   6
   Increase in accounts payable   2
    Total funds provided $38
Use of funds:
   Common stock dividends   20
   Purchase of fixed assets   4
   Increase in inventories   4
   Decrease in long-term debt   2
    Total use of funds $30

Cash balance (April 1, 1997) $10

Difficulty: 3

75. Calculate the following 1997 financial ratios of the Hokie Corporation using the information given in Table 3-9:

current ratio
acid test ratio
debt ratio
return on total assets
return on common equity

Answer:
Current ratio = $46/$28 = 1.64

Acid Test ratio = $20/$28 = 0.71

Debt ratio = $46/$106 = 0.43

Return on total assets = $26/$106 = 0.25

Return on Common Equity = $26/$60 = 0.43
Difficulty: 2

76. S.M., Inc., had total sales of $400,000 in 1997 (70 percent of its sales are credit). The company's gross profit margin is 10 percent, its ending inventory is $80,000, and its accounts receivable is $25,000. What amount of funds can be generated by the company if it increases its inventory turnover ratio to 10.0 and reduces its average collection period to 20 days?

Answer:
Average collection period = accounts receivable/(annual credit sales/360 days)

20 days = accounts receivable/[(400,000 x .70)/360 days]

accounts receivable = 20 x $280,000/360 = $15,556

funds generated by reducing accounts receivable
= $25,000 - $15,556 = $ 9,444

inventory turnover = cost of goods sold/ending inventory

10.0. = ($400,000)(1-.10)/ending inventory

ending inventory = $360,000/10.0 = $36,000

funds generated by reducing inventory = $80,000 - $36,000 = $44,000

Total funds generated = $9,444 + $44,000 = $53,444
Difficulty: 3

77.   T.M.W., Inc. Statement of Income

Net sales	$42,000
Cost of goods sold	27,000
Gross profit	$15,000
Operating expenses:	
Selling expense	$ 1,000
General and administration	5,000
Lease expense	4,000
Earnings before interest and taxes	$ 5,000
Interest expense	1,500
Earnings before taxes	$ 3,500
Income taxes	700
Net income	$ 2,800
Common stock dividend	$ 1,000
Retained earnings	$ 1,800

T.M.W., Inc. paid $200 in principal on a long-term bond during the year. The company had a depreciation expense of $1,000 and has a 20 percent marginal tax rate. Calculate the times-interest-earned ratio.

Answer:

times-interest-earned ratio = EBIT/interest expense

$$= \$5,000/\$1,500 = 3.33$$

cash flow overall coverage ratio

=[EBIT+lease expense+depreciation]/[interest expense+
  lease expense]+[principal payment/(1-marginal tax rate)]

=[$5,000+$4,000+$1,000]/[$1,500+$4,000+[$200/(1-.20)]

$$= \$10,000/\$5,750 = 1.74$$

Difficulty: 2

78. The balance sheet and income statement for Becker, Becker & Becker is presented below.

BALANCE SHEET (000)

Cash	$ 500
Accounts receivable	1,500
Inventories	500
Current assets	$ 2,500
Net fixed assets	5,000
Total Assets	$ 7,500
Accounts payable	$ 1,200
Bank note	300
Total current liabilities	$ 1,500
Long term debt	4,000
Common stock	300
Retained earnings	1,700
Total liabilities and owner's equity	$ 7,500

INCOME STATEMENT (000)

Net sales	$ 8,500
Cost of goods sold	(3,400)
Gross profit	$ 5,100
Operating expenses	(2,900)
Net operating income	$ 2,200
Interest expense	(580)
Earnings before taxes	$ 1,620
Income tax (34%)	(551)
Net income	$ 1,069

a. Compute the following ratios: Current ratio, Acid test ratio, Debt ratio, Total asset turnover, Operating profit margin, Return on total investments, Net profit margin, Times interest earned, Inventory turnover.

b. All other things equal, compute the dollar amount of sales need to achieve an 18% return on total assets for the coming year.

c. Given Becker's inventory turnover ratio, find a way of computing the current level of inventory given this ratio and assuming the current level of inventories is unknown. Set up but do not solve.

Answer:
a. Current ratio   1.67
   Acid test ratio   1.33
   Debt ratio   .73
   Total asset turnover   1.13
   Operating profit margin   .26
   Return on total assets   .14
   Net profit margin   .13
   Times interest earned   3.79
   Inventory turnover   6.80

b. .18 = .13 x sales/7500

    1.3846 = sales/7500

    sales = $10,384,620

c. 6.8 = 3400/inventories

Difficulty: 2

79. The following sets of ratios are industry averages. Given the following three industries, match each industry with a set of matching ratios. Defend your answer.
Industries: employment agency, manufacturer of farm equipment, and gasoline service station.

	1	2	3
Debt	1.8	2.8	1.3
Inventory Turnover	31.0	2.9	---
Current ratio	1.4	1.5	1.7
Sales/Total Assets	6.5	1.7	4.4
Sales/Receivables	73.1	12.3	8.9

Answer:
The actual industry matches are:

gasoline service station - 1
manufacturer of farm equipment - 2
employment agency - 3

The student may have different matches to this problem. It is more important that they can logically defend their answers.

Difficulty: 2

80. Baker & Co. has applied for a loan from the Trust Us Bank in order to invest in several potential opportunities. In order to evaluate the firm as a potential debtor, the bank would like to compare Baker & Co. to the industry. The following are the financial statements given to Trust Us Bank.

Balance Sheet	12/31/96	12/31/97
Cash	$ 305	$ 280
Accounts Receivable	275	290
Inventory	600	580
Current Assets	1,180	1,140
Plant and Equipment	1,700	1,940
Less: Acc Depr	(500)	(600)
Net plant and equipment	1,200	1,340
Total assets	$2,380	$2,480
Liabilities and Owners' Equity		
Accounts payable	$ 150	$ 200
Notes payable	125	0
Current liabilities	275	200
Bonds	500	500
Owners' equity		
Common Stock	175	305
Paid-in-capital	775	775
Retained earnings	665	700
Total owners' equity	1,605	1,850
Total liabilities and owners' equity	$2,380	$2,480
Income Statement (1997)		
Sales (100% credit)	$1,100	$1,330
Cost of Goods Sold	600	760
Gross profit	500	570
Operating expenses	20	30
Depreciation	160	200
Net operating income	320	340
Interest expense	64	57
Net income before taxes	256	283
Taxes	87	96
Net income	$ 169	$ 187

51

Answer:

	1996	1997	Industry Norm	Evaluation
Current Ratio	4.3%	5.7%	5.0%	Satisfactory
Acid-test (Quick) Ratio	2.1%	2.8%	3.0%	Improving
Inventory Turnover	1.0%	1.31%	2.2%	Poor
Average Collection Period	90 days	78.3 days	90 days	Satisfactory
Debt Ratio	33%	28%	33%	Satisfactory
Times Interest	5.0%	6.0%	7.0%	Poor
Total Asset Turnover	.46%	.54%	.75%	Poor
Fixed Asset Turnover	.92%	.99%	1.00%	Satisfactory
Operating Profit Margin	29.1%	25.6%	20.00%	Satisfactory
Net Profit Margin	15.36%	14.06%	12.00%	Poor
Return on Total Assets	7.1%	7.54%	9.00%	Poor
Operating Income Return on Investments	13.45%	13.71%	15.00%	Poor
Return on Equity	10.6%	10.47%	13.43%	Poor
Satisfactory				
Operating Profit Margin	29.1%	25.6%	20.0%	
Satisfactory				
Net Profit Margin	15.36%	14.06%	12.00%	Poor
Return on Total Assets	7.1%	7.54%	9.00%	Poor
Operating Income Return on Investments	13.45%	13.71%	15.00%	Poor
Return on Equity	10.6%	10.47%	13.43%	Poor

Difficulty: 2

81. In reference to the above problem:

    a. What are the firm's financial strengths and weaknesses?
    b. Should the bank make the loan? Why or why not?

Answer:
a.   Financial strengths and weaknesses

The firm's liquidity has improved significantly, as indicated by the current ratio and the acid-test ratio. However, the current ratio is a bit deceiving since it relies on inventory in part for liquidity. Since the inventory is not particularly liquid(low inventory turnover), the quick ratio is a better measure of liquidity, which is still below the industry norm.

Management has done a less-than average job at generating operating profits on its assets (low operating income return on investment). The cause for the low OIROI is the inefficient use of assets (low asset turnover), especially inventory (low inventory turnover). However, this ineffectiveness is countered by efficiencies in keeping operating expenses low (high operating profit margin).

From a balance sheet perspective, the company has less financial risk than the average firm in the industry (slightly lower debt ratio). However, owing to the firm's lower profitability, it is not covering its interest charges as well as the average firm in the industry (low times interest earned).
Owing to the low return on investment, the firm's return on assets and return on equity are low relative to its competition.

b. The answer is not an easy one. The firm has improved its liquidity, but it is still having problems at effectively managing its inventory. It may be that the loan is not needed to the extent thought, but rather management should work at reducing its investment in inventories. The bank would also want to know why the operating profit margin, which is still high, is falling.

Nevertheless, the loan decision could go either way.
Difficulty: 2

82. Lucy Line Cosmetics had a gross profit margin of 27 percent and sales of $10 million. Seventy percent of the firm's sales are on credit while the remainder are cash sales. Lucy Line's current assets equal $1,250,000, its current liabilities equal $200,000, and it has $90,000 in cash plus marketable securities.

    a. If Lucy Line's account receivable balance is $450,000, what is its average collection period?

    b. If Lucy Line reduces its average collection period to 15 days, what will be its new level of accounts receivables?

    c. Lucy Line's inventory turnover ratio is 10 times. What is the level of Lucy Line's inventories?

Answer:
a. Average Col. Pd. = Accounts Receivable/(Credit Sales/360)
          ACP = $450,000/(.70 x $10m/360)
          ACP = 23 days

Note that the ACP is based on credit sales which are 70% of total firm sales.

b. ACP = 15 = [A/R]/[.70 x ($10m/360)]
    Solving for A/R:
        A/R = $291,667

Thus, Lucy Line would reduce its A/R by $450,000-$291,667=158,333

c. Inventory Turnover = Cost of Goods Sold/Inventories
    10 = [(1-.27) x Sales]/Inventories
    Inventories = [.73 x $10m]/10 = $730,000

Difficulty: 2

83. Uncle Bubba's Seafood chain had the following condensed balance sheet at the end of operation for 19X1:

Uncle Bubba's Seafood
Balance Sheet
December 31, 19X1

Cash	$30,000	Current Liabilities	$25,000
Other current assets	60,000	L-T Notes Payable	38,000
	$90,000	Bonds Payable	50,000
Investments	$25,000	Capital Stock	147,000
Fixed assets(net	90,000	Retained earnings	65,000
Land	$120,000		
	$325,000		$325,000

During 19X2, the following occurred

a. Uncle Bubba's sold some of its investments for $12,300 which resulted in a gain of $300.
b. Additional land for a plant expansion was purchased for $22,000.
c. Bonds payable were paid in the amount of $8,500.
d. An additional $25,000 in capital stock was issued.
e. Dividends of $13,000 were paid to stockholders.
f. Net income for 19X2 was $38,000 after allowing for $11,000 in depreciation.
g. A second parcel of land was purchased through the issuance of $10,000 in bonds, and $4,800 in long-term notes payable.

Required:
a. Prepare a statement of changes in financial position for 19X1.
b. Prepare a condensed balance sheet for Uncle Bubba's at December 31, 19X2.

Answer:

Uncle Bubba's, Inc.
Statement of Cash Flow
For the Year Ended December 31, 19X2

Cash flows from operating activities:	
Net Income (from the statement of income)	$38,000
Add (deduct) to reconcile net income to net cash flow:	
Depreciation Expense	11,000
Loss (Gain) from the sale of investments	(300)
Net cash inflow from operating activities	$48,700
Cash flows from investing activities:	
Sale of Investments	12,300
Purchase of Land	(36,800)
Cash flows from financing activities:	
Issuance of capital stock	25,000
Issuance of bonds	10,000
Issuance of notes payable	4,800
Repayment of bonds payable	(8,500)
Dividends	(13,000)
Net increase (decrease) in cash during the period	$42,500

Answer:

Uncle Bubba's, Inc.
Balance Sheet
December 31, 19X2

Cash	$72,500	Current liabilities	$ 25,000
Other current assets	60,000	Long-term notes	42,800
Total current assets	$132,500	payable	
Investments	13,000	Bonds payable	51,500
Fixed assets (net)	79,000	Capital stock	172,000
Land	156,800	Retained earnings	90,000
	$381,300		$381,300

Difficulty: 3

Chapter 4: Financial Forecasting, Budgeting and Planning

TRUE/FALSE

1. The key ingredient in a firm's financial planning is an accurate sales forecast.

   Answer: True Difficulty: 1

2. The only reasonable budgeting period is six months.

   Answer: False Difficulty: 1

3. Depreciation charge can be obtained from the cash budget.

   Answer: False Difficulty: 1

4. It is possible for a firm to have a positive cash flow and yet have negative earnings on an accrual basis.

   Answer: True Difficulty: 2

5. Pro forma statements provide single point estimates of each budgeted item.

   Answer: True Difficulty: 1

6. Pro forma statements are important since they formally report the performance of the firm during the previous reporting period.

   Answer: False Difficulty: 1

7. Traditional financial forecasting takes the sales forecast as given and forecasts the corresponding expenses, assets, and liabilities of the firm.

   Answer: True Difficulty: 1

8. Corporations must include pro forma financial statements in their annual report.

   Answer: False Difficulty: 1

9. A budget is a forecast of future events.

   Answer: True Difficulty: 1

10. The cash budget can be used to provide an estimate of the firm's future financing needs.

    Answer: True Difficulty: 1

11. Accounts payable and accrued expenses are known as discretionary sources of financing needs.

    Answer: False Difficulty: 2

12. The percent-of-sales method is a commonly used method for estimating a firm's financing needs.

    Answer: True Difficulty: 2

13. Most firms prepare longer-range budgets called capital expenditure budgets.

    Answer: True Difficulty: 1

14. One of the virtues of the percent-of-sales method is the precision of the estimate of future financing needs.

    Answer: False Difficulty: 1

15. The cash budget represents a detailed plan of future cash flows.

    Answer: True Difficulty: 1

16. Pro forma financial statements depict the end result of the planning period's operations.

    Answer: True Difficulty: 1

17. Accrued expenses represent a spontaneous form of financing.

    Answer: True Difficulty: 1

18. Discretionary sources of financing are those sources that vary automatically with a firm's level of sales.

    Answer: False Difficulty: 1

19. When fixed expenses change relative to sales it indicates that there is not enough productive capacity to absorb an increase in sales.

    Answer: False Difficulty: 2

20. The budget format used in generating cost and profit budgets is the balance sheet.

    Answer: False Difficulty: 1

21. A set of estimates which corresponds to the worst and best case outcomes is often desired in preparing a financial forecast.

    Answer: True Difficulty: 1

22. Forecasts of revenues and their related expenses are the basis on which firms forecast their future financing needs.

    Answer: True Difficulty: 1

MULTIPLE CHOICE

23. The percent of sales method can be used to forecast:
    a) expenses
    b) assets
    c) liabilities
    d) all of the above

    Answer: d Difficulty: 1

24. A firm's cash position would most likely be helped by:
    a) delaying payment of accounts payable
    b) more liberal credit policies for their customers
    c) purchasing land for investment purposes
    d) holding larger inventories

    Answer: a Difficulty: 1

25. A firm's cash position would most likely be hurt by:
    a) decreasing excess inventory
    b) establishing longer credit terms
    c) retiring outstanding debt
    d) b and c

    Answer: d Difficulty: 2

26. All of the following are found in the cash budget except:
    a) a net change in cash for the period
    b) inventory
    c) cash disbursements
    d) new financing needed

    Answer: b Difficulty: 2

27. Physical budgets include budgets for all of the following except:
    a) inventories
    b) unit sales
    c) physical facilities
    d) production cost

    Answer: d Difficulty: 2

28. The primary purpose of a cash budget is to:
    a) determine the level of investment in current and fixed assets
    b) determine financing needs
    c) provide a detailed plan of future cash flows
    d) determine the estimated income tax for the year

    Answer: c Difficulty: 1

29. Which of the following is always a noncash expense?
    a) income taxes
    b) salaries
    c) depreciation
    d) none of the above

    Answer: c Difficulty: 2

30. A company collects 60% of its sales during the month of sale, 30% one month after the sale, and 10% two months after the sale. The company expects sales of $10,000 in August, $20,000 in September, $30,000 in October, and $40,000 in November. How much money is expected to be collected in October?
    a) $25,000
    b) $15,000
    c) $35,000
    d) none of the above

    Answer: a Difficulty: 2

Table 4-1
Dorian Industries' projected sales for the first six months of 1993 are given below:

Jan.	$200,000	April	$400,000
Feb.	$240,000	May	$320,000
Mar.	$280,000	June	$320,000

25% of sales are collected in cash at time of sale, 50% are collected in the month following the sale, and the remaining 25% are collected in the second month following the sale. Cost of goods sold is 75% of sales. Purchases are made in the month prior to the sales, and payments for purchases are made in the month of the sale. Total other cash expenses are $60,000/month. The company's cash balance as of February 28, 1993 will be $40,000. Excess cash will be used to retire short term borrowing (if any). Dorian has no short term borrowing as of February 28, 1993. Assume that the interest rate on short term borrowing is 1% per month. The company must have a minimum cash balance of $25,000 at the beginning of each month. Round all answers to the nearest $100.

31. Based on the information in Table 4-1, what is Dorian Industries' total cash receipts (collection) for April 1993?
    a) $400,000
    b) $300,000
    c) $100,000
    d) ($60,000)

    Answer: b Difficulty: 2

32. Based on the information in Table 4-1, what is Dorian Industries' total disbursement in May (not including interest on short-term borrowing)?
    a) $300,000
    b) $240,000
    c) $ 25,900
    d) ($60,000)

    Answer: a Difficulty: 2

33. Based on the information in Table 4-1, what is Dorian Industries' ending cash balance (before borrowing) in March?
    a) $10,000
    b) $25,000
    c) $36,000
    d) ($30,000)

    Answer: a Difficulty: 3

34. Based on the information in Table 4-1, what is Dorian's projected cumulative short term borrowing as of April 30, 1993?
    a) $15,000
    b) $60,000
    c) $35,150
    d) none of the above

    Answer: d Difficulty: 3

35. Based on the information in Table 4-1, what is Dorian's projected EBIT for March 1993?
    a) ($10,000)
    b) ($30,000)
    c) $70,000
    d) none of the above

    Answer: b Difficulty: 3

Table 4-2
Fielding Wilderness Outfitters had projected its sales for the first six months of 1993 to be as follows:

Jan.	$ 50,000	April	$180,000
Feb.	$ 60,000	May	$240,000
Mar.	$100,000	June	$240,000

Cost of goods sold is 60% of sales. Purchases are made and paid for two months prior to the sale. 40% of sales are collected in the month of the sale, 40% are collected in the month following the sale, and the remaining 20% in the second month following the sale. Total other cash expenses are $40,000/month. The company's cash balance as of March 1st, 1984 is projected to be $40,000, and the company wants to maintain a minimum cash balance of $15,000. Excess cash will be used to retire short term borrowing (if any exists). Fielding has no short term borrowing as of March 1st, 1984. Assume that the interest rate on short term borrowing is 1% per month.

36. Based on the information contained in Table 4-2, what is Fielding's projected total receipts (collections) for April?
    a) $124,000
    b) $180,000
    c) -$4,000
    d) $ 36,000

    Answer: a Difficulty: 3

37. Based on the information in Table 4-2, what was Fielding's projected loss for March?
    a) $184,000
    b) $110,000
    c) $ 84,000
    d) none of the above

    Answer: d Difficulty: 3

38. Based on the information in Table 4-2, how much short term financing is needed by March 30, 1993?
    a) $110,000
    b) $ 15,000
    c) $ 70,000
    d) $ 85,000

    Answer: d Difficulty: 3

Table 4-3
Thompson Manufacturing Supplies' projected sales for the first six months of 1993 are given below.

Jan.	$250,000	April	$400,000
Feb.	$300,000	May	$450,000
Mar.	$400,000	June	$400,000

40% of sales are collected in the month of the sale, 50% are collected in the month following the sale, and 10% are written off as uncollectible. Cost of goods sold is 70% of sales. Purchases are made the month prior to the sales and are paid during the month the purchases are made (i.e. goods sold in March are bought and paid for in February). Total other cash expenses are $50,000/month. The company's cash balance as of February 1, 1993 will be $40,000. Excess cash will be used to retire short term borrowing (if any). Thompson has no short term borrowing as of February 28, 1993. Assume that the interest rate on short term borrowing is 1% per month. The company must have a minimum cash balance of $25,000 at the beginning of each month. Round all answers to the nearest $100.

39. Based on the information in Table 4-3, what is Thompson's projected total disbursements for April?
    a) $365,000
    b) $315,000
    c) $ 5,000
    d) $ 96,607

    Answer: a Difficulty: 3

40. Based on the information in Table 4-3, what is Thompson's projected gross profit for April?
    a) ($ 5,000)
    b) $85,000
    c) $120,000
    d) none of the above

    Answer: c Difficulty: 3

41. Based on the information in Table 4-3, what is Thompson's projected total receipts (collections) for March?
    a) $400,000
    b) $310,000
    c) ($20,000)
    d) none of the above

    Answer: b Difficulty: 3

42. Based on the information in Table 4-3, what is Thompson's projected cumulative borrowing as of March 1, 1993?
    a) $85,000
    b) $45,000
    c) $70,000
    d) - 0 -

    Answer: c Difficulty: 3

43. Based on the information in Table 4-3, what is Thompson's projected cash balance as of April 1, 1993?
    a) $32,000
    b) $ 4,300
    c) $25,000
    d) none of the above

    Answer: d Difficulty: 3

44. The first step involved in predicting financing needs is:
    a) project the firm's sales revenues and expenses over the planning period
    b) estimating the levels of investment in current and fixed assets that are necessary to support the projected sales
    c) determining the firm's financing needs throughout the planning period
    d) none of the above

    Answer: a Difficulty: 2

45. The firm's cash flow:
    a) is a constant
    b) changes at a given percentage of sales
    c) is a continuous process
    d) has no relevance for budgeting purposes

    Answer: c Difficulty: 2

46. A sales forecast for the coming year would reflect:
    a) any past trend which is expected to continue
    b) the influence of any events that might materially affect that trend
    c) both a and b
    d) neither a nor b

    Answer: c Difficulty: 1

47. The "percentage" used in the percent of sales calculation comes:
    a) from the most recent financial statement item as a percent of current sales
    b) from an average computed over several years
    c) from an analyst's judgment
    d) from all of the above

    Answer: d Difficulty: 1

48. Spontaneous sources of financing include:
    a) accounts payable and accrued expenses
    b) notes payable and mortgages payable
    c) long term debt and capital leases
    d) common stock and paid-in capital

    Answer: a Difficulty: 2

49. A discretionary form of financing would be:
    a) notes payable
    b) accounts payable
    c) accrued expenses
    d) a and b

    Answer: a Difficulty: 2

50. Which of the following would not be found in a cash budget?
    a) interest expense
    b) taxes
    c) depreciation
    d) All of the above would be found in a cash budget

    Answer: c Difficulty: 2

51. A budget for unit sales, personnel, or manpower would most likely be termed a:
    a) physical budget
    b) cost budget
    c) profit budget
    d) fixed budget

    Answer: a Difficulty: 2

52. Which of the following is a spontaneous source of financing?
    a) accrued expenses
    b) notes payable
    c) common stock
    d) paid-in-capital

    Answer: a Difficulty: 2

53. Is it possible for the cash budget and the pro forma income statement to have different results?
    a) Yes, because revenues and expenses included in each statement are different.
    b) Yes, because revenues and expenses are accounted for over different time periods.
    c) No, because they contain the same variables, while just using different formats.
    d) No, because the cash budget and the pro forma income statement provide forecasts for the same time period.

Answer: b Difficulty: 2

54. The cash budget consists of all the following factors except:
    a) cash receipts
    b) cash disbursements
    c) new financing needed
    d) net income

Answer: d Difficulty: 2

ESSAY

55. The balance sheet of the Jackson Company is presented below:

Jackson Company Balance Sheet
March 31, 1997
(Millions of Dollars)

Current assets	$12	Accounts payable	$ 6
Fixed assets	18		
Total	$30	Long-term debt	12
		Common equity	12
		Total	$30

For the year ending March 31, 1997 Jackson had sales of $36 million. The common stockholders receive all net earnings of the firm in the form of cash dividends, leaving no funds from earnings available to the firm for expansion (assume that depreciation expense is just equal to the cost of replacing worn-out assets).

Construct a pro forma balance sheet for March 31, 1998 for an expected level of sales of $45 million. Assume current assets and accounts payable vary as a percent of sales, and fixed assets remain at the present level. Use notes payable as discretionary financing.

Answer:

Jackson Company
Pro Forma Balance Sheet
March 31, 1998

Current assets	$15.0	Accounts payable	$ 7.5
Fixed assets	18.0	Notes payable	1.5
Total	$33.0	Long-term debt	12.0
		Common equity	12.0
		Total	$33.0

Difficulty: 3

56. Frog Hollow Bakery is a new firm specializing in all natural ingredient pastry products. In attempting to determine what the financial position of the firm should be, the financial manager obtained the following average ratios for the baking industry for 1997:

Common equity to total assets	60%
Total asset turnover	3 times
Long-term debt to total capitalization	25%
Current ratio	1.2
Quick ratio	.75
Average collection period (360-day year)	10 days

Complete the accompanying pro forma balance sheet for Frog Hollow Bakery assuming 1998 sales (all credit) are $450,000.

Frog Hollow Bakery Pro Forma Balance Sheet
December 31, 1998

Cash	$_____	Current debt	$_____
Accounts receivable	_____	Long term debt	_____
Inventory	_____		
Total current assets	_____	Common equity	_____
Fixed assets	_____	Total liabilities $_____	
		and equity	
Total assets	_____		

Answer:

Frog Hollow Bakery
Pro Forma Balance Sheet
December 31, 1998

Cash	$ 10,000	Current debt	$ 30,000
Accounts receivable	12,500	Long-term debt	30,000
Inventory	13,500		
Total current assets	$ 36,000	Common equity	90,000
Fixed assets	114,000		
Total assets	$150,000	Total liabilities	$150,000
		and equity	

Difficulty: 3

57. Broad Cloth, Inc. sells its cloth to retail stores on credit terms of 3/15, net 45 (a 3 percent discount is given for payment within 15 days and the net amount is due in 45 days). The firm's average collection period is 30 days.

   a. The vice-president of marketing has projected credit sales of $2.0 million for the coming year. Based on this estimate, project Broad Cloth's accounts receivable level for the year.

   b. The firm is considering changing its discount terms to 2/5, net 45, which it believes will cause the average collection period to increase to 40 days. Project the accounts receivable balance for the coming year on the new credit terms and sales of $2.0 million.

Answer:

a. Average Collection Period $= \dfrac{A/R}{\dfrac{\text{Credit Sales}}{360}}$

$A/R = \dfrac{\$2,000,000}{360} \times 30$

$A/R = \$166,667$

b. $A/R = \dfrac{\$2,000,000}{360} \times 40$

$A/R = \$222,222$

Difficulty: 3

58. The cash budget for Parker Processed Meats, Inc. is given below for the fourth quarter of 1997:

Parker Processed Meats, Inc.
Cash Budget for the Three Months Ending December 31, 1997

Cash receipts	Oct.	Nov.	Dec.
Total collections	$31,050	$ 4,050	$49,950
Cash disbursements:			
Purchases	44,550	48,600	52,650
Wages and salaries	7,425	7,425	7,425
Other expenses	2,025	1,350	675
Taxes			17,415
Total disbursements	$54,000	$57,375	$78,165

The expected sales for the period are as follows:
Oct.: $86,400 Nov.: $91,800 Dec.: $83,700
The total depreciation expense for the period will be $8,775.
An interest payment on outstanding debt of $15,000 will be made in December. Using the information given above, construct a pro forma income statement for the final quarter of 1997 for Parker.

Answer:

Parker Processed Meats, Inc.
Pro Forma Income Statement
For the Quarter Ended December 31, 1997

Sales	$261,900
Less: Cost of goods sold	145,800
Gross profits	$116,100
Less:	
Depreciation expense	$ 8,775
Wages and salaries	22,275
Other expenses	4,050
Net operating income	$ 81,000
Less: interest expense	15,000
Earnings before taxes	$ 66,000
Less: Income taxes	17,415
Net income	$ 48,585

Difficulty: 3

59. The balance sheet for the Long Drive Golf Company on September 30, 1997 is presented below:

Long Drive Golf Company Balance Sheet
September 30, 1997

Cash	$ 528,000	Accounts payable	$1,568,000
Accounts receivable	1,216,000	Notes payable	752,000
Inventory	2,400,000	Total current	
Fixed assets	5,632,000	liabilities	2,320,000
		Long-term debt	2,336,000
Total assets	$9,776,000	Common stock	3,200,000
		Retained earnings	1,920,000
		Total liabilities and stockholders equity	$9,776,000

The treasurer of the firm wants to issue $1,200,000 in long-term bonds to be used as follows:

1. $240,000 to reduce accounts payable
2. $192,000 to retire notes payable
3. $128,000 to increase cash on hand
4. $640,000 to increase inventories

a. Assuming that the loan is obtained, construct a pro forma sheet for December 31, 1997, for Long Drive Golf Company that reflects the use of the funds provided.

b. Was the liquidity of Long Drive Golf Company improved by the loan?

Answer:

a.   Long Drive Golf Co.
                     Pro Forma Balance Sheet
                      December 31, 1997

Assets:	
Cash	$ 656,000
Accounts receivable	1,216,000
Inventory	3,040,000
Total current assets	$ 4,912,000
Fixed assets	5,632,000
Total assets	$10,544,000
Liabilities and owners' equity:	
Accounts payable	$ 1,328,000
Notes payable	560,000
Total current liabilities	$ 1,888,000
Long-term debt	$ 3,536,000
Common stock	3,200,000
Retained earnings	1,920,000
Total liabilities and stockholders' equity	$10,544,000

b.	Current Ratio	Quick Ratio
Before the bond issue	1.79	.75
After the bond issue	2.60	.99

Difficulty: 3

60. The treasurer for Brookdale Clothing must decide how much money the company needs to borrow in July. The balance sheet for June 30, 1997 is presented below:

Brookdale Clothing Balance Sheet
June 30, 1997

Cash	$75,000	Accounts payable	$400,000
Marketable securities	100,000	Long term debt	300,000
Accounts receivable	300,000	Common stock	100,000
Inventory	250,000	Retained earnings	200,000
Total current assets	725,000	Total liabilities and stockholders	
Fixed assets	275,000	equity	$1,000,000
Total assets	$1,000,000		

The company expects sales of $250,000 for July. The company has observed that 25% of its sales is for cash and that the remaining 75% is collected in the following month. The company plans to purchase $400,000 of new clothing. Usually 40% of purchases is for cash and the remaining 60% of purchases is paid in the following month. Salaries are $100,000 per month, lease payments are $50,000 per month, and depreciation charges are $20,000 per month. The company plans to purchase a new building for $200,000 in July and sell its marketable securities for $100,000. If the company must maintain a minimum cash balance of $50,000, how much money must the company borrow in July?

Answer:

Brookdale Clothing
Cash Budget for July, 1997

Cash Inflows	
Reduction in cash	$ 25,000
Sale of marketable securities	100,000
Collection of accounts receivable	300,000
Cash sales (.25)($250,000)	62,500
Total cash inflows	$487,500
Cash Outflows	
Repayment of accounts payable	$400,000
Cash purchases	160,000
Salaries	100,000
Lease payments	50,000
Purchase of building	200,000
Total cash outflows	$910,000
Net Inflow (Outflows)	($422,500)

The company needs to borrow $422,500.

Difficulty: 3

61. The ZYX Corporation is planning to request a line of credit from its bank and wants to estimate its cash needs for the month of September. The following sales forecasts have been made for 1998:

July	$500,000
August	400,000
September	300,000
October	200,000
November	100,000

Collection estimates were obtained from the credit collection department as follows: 20% collected within the month of sale; 70% collected the first month following this sale; and 10% collected the second month following the sale. Payments for labor and raw materials are typically made in the month in which these costs are incurred. Total labor and raw material costs each month are 50% of sales. General administrative expenses are $30,000 per month, lease payments are $10,000 per month, and depreciation charges are $20,000 per month. The corporation tax rate is 40%; however, no corporate taxes are paid in September. Prepare a pro forma income statement and cash budget for September.

Answer:

ZYX Corporation
Pro Forma Income Statement
September, 1998

Sales	$300,000
Total cost of goods sold	150,000
Gross profit	$150,000
Depreciation	(20,000)
General administrative expenses	(30,000)
Lease payments	(10,000)
Operating income	$ 90,000
Taxes	(36,000)
Net income	$ 54,000

ZYX Corporation
Cash Budget
September, 1998

Cash Inflows	
Collections from September sales	$ 60,000
Collections from August sales	280,000
Collections from July sales	50,000
Total cash inflows	$390,000
Cash Outflows	
Labor and raw materials	$150,000
General administrative expenses	30,000
Lease payments	10,000
Total cash outflow	$190,000
Net Cash Inflow	$200,000

Difficulty: 3

62. Amalgamated Enterprises is planning to purchase some new equipment. With this new equipment, the company expects sales to increase from $8,000,000 to $10,000,000. A portion of the financing for the purchase of the equipment will come from a $1,000,000 new common stock issue. The company knows that its current assets, fixed assets, accounts payable, and accrued expenses increase directly with sales. The company's net profit margin on sales is 8 percent, and the company plans to pay 40 percent of its after-tax earnings in dividends. A copy of the company's current balance sheet is given below.

Amalgamated Enterprises Balance Sheet

Current assets	$ 3,000,000
Fixed assets	12,000,000
Total assets	$15,000,000
Accounts payable	$ 4,000,000
Accrued expenses	1,000,000
Long-term debt	3,000,000
Common stock	2,000,000
Retained earnings	5,000,000
Total liabilities and net worth	$15,000,000

Prepare a pro forma balance sheet for Amalgamated for next year.

Answer:

Amalgamated Enterprises
Pro Forma Balance Sheet

	Present Level (Mil)	Percent of Sales	Projected Based on Sales of $10 Mil
Current assets	$ 3	.375	$ 3.75
Fixed assets	12	1.500	15.00
Total assets	$15		$18.75
Accounts payable	$ 4	.50	$ 5.00
Accrued expenses	$ 1	.125	1.25
Long-term debt	3	a.	4.02d
Common stock	2	a.	3.00b
Retained earnings	5	a.	5.48c
Total liabilities and net worth	$15		$18.75

Notes

a. Not applicable. These accounts are assumed not to vary directly with sales.
b. The company issued $1M in new common stock.
c. The increase in retained earnings is equal to net profit minus dividends paid. Increase in retained earnings = $(.08)($10M)(1-.40) = \$.48M$
d. The long-term debt on the projected balance sheet is equal to total assets minus accounts payable, accrued expenses, common stock, and retained earnings.
Long-term debt = $18.75M = $5.0M - $1.25M - $3.0M - $5.48M
           = $ 4.02M

Difficulty: 3

73

63. Lindsey Insurance Co. has current sales of $10 million and predicts next year's sales will grow to $14 million. Current assets are $3 million and fixed assets are $4 million. The firm's net profit margin is 7 percent after taxes. Presently, Lindsey has $900,000 in accounts payable, $1.1 million in long-term debt, and $5 million (including $2.5 million in retained earnings) in common equity. Next year, Lindsey projects that current assets will rise in direct proportion to the forecasted sales, and that fixed assets will rise by $500,000. Lindsey also plans to pay dividends of $400,000 to common shareholders.

    a. What are Lindsey's total financing needs for the upcoming year?

    b. Given the above information, what are Lindsey's discretionary financing needs?

    Answer:

    a. Projected Financing Needs = Projected Total Assets = Projected Current Assets + Projected Fixed Assets = $3m/$10 m X $14m + $4m + $.5m = $8.7m

    b. DFN = Projected Current Assets + Projected Fixed Assets
       - Present LTD - Present Owner's Equity
       -[Projected Net Income-Dividends]-Spontaneous Financing
       = $3m/$10m X $14m + $4.5m - $1.1m - $5m
       - [.07 X $14m - $.4m] - $.9m/$10m X $14m
       DFN = $4.2m + $4.5m - $6.1m - $.58m - $1.26m = $.76m

    Difficulty: 3

64. Hardings' Furniture provides a credit program to his retailers of 2/10 net 30. Because only a portion of its retailers take advantage of this program, Hardings' Furniture has an average collection period of 26 days.

    a. Based upon estimated credit sales of $800,000, predict Hardings' account receivable balance for the upcoming year.

    b. If Hardings' changes its credit terms to 1/10, net 30, it expects the average collection period to rise to 31 days. Estimate Hardings' account receivable balance based on the new credit terms and credit sales of $800,000.

    Answer:

    a. Avg. Col. Pd. = Accounts Rec./(Credit Sales/360)
       26 days = Accounts Rec./($800,000/360)
       Accounts Rec. = $57,778

    b. Accounts Rec. = ($800,000/360 days) X 31 Days = $68,889

    Difficulty: 3

65. CBD Computer Inc. is attempting to estimate its needs for funds during each of the months covering the third quarter of 19X1. Pertinent information is given below:
   a. Past and estimated future sales for 19X1:

April	$80,000	July	$90,000
May	95,000	August	130,000
June	70,000	September	110,000
		October	140,000

   b. Rent expense is $2,500 per month.
   c. A quarterly interest payment on $100,000 in 7% notes payable is to be paid during September, 19X1.
   d. Wages and salaries are estimated as follows:

July	$8,000
August	10,000
September	12,000

   Payments are made within the month in which the wages are earned.
   e. Sixty percent of sales are for cash, with the remaining 40% collected in the month following the sale.
   f. CBD pays 80% of the sales price for merchandise and makes payment in the same month in which the sales occur, although purchases are made in the month prior to the anticipated sales.
   g. CBD plans to pay $7,500 in cash for a new forklift truck in July.
   h. Short-term loans can be obtained at the end of each month at 13% annual interest with interest paid during each month for which the loan is outstanding.
   i. CBD's ending cash balance for June 30, 19X1 is $67,000: the minimum balance the firm wishes to have in any month is $35,000.

   Required: Set up a cash budget for CBD for the quarter ended September 30, 19X1.

Answer:

Worksheet

	June	July	August	September
Sales	$70,000	$90,000	$130,000	$110,000
Cash sales		54,000	78,000	66,000
Collections				
(40% 1 month later)		28,000	36,000	52,000
Total cash collections		$82,000	$114,000	$118,000

Cash Budget

	July	August	September
Cash receipts from sales	$82,000	$114,000	$118,000
Cash disbursements			
Payments on purchases	(72,000)	(104,000)	(88,000)
Rent	(2,500)	(2,500)	(2,500)
Wages and salaries	(8,000)	(10,000)	(12,000)
Interest (0.07 x 100,000 x 1/4)	0	(1,750)	0
Purchase of forklift truck	(7,500)		
Short-term-borrowing interest (0.13)	0	0	0
Total cash disbursement	(90,000)	(118,250)	(102,500)
Net	(8,000)	(4,250)	15,500
Beginning cash balance	67,000	59,000	54,750
Borrowing (repayment)	0	0	0
Ending balance	$59,000	$54,750	$70,250

Difficulty: 3

Chapter 5:   The Time Value of Money

TRUE/FALSE

1. The future value of an investment increases as the number of years of compounding at a positive rate of interest declines.

   Answer: False Difficulty: 1

2. If we invest money for 10 years at 8 percent interest, compounded semi-annually, we are really investing money for 20 six-month periods, during which we receive 4 percent interest each period.

   Answer: True Difficulty: 1

3. Daily compounding allows interest to be earned more frequently than monthly compounding.

   Answer: True Difficulty: 1

4. The compound value interest factor is equal to 1.0 divided by the present value interest factor.

   Answer: True Difficulty: 1

5. The present value of a future sum of money increases as the number of years before the payment is received increases.

   Answer: False Difficulty: 1

6. One characteristic of an annuity is that an equal sum of money is deposited or withdrawn each period.

   Answer: True Difficulty: 1

7. The present value of an annuity increases as the discount rate increases.

   Answer: False Difficulty: 1

8. We can use the present value of an annuity formula to calculate constant annual loan payments.

   Answer: True Difficulty: 1

9. To evaluate and compare investment proposals, we must adjust all cash flows to a common date.

   Answer: True Difficulty: 1

10. A compound annuity involves depositing or investing a single sum of money and allowing it to grow for a certain number of years.

   Answer: False Difficulty: 1

11. A bond paying interest of $120 per year forever is an example of a perpetuity.

   Answer: True Difficulty: 1

12. The formula for calculating the present value of a perpetuity is PV = PP/(1 + i).

   Answer: False Difficulty: 1

13. An example of an annuity is the interest received on long term bonds.

   Answer: True Difficulty: 1

14. When considering unequal cash flows from an investment, one can net the inflows and outflows.

   Answer: False Difficulty: 1

15. A perpetuity is an investment that continues forever but pays a different dollar amount each year.

   Answer: False Difficulty: 1

16. The present value of the future sum of money is inversely related to both the number of years until payment is received and the opportunity rate.

   Answer: True Difficulty: 1

17. The present value of a $100 perpetuity discounted at 5% is $1200.

   Answer: False Difficulty: 2

18. Determining the specified amount of money that you will receive at the maturity of an investment is an example of a future value equation.

   Answer: True Difficulty: 1

19. The same basic formula is used for computing both the computation of future value and present value.

   Answer: True Difficulty: 1

20. When repaying an amortized loan, the interest payments increase over time.

    Answer: False Difficulty: 2

21. The bond value will increase when discounted at a 12% rate rather than at a 7% rate.

    Answer: False Difficulty: 2

MULTIPLE CHOICE

22. The present value of a single future sum:
    a) increases as the number of discount periods increases.
    b) is generally larger than the future sum.
    c) depends upon the number of discount periods.
    d) increases as the discount rate increases

    Answer: c Difficulty: 1

23. The formula for compound value is:
    a) $FV_n = PV(1+i)^n$
    b) $FV_n = (1+i)/PV$
    c) $FV_n = PV/(1+i)^n$
    d) $FV_n = PV(1+i)^{-n}$

    Answer: a Difficulty: 1

24. At 8 percent compounded annually, how long will it take $750 to double?
    a) 6.5 years
    b) 48 months
    c) 9 years
    d) 12 years

    Answer: c Difficulty: 1

25. At what rate must $400 be compounded annually for it to grow to $716.40 in 10 years?
    a) 6 percent
    b) 5 percent
    c) 7 percent
    d) 8 percent

    Answer: a Difficulty: 1

26. If the interest rate is zero:
    a) $PV = FV^n$
    b) $PV = FV^n$
    c) $FV = PV$
    d) $FV = PV/e^n$

    Answer: c Difficulty: 1

27. Assuming two investments have equal lives, a high discount rate tends to favor:
    a) the investment with large cash flow early.
    b) the investment with large cash flow late.
    c) the investment with even cash flow.
    d) neither investment since they have equal lives.

    Answer: a Difficulty: 1

28. You wish to borrow $2,000 to be repaid in 12 monthly installments of $189.12. The annual interest rate is:
    a) 24 percent.
    b) 8 percent.
    c) 18 percent.
    d) 12 percent.

    Answer: a Difficulty: 1

29. A bond maturing in 10 years pays $80 each year and $1,000 upon maturity. Assuming 10 percent to be the appropriate discount rate, the present value of the bond is:
    a) $1,010.84
    b) $925.74
    c) $877.60
    d) $1,000.000

    Answer: c Difficulty: 2

30. If you have $20,000 in an account earning 8 percent annually, what constant amount could you withdraw each year and have nothing remaining at the end of 5 years?
    a) $3,525.62
    b) $5,008.76
    c) $3,408.88
    d) $2,465.78

    Answer: b Difficulty: 1

31. If you invest $750 every six months at 8 percent compounded semi-annually, how much would you accumulate at the end of 10 years?
    a) $10,065
    b) $10,193
    c) $22,334
    d) $21,731

    Answer: c Difficulty: 1

32. You just purchased a parcel of land for $10,000. If you expect a 12 percent annual rate of return on your investment, how much will you sell the land for in 10 years?
    a) $25,000
    b) $31,060
    c) $38,720
    d) $34,310

    Answer: b Difficulty: 2

33. You have just purchased a share of preferred stock for $50.00. The preferred stock pays an annual dividend of $5.50 per share forever. What is the rate of return on your investment?
    a) .055
    b) .010
    c) .110
    d) .220

    Answer: c Difficulty: 2

34. A commercial bank will loan you $7,500 for two years to buy a car. The loan must be repaid in 24 equal monthly payments. The annual interest rate on the loan is 12 percent of the unpaid balance. How large are the monthly payments?
    a) $282.43
    b) $390.52
    c) $369.82
    d) $353.05

    Answer: d Difficulty: 2

35. Your company has received a $50,000 loan from an industrial finance company. The annual payments are $6,202.70. If the company is paying 9 percent interest per year, how many loan payments must the company make?
    a) 15
    b) 13
    c) 12
    d) 19

    Answer: a Difficulty: 2

36. Which of the following provides the greatest annual interest?
    a) 10% compounded annually
    b) 9.5% compounded monthly
    c) 9% compounded daily

    Answer: a Difficulty: 2

37. Which of the following provides the greatest annual interest?
    a) 15% compounded annually
    b) 14.5% compounded annually
    c) 14.0% compounded annually

    Answer: a Difficulty: 2

38. If you place $50 in a savings account with an interest rate of 7% compounded weekly, what will the investment be worth at the end of five years (round to nearest dollar)?
    a) $72
    b) $70
    c) $71
    d) $57

    Answer: c Difficulty: 2

39. If you put $700 in a savings account with a 10% nominal rate of interest compounded quarterly, what will the investment be worth in 21 months (round to the nearest dollar)?
    a) $827
    b) $832
    c) $828
    d) $1,176

    Answer: b Difficulty: 2

40. What is the annual compounded interest rate of an investment with a stated interest rate of 6% compounded quarterly for 7 years (round to the nearest .1%)?
    a) 51.7%
    b) 6.7%
    c) 10.9%
    d) 6.1%

    Answer: d Difficulty: 2

41. You are considering the two investments described below:
    Investment
        A   10% compounded quarterly
        B   r compounded semiannually
    Both investments have equal annual yields. Find r.
    a) 19.875%
    b) 10%
    c) 10.38%
    d) 10.125%

    Answer: d Difficulty: 3

42. If you put $600 in a savings account that yields an 8% rate of interest compounded weekly, what will the investment be worth in 37 weeks (round to the nearest dollar)?
    a) $648
    b) $635
    c) $634
    d) $645

    Answer: b Difficulty: 2

43. You are considering two investments. Investment A yields 12% compounded quarterly. Investment B yields r percent compounded semiannually. Both A and B have the same annual yield. Find r.
    a) 11.82%
    b) 12.0%
    c) 12.18%
    d) 12.55%

    Answer: c Difficulty: 3

44. What is the value of $750 invested at 7.5% compounded quarterly for 4.5 years (round to nearest $1)?
    a) $1,048
    b) $1,010
    c) $1,038
    d) $808

    Answer: a Difficulty: 2

45. Shorty Jones wants to buy a one way ticket to Mule-Snort, Pennsylvania. The bus ticket costs $142 but Mr. Jones only has $80. If Shorty puts the money in an account that pays 9% interest compounded monthly, how many months must Shorty wait until he has his $142 (round to nearest month)?
    a) 73 months
    b) 75 months
    c) 77 months
    d) 79 months

    Answer: c Difficulty: 3

46. If you put $900 in a savings account that yields 10% compounded semi-annually, how much money will you have in the account in three years (round to nearest dollar)?
    a) $1,340
    b) $1,170
    c) $1,227
    d) $1,206

    Answer: d Difficulty: 2

47. If you put $1300 in a savings account that yields 8% compounded quarterly, how much money will you have in the account in 10 years (round to nearest $10)?
    a) $2,800
    b) $2,810
    c) $2,870
    d) $2,340

    Answer: c Difficulty: 2

48. Which of the following provides the greatest annual yield?
    a) 16% compounded quarterly
    b) 15.2% compounded monthly
    c) 15.2% compounded daily
    d) cannot be determined

    Answer: c Difficulty: 2

49. If you put $1,000 in an investment that returns 24 percent compounded monthly what would you have after 2 years?
    a) 2,684
    b) 1,538
    c) 1,458
    d) 1,608

    Answer: d Difficulty: 2

50. How much would $1,000 in an account paying 14 percent interest compounded semi-annually accumulate to in 10 years?
    a) $2,140
    b) $3,707
    c) $1,647
    d) $3,870

    Answer: d Difficulty: 2

51. If you want to have $1700 in seven years, how much money must you put in a savings account today? Assume that the savings account pays 6% and it is compounded quarterly (round to the nearest $10).
    a) $1,120
    b) $1,130
    c) $1,110
    d) $1,140

    Answer: a Difficulty: 2

52. If you want to have $90 in four years, how much money must you put in a savings account today? Assume that the savings account pays 8.5% and it is compounded monthly (round to the nearest $1).
    a) $64
    b) $65
    c) $66
    d) $71

    Answer: a Difficulty: 2

53. What is the present value of $1000 to be received 10 years from today? Assume that the savings account pays 8.5% and it is compounded monthly (round to the nearest $1).
    a) $893
    b) $3,106
    c) $429
    d) $833

    Answer: c Difficulty: 2

54. What is the present value of $12,500 to be received 10 years from today? Assume a discount rate of 8% compounded annually and round to the nearest $10.
    a) $5,790
    b) $11,574
    c) $9,210
    d) $17,010

    Answer: a Difficulty: 2

55. How much money must be put into a bank account yielding 5.5% (compounded annually) in order to have $250 at the end of 5 years (round to nearest $1)?
    a) $237
    b) $191
    c) $187
    d) $179

    Answer: b Difficulty: 2

56. If you want to have $1,200 in 27 months, how much money must you put in a savings account today? Assume that the savings account pays 14% and it is compounded monthly (round to nearest $10).
    a) $910
    b) $890
    c) $880
    d) $860

    Answer: c Difficulty: 2

57. If you want to have $875 in 32 months, how much money must you put in a savings account today? Assume that the savings account pays 16% and it is compounded quarterly (round to nearest $10).
    a) $630
    b) $580
    c) $650
    d) $660

    Answer: b Difficulty: 2

58. If you want to have $2,100 in 3 years, how much money must you put in a savings account today? Assume that the savings account pays 7% and it is compounded quarterly.
    a) $1,656
    b) $1,710
    c) $1,674
    d) $1,697

    Answer: a Difficulty: 2

59. If you want to have $1,400 in 5 years, how much money must you put in a savings account today? Assume that the savings account pays 10% and it is compounded semi-annually (round to nearest $10).
    a) $780
    b) $860
    c) $870
    d) $840

    Answer: b Difficulty: 2

60. What is the present value of an annuity of $27 received at the beginning of each year for the next six years? The first payment will be received today, and the discount rate is 10% (round to nearest $10).
    a) $120
    b) $130
    c) $100
    d) $110

    Answer: b Difficulty: 2

61. What is the present value of $150 received at the beginning of each year for 16 years? The first payment is received today. Use a discount rate of 9% and round your answer to the nearest $10.
    a) $1,360
    b) $1,480
    c) $1,250
    d) $1,210

    Answer: a Difficulty: 2

62. What is the present value of $250 received at the beginning of each year for 21 years. Assume that the first payment is received today. Use a discount rate of 12%, and round your answer to the nearest $10.
    a) $1,870
    b) $2,090
    c) $2,120
    d) $2,200

    Answer: c Difficulty: 2

63. What is the present value of an annuity of $12 received at the end of each year for seven years? Assume a discount rate of 11%. The first payment will be received one year from today (round to nearest $1).
    a) $25
    b) $40
    c) $57
    d) $118

    Answer: c Difficulty: 2

64. What is the present value of an annuity of $100 received at the end of each year for seven years? The first payment will be received one year from today (round to nearest $10). The discount rate is 13%.
    a) $440
    b) $43
    c) $500
    d) $1,040

    Answer: a Difficulty: 2

65. What is the present value of $27 received at the end of each year for 5 years? Assume a discount rate of 9%. The first payment will be received one year from today (round to nearest $1).
    a) $42
    b) $114
    c) $88
    d) $105

    Answer: d Difficulty: 2

66. What is the present value of annuity of an $50 received at the end of each year for 3 years? Assume a discount rate of 11%. The first payment will be received one year from today (round to nearest $1).
    a) $68
    b) $122
    c) $136
    d) $110

    Answer: b Difficulty: 2

67. What is the present value of an annuity of $160 received at the end of each year for 6 years? Assume a discount rate of 7%. The first payment will be received one year from today (round to nearest $10).
   a) $760
   b) $820
   c) $660
   d) $640

   Answer: a Difficulty: 2

68. You are considering two investments: A & B. Both investments provide a cash flow of $100 per year for n years. However, investment A receives the cash flow at the beginning of each year, while investment B receives the cash at the end of each year. If the present value of cash flows from investment A is P, and the discount rate is r, what is the present value of the cash flows from investment B?
   a) $P/(1+r)$
   b) $P(1+r)$
   c) $P/(1+r)^n$
   d) $P(1+r)^n$

   Answer: a Difficulty: 2

69. What is the present value of $300 received at the beginning of each year for 5 years? Assume that the first payment is not received until the beginning of the third year (thus the last payment is received at the beginning of the 7th year). Use a 10% discount rate and round your answer to the nearest $100.
   a) $1,100
   b) $1,000
   c) $900
   d) $1,200

   Answer: b Difficulty: 3

70. What is the value on 1/1/85 of the following cash flows:

Date Cash Received	Amount of Cash
1/1/87	$100
1/1/88	$200
1/1/89	$100
1/1/90	$100
1/1/91	$100

   Use a 10% discount rate, and round your answer to the nearest $10.
   a) $490
   b) $460
   c) $420
   d) $450

   Answer: c Difficulty: 2

71. Consider the following cash flows:

Date Cash Received   Amount of Cash
    1/1/87 $100
    1/1/88 $100
    1/1/89 $500
    1/1/90 $100

What is the value on 1/1/85 of the above cash flows? Use an 8% discount rate and round your answer to the nearest $10.
a) $600
b) $620
c) $630
d) $650

Answer: a   Difficulty: 2

72. Charlie Stone wants to retire in 30 years, and he wants to have an annuity of $1000 a year for 20 years after retirement. Charlie wants to receive the first annuity payment at the end of the 30th year. Using an interest rate of 10%, how much must Charlie invest today in order to have his retirement annuity (round to nearest $10).
a) $500
b) $490
c) $540
d) $570

Answer: c   Difficulty: 2

73. It is January 1st and Darwin Davis has just established an IRA (Individual Retirement Account). Darwin will put $1000 into the account on December 31st of this year and at the end of each year for the following 39 years (40 years total). How much money will Darwin have in his account at the beginning of the 41st year? Assume that the account pays 12% interest compounded annually and round to nearest $1000.
a) $93,000
b) $766,000
c) $767,000
d) $850,000

Answer: d   Difficulty: 2

74. If you put $510 in a savings account at the beginning of each year for 30 years, how much money will be in the account at the end of the 30th year? Assume that the account earns 5% and round to the nearest $100.
a) $33,300
b) $32,300
c) $33,900
d) none of the above

Answer: d   Difficulty: 2

75. If you put $10 in a savings account at the beginning of each year for 11 years, how much money will be in the account at the end of the 11th year? Assume that the account earns 11% and round to the nearest $10.
    a) $220
    b) $200
    c) $190
    d) $180

    Answer: a Difficulty: 2

76. If you put $310 in a savings account at the beginning of each year for 10 years, how much money will be in the account at the end of the 10th year? Assume that the account earns 5.5% and round to the nearest $100.
    a) $3,800
    b) $3,900
    c) $4,000
    d) $4,200

    Answer: d Difficulty: 2

77. If you put $200 in a savings account at the beginning of each year for 10 years and then allow the account to compound for an additional 10 years, how much will be in the account at the end of the 20th year? Assume that the account earns 10% and round to the nearest $100.
    a) $8,300
    b) $9,100
    c) $8,900
    d) $9,700

    Answer: b Difficulty: 3

78. How much money must you pay into an account at the beginning of each of 30 years in order to have $10,000 at the end of the 30th year? Assume that the account pays 11% per annum, and round to the nearest $1.
    a) $39
    b) $46
    c) $50
    d) none of the above

    Answer: d Difficulty: 3

79. How much money must you pay into an account at the beginning of each of 20 years in order to have $10,000 at the end of the 20th year? Assume that the account pays 12% per annum, and round to the nearest $1.
    a) $1,195
    b) $111
    c) $124
    d) $139

    Answer: c Difficulty: 2

80. How much money must you pay into an account at the beginning of each of 5 years in order to have $5,000 at the end of the 5th year? Assume that the account pays 12% per year, and round to the nearest $10.
    a) $700
    b) $1,390
    c) $1,550
    d) $790

    Answer: a Difficulty: 2

81. How much money must you pay into an account at the beginning of each of 11 years in order to have $5,000 at the end of the 11th year? Assume that the account pays 8% per year, and round to the nearest $1.
    a) $700
    b) $257
    c) $300
    d) $278

    Answer: d Difficulty: 2

82. You are going to pay $800 into an account at the beginning of each of 20 years. The account will then be left to compound for an additional 20 years. At the end of the 41st year you will begin receiving a perpetuity from the account. If the account pays 14%, how much each year will you receive from the perpetuity (round to nearest $1,000)?
    a) $140,000
    b) $150,000
    c) $160,000
    d) $170,000

    Answer: c Difficulty: 3

83. You are going to pay $100 into an account at the beginning of each of the next 40 years. At the beginning of the 41st year you buy a 30 year annuity whose first payment comes at the end of the 41st year (the account pays 12%). How much money will be in the account at the end of year forty (nearest $1,000)?
    a) $77,000
    b) $86,000
    c) $69,000
    d) $93,000

    Answer: b Difficulty: 3

84. You are going to pay $100 into an account at the beginning of each of the next 40 years. At the beginning of the 41st year you buy a 30 year annuity whose first payment comes at the end of the 41st year (the account pays 12%). How much will you receive at the end of the 41st year (i.e. the first annuity payment). Round to nearest $100.
    a) $93,000
    b) $7,800
    c) $11,400
    d) $10,700

    Answer: d Difficulty: 3

85. A retirement plan guarantees to pay you or your estate a fixed amount for 20 years. At the time of retirement you will have $31,360 to your credit in the plan. The plan anticipates earning 8% interest annually over the period you receive benefits. How much will your annual benefits be assuming the first payment occurs 1 year from your retirement date?
    a) $682
    b) $6,272
    c) $2,000
    d) $3,194

    Answer: d Difficulty: 3

86. A 20-year bond pays 6% on a face value of $1,000. If similar bonds are currently yielding 8%, what is the market value of the bond?
    a) over $1,000
    b) under $1,000
    c) over $1,200
    d) over $1,300

    Answer: b Difficulty: 2

87. A bond maturing in 10 years pays $50 semi-annually and $1,000 upon maturity. Assuming 10% to be the appropriate market discount rate, what is the present value of the bond (round to nearest $10)?
    a) $1,010
    b) $925
    c) $880
    d) $1,000

    Answer: d Difficulty: 2

88. Amax Inc. deposited $2,000 in a bank account that pays 12% interest annually. What will the dollar amount be in four years?
    a) 2,800
    b) 3,100
    c) 3,111
    d) 3,148

    Answer: d Difficulty: 2

89. Amax Inc. deposited $2,000 in a bank account that pays 12% interest annually. What will the dollar amount be if the interest is compounded semi-annually for those four years?
    a) $3,100
    b) $3,188
    c) $3,248
    d) $3,290

    Answer: b Difficulty: 2

90. Amax Inc. deposited $2,000 in a bank account that pays 12% interest annually. How many periods would it take for the deposit to grow to $6,798 if the interest is compounded semi-annually?
    a) 17
    b) 19
    c) 21
    d) 25

    Answer: c Difficulty: 2

91. Amax Inc. deposited $2,000 in a bank account that pays 12% interest annually compounded semi-annually. How much money will be in the account at the end of 20 years?
    a) $20,571
    b) $20,704
    c) $20,900
    d) $21,113

    Answer: a Difficulty: 2

92. An investment is expected to yield $300 in three years, $500 in five years, and $300 in seven years. What is the present value of this investment if our opportunity rate is 5%?
    a) $735
    b) $865
    c) $885
    d) $900

    Answer: b Difficulty: 2

93. The time value of money is created by:
    a) the existence of profitable investment alternatives and interest rates
    b) the fact that the passing of time increases the value of money
    c) the elimination of the opportunity cost as a consideration
    d) the fact that the value of saving money for tomorrow could be more or less than spending it today

    Answer: a Difficulty: 2

94. All else constant, the future value of an investment will increase if:
    a) the investment involves more risk
    b) the investment is compounded for more years
    c) the investment is compounded at a higher interest rate
    d) both b and c

    Answer: d Difficulty: 2

95. To compound $100 quarterly for 20 years at 8%, we must use:
    a) 40 periods at 4%
    b) 5 periods at 12%
    c) 10 periods at 4%
    d) 80 periods at 2%

    Answer: d Difficulty: 2

96. How much money do I need to place into a bank account which pays a 6% rate in order to have $500 at the end of 7 years?
    a) $332.53
    b) $751.82
    c) $463.77
    d) $629.52

    Answer: a Difficulty: 2

97. Bobby's grandmother deposited $100 in a savings account for him when he was born. The money has been earning an annual rate of 12% interest, compounded quarterly for the last twenty five years. He is getting married and would like to take his new bride on a fabulous honeymoon. How much does he have in this account to use?
    a) $4,165
    b) $1,700
    c) $5,051
    d) $1,922

    Answer: d Difficulty: 2

98. George and Barbara will be retiring in four years and would like to buy a lakehouse. They estimate that they will need $150,000 at the end of four years to buy this house. They want to make four equal annual payments into an account at the end of each year. If they can earn 16% on their money, compounded annually, over the next four years, how much must they invest at the end of each year for the next four years to have accumulated $150,000 by retirement?
    a) $25,523
    b) $29,606
    c) $46,212
    d) $43,500
    e) $37,500

    Answer: b Difficulty: 2

99. You have been accepted to study gourmet cooking at the Cordon-Bleu Cooking School in Paris, France. You will need $15,000 every 6 months (beginning 6 months from now) for the next three years to cover tuition and living expenses. Mom and Dad have agreed to pay for your education. They want to make one deposit now in a bank account earning 6% interest, compounded semi-annually, so that you can withdraw $15,000 every 6 months for the next 3 years. How much must they deposit now?
    a) $97,026
    b) $73,760
    c) $90,000
    d) $81,258

    Answer: d Difficulty: 3

100. You bought a painting 10 years ago as an investment. You originally paid $85,000 for it. If you sold it for $484,050, what was your annual return on investment?
    a) 47%
    b) 4.7%
    c) 19%
    d) 12.8%

    Answer: c Difficulty: 2

101. Slick Corporation bonds have a coupon rate of 12%, paid semi-annually, a par value of $1,000, and mature at the end of 20 years. What is the current price on this bond if its yield to maturity is 10%?
    a) $850
    b) $1,172
    c) $608
    d) $1,133

    Answer: b Difficulty: 2

102. You are thinking of buying a miniature golf course. It is expected to generate cash flows of $40,000 per year in years 1 through 4 and $50,000 per year in years 5 through 8. If the appropriate discount rate is 10%, what is the present value of these cash flows?
    a) $285,288
    b) $167,943
    c) $235,048
    d) $828,230

    Answer: c Difficulty: 3

103. You have been depositing money at the end of each year into an account drawing 8% interest. What is the balance in the account at the end of year four if you deposited the following amounts?

Year	End of Year Deposit
1	$350
2	$500
3	$725
4	$400

a) $1,622
b) $2,207
c) $2,384
d) $2,687

Answer: b Difficulty: 3

104. Horace and Myrtle want to buy a house. Their banker offered them a fully amortizing $95,000 loan at a 12% annual rate for 20 years. What will their monthly payment be if they make equal <u>monthly</u> installments over the next 20 years?
a) $1,046
b) $749
c) $8,722
d) $1,346

Answer: a Difficulty: 2

105. You are considering the purchase of XYZ Company's perpetual preferred stock which pays a perpetual annual dividend of $8 per share. If the appropriate discount rate for this investment is 14%, what is the price of one share of this stock?
a) $7.02
b) $57.14
c) $36.43
d) Cannot be determined without maturity date.

Answer: b Difficulty: 2

106. You bought a race horse which has had a winning streak for four years, bringing in $500,000 per year before dying of a heart attack. If you paid $1,518,675 for the horse 4 years ago, what was your annual return over this 4 year period?
a) 8%
b) 33%
c) 18%
d) 12%

Answer: d Difficulty: 2

107. You deposit $500 in a savings account earning an 8% annual rate compounded semi-annually. How much will you have in your account at the end of five years?
a) $743
b) $544
c) $625
d) $680

Answer: a Difficulty: 2

108. You want to travel to Europe to visit relatives when you graduate from college three years from now. The trip is expected to cost a total of $10,000 at that time. Your parents have deposited $5,000 for you in a CD paying 6% interest annually, maturing three years from now. Aunt Hilda has agreed to finance the balance. If you are going to put Aunt Hilda's gift in an investment earning 10% over the next three years, how much must she deposit now, so you can visit your relatives at the end of three years?
a) $3,757
b) $3,039
c) $5,801
d) $3,345

Answer: b Difficulty: 3

109. As a part of your savings plan at work, you have been depositing $250 per quarter in a savings account earning 8% interest compounded quarterly for the last ten years. You will retire in 15 years and want to increase your contribution each year from $1,000 to $2,000 per year, by increasing your contribution every four months from $250 to $500. Additionally, you have just inherited $10,000, which you plan to invest now to earn interest at 12% compounded annually for the next 15 years. How much money will you have in savings when you retire 15 years from now?
a) $126,862
b) $73,012
c) $161,307
d) $194,415

Answer: c Difficulty: 3

110. Ronald Slump purchased a real estate investment with the following end of year cash flows.

Year	EOY Cash Flow
1	200
2	-350
3	-430
4	950

What is the PV of these cash flows if the appropriate discount rate is 20%?
a) 178
b) 160
c) 133
d) 767

Answer: c Difficulty: 3

111. You have just won a magazine sweepstakes and have a choice between three alternatives. You can get $100,000 now, or $10,000 per year in perpetuity, or $50,000 now and $150,000 at the end of 10 years. If the appropriate discount rate is 12%, which option should you choose?
a) $100,000 now
b) $10,000 in perpetuity
c) $50,000 now and $150,000 in 10 years

Answer: a Difficulty: 3

112. You buy a zero coupon bond which pays no annual coupon interest payments. It matures at the end of five years with a face value (par) of $1,000. What is the current price on the bond if it is priced to yield 8%?
a) $1,000
b) $1,469
c) $80
d) $681

Answer: d Difficulty: 2

113. Harry just bought a new Jeep Cherokee four wheel drive for his lumber business. The price of the vehicle was $35,000 of which he made a $5,000 downpayment and took out an amortized loan for the rest. His local bank made the loan at 12% interest for five years. He is to pay back the principal and interest in five equal annual installments beginning one year from now. Determine the amount of Harry's annual payment.
a) $8,322
b) $9,600
c) $9,709
d) $6,720

Answer: a Difficulty: 3

114. Middletown USA currently has a population of 1.5 million people. It has been one of the fastest growing cities in the nation, growing by an average of 4% per year for the last five years. If this city's population continues to grow at 4% per year, what will the population be 10 years from now?
    a) 1,560,000
    b) 2,220,366
    c) 2,100,000
    d) 1,824,979

    Answer: b Difficulty: 2

115. You have $1,000 you don't need for 1 year. You can get a certificate of deposit paying 8% compounded quarterly or a savings bond paying 8 1/8% compounded annually. Which alternative should you take?
    a) 8 1/8% compounded annually
    b) 8% compounded quarterly
    c) They are both equal.

    Answer: b Difficulty: 2

116. You deposit $5,000 today in an account drawing 12% compounded quarterly. How much will you have in the account at the end of 2 1/2 years?
    a) $7,401
    b) $5,523
    c) $7,128
    d) $6,720

    Answer: d Difficulty: 3

ESSAY

117. If you deposit $1,000 each year in a savings account earning 4 percent compounded annually, how much will you have in 10 years?

    Answer:

    $FV_{10} = \$1,000(12.006) = \$12,006$
    Difficulty: 2

118. If you have an opportunity cost of 10 percent, how much are you willing to invest each year to have $4,000 accumulated in 10 years?

    Answer:

    $\$4,000 = A(15.937)$
    $A = \$250.99$
    Difficulty: 2

119. Consider an investment that has cash flows of $500 the first year and $400 for the next 4 years. If your opportunity cost is 10 percent, how much is this investment worth to you?

Answer:

$$PV = \$500(.909) \qquad = \$454.50$$
$$PV = \$400(3.170)(.909) = 1,152.61$$
$$\phantom{PV = \$400(3.170)(.909) = }\$1,607.11$$

Difficulty: 2

120. Your bank has agreed to loan you $3,000 if you agree to pay a lump sum of $5,775 in 5 years. What annual rate of interest will you be paying?

Answer:

$$FVIF_{?\ \%,\ 5\ yr}\ \$3,000 = \$5,775$$
$$FVIF_{?\ \%,\ 5\ yr} = \$5,775$$
$$i = 14\%$$

Difficulty: 2

121. If your opportunity cost is 12 percent, how much will you pay for a bond that pays $100 per year forever?

Answer: $PV = \$100/.12 = \$833.33$ Difficulty: 2

122. If you invest $450 today and it increases to $6,185 at the end of 20 years, what rate of return have you earned?

Answer:

$$\$6,185 = \$450\ FVIF_{?\ \%,\ 20\ yr}$$
$$13.743 = FVIF_{?\ \%,\ 20\ yr}$$
$$i = 14\%$$

Difficulty: 2

123. If your opportunity cost is 10 percent, how much are you willing to pay for an investment promising $750 per year for the first four years and $450 for the next six years?

Answer:

$$PV = \$750(3.17) \qquad = \$2,377.50$$
$$PV = \$450(4.355)(.683) = 1,338.51$$
$$\phantom{PV = \$450(4.355)(.683) = }\$3,716.01$$

Difficulty: 2

124. You have just received an endowment of $32,976. You plan to put the entire amount in an account earning 8 percent compounded annually and to withdraw $4000 at the end of each year. How many years can you continue to make the withdrawals?

Answer:

$32,976 = $4,000 \text{ PVIFA}_{8\%, \ ? \ yr}$
$8.244 = \text{PVIFA}_{8\%, \ ? \ yr}$
14 years

Difficulty: 2

125. Earnings per share for XYZ, INC. grew constantly from $7.99 in 1974 to $12.68 in 1980. What was the compound annual growth rate in earnings-per-share over the period?

Answer:

$ 12.68 = $7.99 \text{ FVIF}_{? \ \%, \ 6 \ yr}$
$1.587 = \text{FVIF}_{? \ \%, \ 6 \ yr}$
$g = 8\%$

Difficulty: 2

126. To repay a $2,000 loan from your bank, you promise to make equal payments every six months for the next five years totaling $3,116.20. What annual rate of interest will you be paying?

Answer:

Total payments of $3,116.20 indicates that each payment is $311.62.
$2,000 = $311.62

$\text{PVIFA}_{? \ \%, \ 10 \ periods}$
$6.418 = \text{PVIFA}_{? \ \%, \ 10 \ periods}$
$i = 9\%$

Annual interest rate = $(.09)(2) = .18$

Difficulty: 2

127. You have been offered the opportunity to invest in a project which will pay $1,000 per year at the end of years one through 10 and $2,000 per year at the end of years 21 through 30. If the appropriate discount rate is 8 percent, what is the present value of this cash flow pattern?

Answer:

Present value of
$1,000 per year for
years 1 through 10 = $1,000(6.710) = $6,710   i = 8%

Value in year 20 of annuity of
$2,000 per year for years 21 through 30 = $2,000(6.710) = $13,420

Present value of annuity of $2,000 per
year for years 21 through 30 = $13,420(.215) = $2,885.30

Total present value = $6,710 + $2,885.30 = $9,595.30
Difficulty: 3

128. You are saving money to buy a house. You will need $7,473.50 to make the down payment. If you can deposit $500 per month in a savings account which pays 1 percent per month, how long will it take you to save the $7,473.50?

Answer:

$7,473.50 = \$500 \text{ FVIFA}_{1\%, \text{ n periods}}$
$14.947 = \text{FVIFA}_{1\%, \text{ n periods}}$
$n = 14 \text{ months}$

Difficulty: 3

129. You are currently making annual payments to a local bank of $1,200 per year. Your loan with the bank has a remaining life of 5 years. The interest rate on the loan is 15 percent per year. If you decide to repay the entire loan today, how much would you pay the bank?

Answer:

$PV = \$1,200 \text{ PVIFA}_{15\%, \text{ 5 yr}}$
$= \$1,200 (3.352) = \$4,022.40$
Difficulty: 2

130. You are considering purchasing common stock in AMZ Corporation. You anticipate that the company will pay dividends of $5.00 per share next year and $7.50 per share in the following year. You also believe that you can sell the common stock two years from now for $30.00 per share. If you require a 14 percent rate of return on this investment, what is the maximum price that you would be willing to pay for a share of AMZ common stock?

Answer:

$$PV = \$5.00 \ PVIF_{14\%, \ 1 \ yr} + (\$7.50 + \$30.00) \ PVIF_{14\%, \ 2 \ yr}$$
$$= \$5.00 \ (.877) + (\$37.50)(.769)$$
$$= \$33.22$$

Difficulty: 3

131. You are planning to sell a corporate bond which has three years to maturity. The bond has a face value of $5,000 and has a 10 percent coupon rate. Interest is paid semi-annually. What is the selling price for this bond if the market discount rate is 8 percent compounded semi-annually?

Answer:

Semiannual interest payments = $(.10)(\$5,000)(.5) = \$250$
Price of bond = $\$250 \ PVIFA_{4\%, 6 \ periods} + \$5,000 \ PVIF_{4\%, 6 \ periods}$
$$= \$250(5.242) + \$5,000(.79)$$
$$= \$1,310.50 + \$3,950 = \$5,260.50$$

Difficulty: 2

132. If you deposit $700 today into a bank account, how much will you have in 4.5 years if the account pays 12 percent interest compounded quarterly?

Answer:

$$FV = \$700 \ FVIF_{3\%, \ 18 \ periods}$$
$$= \$700(1.702) = \$1,191.40$$

Difficulty: 2

133. You are planning to deposit $10,000 today into a bank account. Five years from today you expect to withdraw $7,500. If the account pays 5 percent interest per year, how much will remain in the account eight years from today?

Answer:

FV = $10,000 FVIF$_{5\%, 5 yr}$
   = $10,000(1.276) = $12,760

Amount to invest in remaining 3 years = $12,760 - $7,500 = $5,260

FV = $5,260 FVIF$_{5\%, 3 yr}$
   = $5,260(1.158) = $6,091.08

Difficulty: 3

134. Fred borrowed $10,000 from a local finance company. He is required to pay $2,191 per year for seven years. What is the annual interest rate on the loan?

Answer:

$10,000 = $2,191 PVIFA$_{? \%, 7 yr}$
$\frac{\$10,000}{\$2,191}$ = 4.564 = PVIFA$_{? \%, 7 yr}$ i = 12%

Difficulty: 2

135. Suppose you are 40 years old and plan to retire in exactly 20 years. Twenty-one years from now you will need to withdraw $5,000 per year from a retirement fund to supplement your social security payments. You expect to live to the age of 85. How much money should you place in the retirement fund each year for the next 20 years to reach your retirement goal if you can earn 12 percent interest per year from the fund?

Answer:

Amount in fund at age 60 = $5,000 'PVIFA' sub '12%, 25 yr'
                         = $5,000(7.843) = $39,215

$39,215 = (annual contribution) 'FVIFA' sub '12%, 20 yr'

$39,215 = (annual contribution) (72.052)

annual contribution = $39,215/72.052 = $544.26

Difficulty: 3

136. You have just purchased a car from "Friendly Sam." The selling price of the car is $6,500. If you pay $500 down, then your monthly payments are $317.22. The annual interest rate is 24 percent. How many payments must you make?

Answer:
$ 6,000 = $317.22 $\text{PVIFA}_{2\%, \text{ ? periods}}$ n = 24 months
18.914 = $\text{PVIFA}_{2\%, \text{ ? periods}}$
Difficulty: 2

137. An investment will pay $500 in three years, $700 in five years and $1000 in nine years. If your opportunity rate is 6%, what is the present value of this investment?

Answer:

$\text{PV} = 500(1/(1.06)^3) + 700(1/(1.06)^5) + 1000(1/(1.06)^9)$
$\text{PV} = 500(.840) + 700(.747) + 1000(.592)$
$= 420.00 + 522.90 + 592.00$
$= \$1,534.90$

Difficulty: 3

138. a. If Sparco Inc. deposits $150 at the end of each year for the next eight years in an account that pays 5% interest, how much money will Sparco have at the end of eight years?

    b. Suppose Sparco decides that they need to have $5,300 at the end of the eight years. How much will they have to deposit at the end of each year?

Answer:

a. FV = 150 (9.549)
    = $1,432.35

b. 5300 = A(9.549)
    A = $555.03

Difficulty: 2

105

139. What is the value (price) of a bond that pays $400 semi-annually for ten years and returns $10,000 at the end of ten years? The market discount rate is 10% paid semi-annually.

Answer:

$$\text{Bond value} = 400 \left[\sum_{t=1}^{20} \frac{1}{(1 + .05)^t} \right] + 10,000 \left[\frac{1}{(1 + .05)^{20}} \right]$$

= 400 [12.462] + 10.000 [.377]
= 4984.80 + 3770 = $8754.80

Difficulty: 2

140. Frank Zanca is considering three different investments that his broker has offered to him. The different cash flows are as follows:

End of Year	A	B	C
1	300		400
2	300		
3	300		
4	300	300	600
5		300	
6		300	
7		300	
8	300	600	

Because Frank only has enough savings for one investment, his broker has proposed the third alternative to be, according to his expertise, "the best in town." However, Frank questions his broker and wants to eliminate the present value of each investment. Assuming a 15% discount rate, what is Frank's best alternative?

Answer:

Investment A
PV = $300 pymt, 4 years, 15%
PV = $856.49

Investment B
PV = $300 pymt beginning at the end of the fourth year, 5 years, 15%
PV = $1,346.2 - $684.97
PV = $661.23

Investment C
PV = ($400, 1 year, 15%) + ($600, 4 years 15%) + ($600, 8 years, 15%)
PV = $348 + $343.05 + $196.14
PV = $887.19

Thus, investment C is the best as it has the highest NPV.

Difficulty: 2

141. What is the present value of the following perpetuities?

   a. $600 discounted at 7%
   b. $450 discounted at 12%
   c. $1,000 discounted at 6%
   d. $880 discounted at 9%

   Answer:

   a. PV = $600/.07
      PV = $8,571.43

   b. PV = $450/.12
      PV = $3,750

   c. PV = $1,000/.06
      PV = $16,666.67

   d. PV = $880/.09
      PV = $9,777.78

   Difficulty: 3

142. Leigh Delight Candy, Inc. is choosing between two bonds in which to invest their cash. One is being offered from Hershey's and will mature in 10 years that pays 12% per year compounded quarterly. The other alternative is a Mars' bond that will mature in 20 years that pays 12% per year compounded quarterly. What would be the present value of each bond if the discount rate is 10%?

   Answer:

   Bond A
   PV = $1,000, 10 years, 12% interest compounded quarterly, 10% discount rate
   PV = $1,125.51

   Bond B
   PV = $1,000, 20 years, 12% interest compounded quarterly, 10% discount rate
   PV = $1,172.26

   Difficulty: 3

143. In order to send your oldest child to Law School when the time comes, you want to accumulate $40,000 at the end of 18 years. Assuming that your savings account will pay 6% compounded annually, how much would you have to deposit if:
    a. you want to deposit an amount annually at the end of each year?
    b. you want to deposit one large lump sum today?

Answer:

$40,000, 18 years, 6%

a. Pymt   = $1,294.26

b. Pymt   = $14,019.75

Difficulty: 2

Chapter 6: Valuation & Characteristics of Fixed Income Securities

TRUE/FALSE

1. So long as a bond sells for an amount above its par value, the coupon interest rate and yield to maturity remain equal.

   Answer: False Difficulty: 1

2. Bonds generally have a maturity date while preferred stocks do not.

   Answer: True Difficulty: 1

3. Bond prices decrease when market interest rates increase.

   Answer: True Difficulty: 1

4. The liquidation value of an asset is determined from the firm's overall market value.

   Answer: False Difficulty: 1

5. Book value represents the sum of an asset's market value and liquidation value.

   Answer: False Difficulty: 1

6. If a firm went out of business and sold its assets to the highest bidder, the sale price of those assets would be equal to their book value.

   Answer: False Difficulty: 1

7. An efficient market may be defined as one in which the values of all securities at any instant in time fully reflect all available information.

   Answer: True Difficulty: 1

8. Unlike market value, the intrinsic value of an asset is estimated independently of risk.

   Answer: False Difficulty: 1

9. The par value of a corporate bond indicates the level of interest payments that will be paid to investors.

   Answer: False Difficulty: 1

10. When referring to bonds, expected rate of return and yield to maturity are often used interchangeably.

    Answer: True Difficulty: 1

11. The present value of an investment's expected future cash flows is also known as the intrinsic value.

    Answer: True Difficulty: 1

12. The intrinsic value should necessarily be below the market value in order to make it desirable in the eyes of an investor.

    Answer: False Difficulty: 2

13. The dollars of interest a bond pays is found by multiplying the bond's coupon rate by its par value.

    Answer: True Difficulty: 2

14. An indenture contains the current yield at which a bond will sell.

    Answer: False Difficulty: 2

15. Yield to maturity is a bond's internal rate of return.

    Answer: True Difficulty: 2

16. As the riskless rate of interest fluctuates, approximately parallel movement in the yields of corporate bonds can be expected.

    Answer: True Difficulty: 1

17. A mortgage bond is secured by a lien on real property.

    Answer: True Difficulty: 1

18. One way to obtain a continuous source of debt financing is through a sinking fund.

    Answer: False Difficulty: 1

19. Bonds with the highest bond rating have the least risk.

    Answer: False Difficulty: 1

20. The highest rating that a bond can have is AAA.

    Answer: True Difficulty: 1

21. A bond rating of A is lower than a bond rating of AA.

   Answer: True Difficulty: 1

22. A bond's call provision offers an advantage to the firm's bondholders but not to the firm's stockholders.

   Answer: False Difficulty: 1

23. A bond is any long term promissory note issued by the firm.

   Answer: True Difficulty: 1

24. The yield-to-maturity is the discount rate that equates the present value of the interest and principal payments with the face value of the bond.

   Answer: False Difficulty: 1

25. Bond ratings are favorably affected by a little use of subordinated debt.

   Answer: True Difficulty: 1

26. The less risky the bond, or the higher the bond rating, the lower will be the yield on the bond.

   Answer: True Difficulty: 1

27. In the case of insolvency, the claims of debt are honored prior to those of both common and preferred stock.

   Answer: True Difficulty: 1

28. The main difference between a debenture bond and an indenture bond is that the former is unsecured, but the latter is secured by future income.

   Answer: False Difficulty: 1

29. When investors require a call provision, it causes the issuing price of a bond to be higher than would otherwise be the case.

   Answer: False Difficulty: 2

30. Different bonds can have different maturities.

   Answer: True Difficulty: 1

31. An incentive is only valid for five years.

    Answer: False   Difficulty: 2

32. Zero coupon bonds allow a firm to delay principal repayment for many years, but because of the absence of interest a firm realizes no tax benefits from issuing the securities.

    Answer: False   Difficulty: 2

33. The presence of a sinking fund means that a firm must repay a certain amount of principal each year; this increases the risk and lowers the price of a bond issue.

    Answer: False   Difficulty: 1

34. Par value is the present value of all future cash flows due to be received from a bond.

    Answer: False   Difficulty: 1

35. The yield to maturity is simply a bond's coupon rate.

    Answer: False   Difficulty: 2

36. The yield to maturity is the discount rate that equates the present value of the interest and principal payments with the current market price of the bond.

    Answer: True   Difficulty: 2

37. A firm's bond rating would be favorably affected if they have a low use of financial leverage.

    Answer: True   Difficulty: 1

38. The term debenture applies to any long-term debt -- secured or unsecured.

    Answer: False   Difficulty: 2

39. The coupon interest rate refers to the ratio of the annual interest payment on the bond's market price.

    Answer: False   Difficulty: 2

40. A disadvantage of junk bonds is that they are not callable and can only be retired at maturity.

    Answer: False   Difficulty: 1

MULTIPLE CHOICE

41. The yield to maturity on a bond:
    a) is fixed in the indenture
    b) is lower for higher risk bonds
    c) is the required return on the bond
    d) is generally equal to the coupon interest rate

    Answer: c Difficulty: 1

42. A $1,000 par value 10-year bond with a 10 percent coupon rate recently sold for $900. The yield to maturity is:
    a) 10 percent
    b) greater than 10 percent
    c) less than 10 percent
    d) cannot be determined

    Answer: b Difficulty: 2

43. All of the following affect the value of a bond except:
    a) investors' required rate of return
    b) the recorded value of the firm's assets
    c) the coupon rate of interest
    d) the maturity date of the bond

    Answer: b Difficulty: 1

44. In an efficient securities market the market value of a security is equal to:
    a) its liquidation value
    b) its book value
    c) its intrinsic value
    d) none of the above

    Answer: c Difficulty: 1

45. The liquidation value of a firm is equal to:
    a) the firm's net worth
    b) the firm's value as an ongoing concern
    c) the book value of its plant and equipment
    d) none of the above

    Answer: d Difficulty: 1

46. The interest on corporate bonds is typically paid:
    a) semi-annually
    b) annually
    c) quarterly
    d) monthly

    Answer: a Difficulty: 1

47. If the market price of a bond decreases, then:
    a) the yield to maturity decreases
    b) the coupon rate increases
    c) the yield to maturity increases
    d) b and c

Answer: c Difficulty: 2

48. What is the name given to the value placed on an asset based upon the future cash flows to be realized from the investment, the investors required rates of return, and the riskiness of the asset?
    a) book value
    b) liquidation value
    c) market value
    d) intrinsic value

Answer: d Difficulty: 2

49. Market efficiency implies which of the following?
    a) book value = liquidation value
    b) book value = market value
    c) liquidation value = market value
    d) none of the above

Answer: d Difficulty: 1

50. Market efficiency implies which of the following?
    a) book value = intrinsic value
    b) market value = intrinsic value
    c) book value = market value
    d) liquidation value = book value

Answer: b Difficulty: 1

51. Which of the following affect an asset's value to an investor?
    I. Amount of an asset's expected cash flow
    II. The riskiness of the cash flows
    III. Timing of an asset's cash flows
    IV. Investor's required rate of return
    a) I, II, III
    b) I, III, IV
    c) I, II, IV
    d) I, II, III, IV

Answer: d Difficulty: 2

52. What is the yield to maturity of a 9 year bond that pays a coupon rate of 20% per year, has a $1,000 par value, and is currently priced at $1,407? Round your answer to the nearest whole percent and assume annual coupon payments.
    a) 5%
    b) 14%
    c) 12%
    d) 11%

    Answer: c Difficulty: 2

53. What is the expected rate of return on a bond that matures in 7 years, has a par value of $1,000, a coupon rate of 14%, and is currently selling for $911? Round your answer to the nearest whole percent, and assume annual coupon payments.
    a) 15%
    b) 14%
    c) 2%
    d) 16%

    Answer: d Difficulty: 2

54. What is the expected rate of return on a bond that pays a coupon rate of 9%, has a par value of $1,000, matures in 5 years, and is currently selling for $714? Round your answer to the nearest whole percent, and assume annual coupon payments.
    a) 18%
    b) 13%
    c) 16%
    d) 17%

    Answer: a Difficulty: 2

55. What is the value of a bond that has a par value of $1,000, a coupon of $80 (annually), and matures in 11 years? Assume a required rate of return of 11%, and round your answer to the nearest $10.
    a) $320
    b) $500
    c) $810
    d) $790

    Answer: c Difficulty: 2

56. What is the value of a bond that matures in 60 years, has an annual coupon rate of $60, and a par value of $1,000? Assume a required rate of return of 12%, and round your answer to the nearest $10.
    a) $410
    b) $490
    c) $500
    d) $520

    Answer: c Difficulty: 2

57. What is the value of a bond that matures in 3 years, has an annual coupon rate of $110, and a par value of $1,000? Assume a required rate of return of 11%, and round your answer to the nearest $10.
    a) $970
    b) $1,330
    c) $330
    d) $1,000

    Answer: d Difficulty: 2

58. Which type of value is shown on the firm's balance sheet?
    a) book value
    b) liquidation value
    c) market value
    d) intrinsic value

    Answer: a Difficulty: 1

59. When the intrinsic value of an asset exceeds the market value
    a) the asset is undervalued to the investor
    b) the asset is overvalued to the investor
    c) market value and intrinsic value are the same; therefore, this could not happen

    Answer: a Difficulty: 1

60. In terms of interest rate risk, long-term government bonds have become as risky as:
    a) corporate bonds
    b) intermediate-term government bonds
    c) U.S. Treasury Bills
    d) common stock of large companies

    Answer: a Difficulty: 2

61. The present value of the expected future cash flows of an asset represent the asset's _____.
    a) liquidation value
    b) book value
    c) intrinsic value
    d) par value

    Answer: c Difficulty: 2

62. As interest rates, and consequently investors' required rates of return, change over time the _____ of outstanding bonds will also change.
    a) maturity date
    b) coupon interest payment
    c) par value
    d) price

    Answer: d Difficulty: 2

63. Zoro Sword Company bonds pay an annual coupon of 9 1/2%. They have 8 years to maturity and face value, or par, of $1,000. Compute the value of Zoro bonds if investors' required rate of return is 10%.
   a) $1,516.18
   b) $973.33
   c) $1,027.17
   d) $950.00

   Answer: b Difficulty: 2

64. Cassel Corp. bonds pays an annual coupon rate of 10%. If investors' required rate of return is now 8% on these bonds, they will be priced at:
   a) Par value
   b) A premium to par value
   c) A discount to par value
   d) Cannot be determined from information given

   Answer: b Difficulty: 2

65. Terminator Bug Company bonds have a 14% coupon rate. Interest is paid semi-annually. The bonds have a par value of $1,000 and will mature 10 years from now. Compute the value of Terminator Bonds if investors' required rate of return is 12%.
   a) $1,114.70
   b) $1,149.39
   c) $894.06
   d) $1,000.00

   Answer: a Difficulty: 2

66. Odor Eaters Corporation bonds are currently priced at $953.77. They have a par value of $1,000 and 6 years to maturity. They pay an annual coupon rate of 7%. Compute the required return on this bond or yield to maturity.
   a) 4%
   b) 6 1/2%
   c) 19%
   d) 8%

   Answer: d Difficulty: 2

67. Cowtown Cellular bonds mature in 1 1/2 years with a face value of $1,000. They pay a coupon rate of 12% distributed semi-annually. If the required rate of return on these bonds is 14% what is the bond's value?
   a) $1,026.73
   b) $973.76
   c) $1,022.74
   d) $814.26

   Answer: b Difficulty: 2

68. The yield to maturity on long-term debt:
    a) can never equal the current yield
    b) is the coupon rate on the bond
    c) is the net present value of the bond
    d) is the internal rate of return on the bond

    Answer: d Difficulty: 2

69. A bond's yield to maturity depends upon:
    a) the bond rating
    b) the maturity of the bond
    c) the coupon rate
    d) all of the above

    Answer: d Difficulty: 2

70. A bond indenture:
    a) contains the provisions of the security agreement
    b) states the bond's current rating
    c) states the yield to maturity of the bond
    d) all of the above

    Answer: a Difficulty: 2

71. A sinking fund:
    a) is beneficial to bondholders
    b) is set up by firms about to issue common stock through a rights offering
    c) provides for the refunding of outstanding bonds
    d) a and c

    Answer: d Difficulty: 2

72. Which of the following bonds provides the least protection to bondholders?
    a) zero coupon bonds
    b) mortgage bonds
    c) income bonds
    d) treasury bonds

    Answer: c Difficulty: 2

73. Which of the following organizations rate bonds?
    a) Moody's
    b) Dun and Bradstreet
    c) Robert Morris Associates
    d) all of the above

    Answer: a Difficulty: 2

ESSAY

74. Triangle bonds' par value is $1,000. The bonds pay $60 in interest every six months and will mature in 10 years.

    a. Calculate the price if the yield to maturity on the bonds is 14 percent.

    b. Explain the impact on price if the required rate of return decreases.

Answer:

a. $P^o = \$60(10.594) + \$1,000(0.258) = \$893.64$

b. The price of the bond will increase.

Difficulty: 2

75. BCD's $1,000 par value bonds currently sell for $798.50. The coupon rate is 10 percent, paid semi-annually. If the bonds have 5 years before maturity, what is the yield to maturity or expected rate of return?

Answer:

$\$798.50 = \$50(PVFA) + \$1,000(PVIF)$

By trial and error try 8 percent.

$\$798.50 = \$50 \times 6.710 + \$1,000 \times .463$

$\$798.50 = \$798.50$

Yield to maturity = $(.08)(2) = .16$
Difficulty: 2

76. If you are willing to pay $1,392.05 for a 15-year $1,000 par value bond that pays 10 percent interest semi-annually, what is your expected rate of return?

Answer:

Try 3 percent

$\$1,392.05 = \$50 \times 19.601 + \$1,000 \times 0.412$

Required rate of return = $(.03)(2) = .06$
Difficulty: 3

77. Vertex bonds have a maturity value of $1,000. The bonds carry a coupon rate of 14 percent. Interest is paid semi-annually. The bonds will mature in seven years. If the current market price is $1,092.65, what is the yield to maturity on the bond?

Answer:
$$\$1,092.65 = \$70 \text{ PVIFH}_{R,14} + \$1,000 \text{ PVIF}_{R,14}$$

$R = 6.00\%$

Yield to maturity = 12.00%

Difficulty: 3

78. DAH, Inc. has issued a 12% bond that is to mature in 9 years. The bond had a $1,000 par value and interest is due to be paid semi-annually. If your required rate of return is 10%, what price would you be willing to pay for the bond?

Answer:

$V = 60(11.69) + 1000(.416)$
$V = 701.40 + 416$
$V = \$1117.40$

Difficulty: 3

79. Calculate the value of a bond that is expected to mature in 13 years with a $1,000 face value. The interest coupon rate is 8%, and the required rate of return is 10%. Interest is paid annually.

Answer:

V = PV of interest payments as an annuity + PV of maturity value.
$V = 568.27 + 289.66$
$V = \$857.93$

Difficulty: 3

Chapter 7: Valuation and Characteristics of Common Stock

TRUE/FALSE

1. A firm's common equity as reported in its balance sheet determines the market price of that firm's common stock.

   Answer: False Difficulty: 1

2. Common stock cannot be worth less than its book value.

   Answer: False Difficulty: 1

3. A security's value equals the compound value of dividends investors expect to receive.

   Answer: False Difficulty: 1

4. The higher the expected growth in dividends for a share of common stock, the lower its required rate of return.

   Answer: False Difficulty: 1

5. The stock valuation model $D_1/(R_c - g)$ requires $R_c > G$.

   Answer: True Difficulty: 1

6. When a firm decides to retain a portion of its earnings, the stockholders are indirectly investing in the firm.

   Answer: True Difficulty: 1

7. While cash flows are quite important in the valuation of common stock, it matters little in bond valuation since the coupon interest rate is known.

   Answer: False Difficulty: 1

8. The common stock of a non-growth firm is valued in the same manner as its preferred stock.

   Answer: True Difficulty: 2

9. Common stock does not mature.

   Answer: True Difficulty: 1

10. Like common stock, preferred stock pays a dividend that varies with earnings.

    Answer: False Difficulty: 1

11. Preferred stock has priority over common stock with respect to its claims on income for dividends.

    Answer: True Difficulty: 1

12. A call provision allows the issuing firm to take advantage of rising interest rates.

    Answer: False Difficulty: 1

13. Common stock represents ownership of the firm.

    Answer: True Difficulty: 1

14. Preferred shareholders have preemptive rights which allow them to receive a stated dividend before common stockholders are paid.

    Answer: False Difficulty: 1

15. If a firm does not have enough money to pay any common stock dividends, it is technically in default to the common shareholders.

    Answer: False Difficulty: 1

16. A call provision on common stock helps allow management to avoid proxy fights.

    Answer: False Difficulty: 1

17. Common stock has priority over preferred stock in regard to a claim on assets in the instance of a firm's bankruptcy.

    Answer: False Difficulty: 1

18. Preferred stock is considered riskier than corporate bonds.

    Answer: True Difficulty: 1

19. Common stockholders have priority over both the preferred stockholders and bond owners in the case of a firm's bankruptcy.

    Answer: False Difficulty: 1

MULTIPLE CHOICE

20. Preferred stock valuation usually treats the preferred stock as a:
    a) capital asset
    b) perpetuity
    c) common stock
    d) long-term bond

    Answer: b Difficulty: 1

21. All of the following affect the value of a share of common stock except:
    a) the par value of stock
    b) the risk-free rate
    c) the future growth in dividends
    d) the future dividends

    Answer: a Difficulty: 1

22. The XYZ Company, whose common stock is currently selling for $40 per share, is expected to pay a $2.00 dividend in the coming year. If investors believe that the expected rate of return on XYZ is 14 percent, what growth rate in dividends must be expected?
    a) 5 percent
    b) 14 percent
    c) 9 percent
    d) 6 percent

    Answer: c Difficulty: 2

23. The expected rate of return on a share of common stock whose dividends are growing at a constant rate (g) is which of the following?
    a) $(D_1 + g)/Vc$
    b) D_1/Vc
    c) D_1/g
    d) none of the above

    Answer: d Difficulty: 1

24. Style Corp. preferred stock pays $3.15. What is the value of the stock if your required rate of return is 8.5% (round your answer to the nearest $1, and assume no transaction costs).
    a) $33
    b) $23
    c) $27
    d) $37

    Answer: d Difficulty: 1

25. Solitron Manufacturing Company preferred stock is selling for $14. If it has a yearly dividend of $1, what is your expected rate of return if you purchase the stock at its market price (round your answer to the nearest 1% and assume no transaction costs)?
    a) 25.0%
    b) 14.2%
    c) 7.1%
    d) 9.3%

    Answer: c Difficulty: 1

26. Bell Corp. has a preferred stock that pays a dividend of $2.40. If you are willing to purchase the stock at $11 or below, what is your required rate of return (round your answer to the nearest .1% and assume that there are no transaction costs)?
    a) 21.8%
    b) 11.0%
    c) 9.1%
    d) 20.1%

    Answer: a Difficulty: 1

27. What is the value of a preferred stock that pays a $2.10 dividend to an investor with a required rate of return of 11% (round your answer to the nearest $1)?
    a) $19
    b) $23
    c) $17
    d) $21

    Answer: a Difficulty: 1

28. How is preferred stock affected by a decrease in the required rate of return?
    a) the value of a share of preferred stock decreases
    b) the dividend increases
    c) the dividend decreases
    d) none of the above

    Answer: d Difficulty: 1

29. An example of the growth factor in common stock is:
    a) acquiring a loan to fund an investment in East Germany
    b) retaining profits in order to reinvest into the firm
    c) issuing new stock to provide capital for future growth
    d) two strong companies merging together to increase their economy of scale

    Answer: b Difficulty: 2

30. Preferred stock is similar to a bond in the following way:
    a) preferred stock always contains a maturity date
    b) both investments provide a constant income
    c) both contain a growth factor similar to common stock
    d) none of the above

    Answer: b Difficulty: 1

31. The common stockholders are most concerned with:
    a) the percentage of profits retained
    b) the size of the firm's beginning earnings per share
    c) the riskiness of the investment
    d) the spread between the return generated on new investments and the investor's required rate of return

    Answer: d Difficulty: 2

32. Tri State Pickle Company preferred stock pays a perpetual annual dividend of 2 1/2% of its par value. Par value of TSP preferred stock is $100 per share. If investors' required rate of return on this stock is 15%, what is the value per share?
    a) $37.50
    b) $15.00
    c) $16.67
    d) $6.00

    Answer: c Difficulty: 2

33. Petrified Forest Skin Care Inc. pays an annual perpetual dividend of $1.70 per share. If the stock is currently selling for $21.25 per share, what is the expected rate of return on this stock?
    a) 36.13%
    b) 12.5%
    c) 8%
    d) 13.6%

    Answer: c Difficulty: 1

34. You are considering the purchase of a share of AFZ Corporation common stock. You expect to sell it at the end of 1 year for $32.00. You will also receive a dividend of $2.50 at the end of the year. AFZ just paid a dividend of $2.25. If your required return on this stock is 12%, what is the most you would be willing to pay for it now?
    a) $28.57
    b) $33.05
    c) $20.83
    d) $30.80

    Answer: d Difficulty: 2

35. Little Feet Shoe Co. just paid a dividend of $1.65 on its common stock. This company's dividends are expected to grow at a constant rate of 3% indefinitely. If the required rate of return on this stock is 11%, compute the current value per share of LFS stock.
    a) $20.63
    b) $21.24
    c) $15.00
    d) $55.00

    Answer: b Difficulty: 2

36. XLNT Corp. just paid a dividend of $2.15 on its common stock. The dividends of XLNT are expected to grow at about 4% per year indefinitely. If the risk free rate is 5% and investors' risk premium on this stock is 7 1/2%, estimate the value of XLNT stock 3 years from now.
    a) $71.71
    b) $28.47
    c) $37.23
    d) $29.65

    Answer: d Difficulty: 3

37. Moo Moo Land Dairy Co. has net income of $450,000 this year. The book value of MML common stock is $3 million dollars. The company's dividend payout ratio is 60% and is expected to remain this way. What is Moo Moo Land Dairy's sustainable growth rate?
    a) 3%
    b) 9%
    c) 6%
    d) 10%

    Answer: c Difficulty: 3

38. Newbanks Corporation net income this year is $800,000. The company generally retains 35% of net income for reinvestment. The company's common stock currently has a book value of $5,000,000. They just paid a dividend of $1.37, and the required rate of return on this stock is 12%. Compute the value of this stock if dividends are expected to continue growing indefinitely at the company's sustainable growth rate.
    a) $22.61
    b) $11.42
    c) $15.63
    d) $4.35

    Answer: a Difficulty: 3

39. Marble Corporation's ROE is 17%. Their dividend payout ratio is 20%. The last dividend, just paid, was $2.58. If dividends are expected to grow by the company's sustainable growth rate indefinitely, what is the current value of Marble common stock if its required return is 18%?
    a) $14.33
    b) $18.27
    c) $47.67
    d) $66.61

    Answer: d Difficulty: 3

40. Fris B. Corporation stock is currently selling for $42.86. It is expected to pay a dividend of $3.00 at the end of the year. Dividends are expected to grow at a constant rate of 3% indefinitely. Compute the required rate of return on FBC stock.
    a) 10%
    b) 33%
    c) 7%
    d) 4.3%

    Answer: a Difficulty: 3

41. Cumulative preferred stock:
    a) requires dividends in arrears to be carried over into the next period
    b) has a right to vote cumulatively
    c) has a claim to dividends after common stock
    d) generally has the right to vote

    Answer: a Difficulty: 2

42. Preferred stock differs from common stock in that
    a) preferred stock usually has a maturity date
    b) preferred stock can never be called
    c) preferred stock dividends are fixed
    d) none of the above

    Answer: c Difficulty: 2

ESSAY

43. Texon's preferred stock sells for $85 and pays $11 each year in dividends. What is the expected rate of return?

    Answer:
    $$\text{Required rate of return} = \frac{\$11}{\$85} = 0.129$$

    Difficulty: 2

44. Draper Company's common stock paid a dividend LAST year of $3.70. You believe that the long-term growth in the dividends of the firm will be 8 percent per year. If your required return for Draper is 14 percent, how much are you willing to pay for the stock?

Answer:

$$P_0 = \frac{\$3.70\ (1 + .08)}{0.14 - 0.08} = \frac{\$3.996}{0.06} = \$66.60$$

Difficulty: 3

45. The price of Ellet Corporation stock is expected to be $68 in 5 years. Dividends are anticipated to increase at an annual rate of 20 percent from the most recent dividend of $2.00. If your required rate of return is 16 percent, how much are you willing to pay for Ellet stock?

Answer:

Year	D	PV
0	$2.00	$ -0-
1	2.40	2.07
2	2.88	2.14
3	3.46	2.22
4	4.15	2.29
5	4.98	2.37
		$11.09

P = $11.09 + $68 x .476
P = $43.46
Difficulty: 2

46. You are considering the purchase of AMDEX Company stock. You anticipate that the company will pay dividends of $2.00 per share next year and $2.25 per share the following year. You believe that you can sell the stock for $17.50 per share two years from now. If your required rate of return is 12 percent, what is the maximum price that you would pay for a share of AMDEX Company stock?

Answer:

$$V_C = \$2.00\ PVIF_{12\%,1} + \$19.75\ PVIF_{12\%,2}$$

$$= (\$2.00)(.893) + (\$19.75)(.797)$$

$$= \$17.53$$

Difficulty: 2

47. You can purchase one share of Sumter Company common stock for $80 today. You expect the price of the common stock to increase to $85 per share in one year. The company pays an annual dividend of $3.00 per share. What is your expected rate of return for Sumter stock?

Answer:
$$\$80.00 = \frac{\$3.00}{1 + R} + \frac{\$85.00}{(1 + R)}$$

$$\$80.00(1 + R) = \$88.00$$
$$(1 + R) = \frac{\$88.00}{\$80.00} = \$1.10$$
$$R = .10$$

Difficulty: 3

48. Dink and Company's preferred stock pays an annual dividend of $2.80. The shares have no maturity date. You as an investor require a 7% return. What is the value of Dink's preferred stock to you?

Answer:
$$V = \frac{\$2.80}{.07} = \$40$$

Difficulty: 1

49. Tannerly Worldwide's common stock is currently selling for $48 a share. If the expected dividend at the end of the year is $2.40 and last year's dividend was $2.00, what is the rate of return implicit in the current stock price?

Answer:

$$R_c = 2.40/48 + (2.40 - 2.00)/2.00$$
$$= .05 + .20$$
$$= 25\%$$

Difficulty: 3

50. Miller/Hershey's preferred stock is selling at $54 on the market and pays an annual dividend of $4.20 per share.
    a. What is the expected rate of return on the stock?
    b. If an investor's required rate of return is 9%, what is the value of the stock for that investor?
    c. Considering the investor's required rate of return, does this stock seem to be a desirable investment?

    Answer:

    a. R = D/V
        R = $4.20/54
        R = 7.78%

    b. V = D/R
        V = $4.20/.09
        V = $46.66

    c. No, it is not a desirable investment.
    Difficulty: 3

51. The common stock of Cranberry Inc. is selling for $26.75 on the open market. A dividend of $3.68 is expected to be distributed, and the growth rate of this company is estimated to be 5.5%. If Richard Dean, an average investor, is considering purchasing this stock at the market price, what is his expected rate of return?

    Answer:

    R = (D/V) + g
    R = ($3.68/$26.75) + .055
    R = 19.26%
    Difficulty: 3

Chapter 8:   The Meaning and Measurement of Risk and Return

TRUE/FALSE

1. Variation in the rate of return of an investment is a measure of the riskiness of that investment.

   Answer: True Difficulty: 1

2. The security market line reflects individual investors' attitudes toward risk.

   Answer: False Difficulty: 2

3. By investing in different securities, an investor can lower his exposure to risk.

   Answer: True Difficulty: 1

4. Total risk equals unique security risk times systematic risk.

   Answer: False Difficulty: 1

5. A security with a beta of zero has a required rate of return equal to the overall market rate of return.

   Answer: False Difficulty: 2

6. Unique security risk can be eliminated from an investor's portfolio by diversification.

   Answer: True Difficulty: 1

7. The market value of an asset is determined by the demand and supply forces working together in the market.

   Answer: True Difficulty: 1

8. The required rate of return for an asset is equal to the risk-free rate plus a risk premium.

   Answer: True Difficulty: 1

9. Beta is a measurement of the relationship between a security's returns and the general market's returns.

   Answer: True Difficulty: 1

10. In general, the required rate of return is a function of (1) the time value of money, (2) the risk of an asset, and (3) the investor's attitude toward risk.

    Answer: True Difficulty: 1

11. The total risk of a security is equal to systematic risk plus unsystematic risk.

    Answer: True   Difficulty: 1

12. The CAPM designates the risk-return tradeoff existing in the market, where risk is defined in terms of beta.

    Answer: True   Difficulty: 2

13. As the required rate of return of a bond decreases, the market price of the bond decreases.

    Answer: False   Difficulty: 2

14. The relevant risk to an investor is that portion of the variability of returns that cannot be diversified away.

    Answer: True   Difficulty: 1

15. The expected cash flow of an investment takes the condition of the economy into consideration.

    Answer: True   Difficulty: 2

16. Elimination of all variations in returns is simply achieved by diversifying into securities that do not have positive correlation.

    Answer: False   Difficulty: 2

MULTIPLE CHOICE

17. The capital asset pricing model:
    a) provides a risk-return trade off in which risk is measured in terms of the market volatility.
    b) provides a risk-return trade off in which risk is measured in terms of beta.
    c) measures risk as the coefficient of variation between security and market rates of return
    d) depicts the total risk of a security

    Answer: b   Difficulty: 2

18. The appropriate measure for risk according to the capital asset pricing model is:
    a) the standard deviation of a firm's cash flows
    b) alpha
    c) the coefficient of variation of a firm's cash flows
    d) none of the above

    Answer: d   Difficulty: 2

19. The risk-return relationship for each financial asset is shown on:
    a) the capital market line
    b) the New York Stock Exchange market line
    c) the security market line
    d) none of the above

    Answer: c Difficulty: 2

20. You have invested in a project that has the following payoff schedule:

Payoff	Probability of Occurrence
$40	.15
$50	.20
$60	.30
$70	.30
$80	.05

    What is the expected value of the investment's payoff? (Round to the nearest $1)
    a) $60
    b) $65
    c) $58
    d) $70

    Answer: d Difficulty: 1

21. Which of the following investments is clearly preferred to the above:

Investment	$\bar{R}$	σ
A	18%	20%
B	20%	20%
C	20%	18%

    a) Investment A
    b) Investment B
    c) Investment C
    d) Cannot be determined without information regarding the risk adversion of the investor.

    Answer: c Difficulty: 1

22. Which of the following investments is clearly preferred to the others:

Investment	$\bar{R}$	σ
A	14%	12%
B	22%	20%
C	18%	16%

    a) Investment A
    b) Investment B
    c) Investment C
    d) Cannot be determined

    Answer: d Difficulty: 1

23. You are considering investing in Ford Motor Company. Which of the following are examples of diversifiable risk?

    I. Risk resulting from possibility of a stock market crash.
    II. Risk resulting from uncertainty regarding a possible strike against Ford.
    III. Risk resulting from an expensive recall of a Ford product.
    IV. Risk resulting from interest rates decreasing.
    a) I only
    b) I and IV
    c) I, II, III, IV
    d) II, III

    Answer: d Difficulty: 2

24. You are considering investing in U.S. Steel. Which of the following are examples of non-diversifiable risks?

    I. Risk resulting from foreign expropriation of U.S. Steel property.
    II. Risk resulting from oil exploration by Marathan Oil (a U.S. Steel subsidy).
    III. Risk resulting from a strike against U.S. Steel.
    a) I and II
    b) II and III
    c) I, II, and III
    d) none of the above

    Answer: d Difficulty: 2

25. You are considering buying some stock in Continental Grain. Which of the following are examples of non-diversifiable risks?

    I. Risk resulting from a general decline in the stock market.
    II. Risk resulting from a possible increase in income taxes.
    III. Risk resulting from an explosion in a grain elevator owned by Continental.
    IV. Risk resulting from an impending lawsuit against Continental.
    a) I and II
    b) III and IV
    c) I only
    d) II, III, and IV

    Answer: a Difficulty: 2

26. Sterling Incorporated has a beta of 1.0. If the expected return on the market is 12%, what is the expected return on Sterling Incorporated's stock?
a) 9%
b) 10%
c) 12%
d) insufficient information is provided

Answer: c Difficulty: 2

27. Siebling Manufacturing Company's common stock has a beta of .8. If the expected risk free return is 7% and the market offers a premium of 8% over the risk free rate, what is the expected return on Siebling's common stock?
a) 7.8%
b) 13.4%
c) 14.4%
d) 8.7%

Answer: b Difficulty: 2

28. Huit Industries' common stock has an expected return of 14.4% and a beta of 1.2. If the expected risk free return is 8%, what is the expected return for the market (round your answer to the nearest .1%)?
a) 7.7%
b) 9.6%
c) 12.0%
d) 13.3%

Answer: d Difficulty: 2

29. Tanzlin Manufacturing's common stock has a beta of 1.5. If the expected risk free return is 9% and the expected return on the market is 14%, what is the expected return on the stock?
a) 13.5%
b) 21.0%
c) 16.5%
d) 21.5%

Answer: c Difficulty: 2

30. Which of the following has a beta of zero?
a) a risk free asset
b) the market
c) all assets have a beta greater than zero
d) none of the above

Answer: a Difficulty: 2

31. Which of the following has a beta of one?
    a) a risk free asset
    b) the market
    c) all assets have a beta greater than one
    d) all assets have a beta less than one

    Answer: b Difficulty: 2

32. If there is a 20% chance we will get a 16% return, a 30% chance of getting a 14% return, a 40% chance of getting a 12% return, and a 10% chance of getting an 8% return, what is the expected rate of return?
    a) 12%
    b) 13%
    c) 14%
    d) 15%

    Answer: b Difficulty: 1

33. The standard deviation for the above investment would be:
    a) 2.24
    b) 2.56
    c) 2.87
    d) 2.98

    Answer: a Difficulty: 3

34. The required rate of return to an investor is a function of what things:
    a) the time value of money
    b) the variability of returns of the asset
    c) the investor's attitude toward risk
    d) a and b
    e) a, b, and c

    Answer: e Difficulty: 2

35. Beta is a statistical measure of
    a) unsystematic risk
    b) total risk
    c) the standard deviation
    d) the relationship between an investment's returns and the market return

    Answer: d Difficulty: 2

36. Given the capital asset pricing model, a security with a beta of 1.5 should return what, if the risk-free rate is 6% and the market return is 11%:
   a) 13.5%
   b) 14.0%
   c) 14.5%
   d) 15.0%

   Answer: a Difficulty: 2

37. You are considering investing in a project with the following possible outcomes:

States	Probability of Occurrence	Investment Returns
State 1: Economic boom	15%	16%
State 2: Economic growth	45%	12%
State 3: Economic decline	25%	5%
State 4: Depression	15%	-5%

   Calculate the expected rate of return and standard deviation of returns for this investment.
   a) 9.8%, 7.0%
   b) 7%, 43.6%
   c) 8.3%, 6.6%
   d) 8.3%, 16.1%

   Answer: c Difficulty: 2

38. A stock's beta is a measure of its:
   a) Systematic risk
   b) Unsystematic risk
   c) Company specific risk
   d) Diversifiable risk

   Answer: a Difficulty: 2

39. If you hold a portfolio made up of the following stocks:

	Investment Value	Beta
Stock A	$2,000	1.5
Stock B	$5,000	1.2
Stock C	$3,000	.8

   What is the beta of the portfolio?
   a) 1.17
   b) 1.14
   c) 1.32
   d) Can't be determined from information given.

   Answer: b Difficulty: 3

137

40. You are going to invest all of your funds in one of three projects with the following distribution of possible returns:

PROJECT 1

Probability	Return	Standard Deviation
50% Chance	20%	12%
50% Chance	-4%	

PROJECT 2

Probability	Return	Standard Deviation
30% Chance	30%	19.5%
40% Chance	10%	
30% Chance	-20%	

PROJECT 3

Probability	Return	Standard Deviation
10% Chance	30%	12%
40% Chance	15%	
40% Chance	10%	

If you a risk averse investor, which one should you choose?
a) Project 1
b) Project 2
c) Project 3

Answer: c Difficulty: 3

41. If we are able to fully diversify, what is the appropriate measure of risk to use?
a) Expected Return
b) Standard Deviation
c) Beta
d) All of the above

Answer: c Difficulty: 2

42. Changes in the general economy, like changes in interest rates or tax laws represent what type of risk?
a) Firm specific risk
b) Market risk
c) Unsystematic risk
d) Diversifiable risk

Answer: b Difficulty: 2

43. Zip Corporation zero coupon bonds are currently selling for $712.99. They have five years to maturity and a par value of $1,000. If the current rate on 6 month Treasury bills is currently 4%, estimate the risk premium required by Zip Corporation bondholders.
a) 8%
b) 3%
c) 4%
d) 7%

Answer: b Difficulty: 3

44. The Elvisalive Corporation, makers of Elvis memorabilia has a beta of 2.35. The return on the market portfolio is 13% and the riskfree rate is 7%. According to CAPM, what is the risk premium on a stock with a beta of 1?
    a) 11.75%
    b) 18.75%
    c) 6%
    d) 13%

    Answer: c Difficulty: 2

45. Bell Weather Inc. has a beta of 1.25. The return on the market portfolio is 12.5% and the riskfree rate is 5%. According to CAPM, what is the required return on this stock?
    a) 20.62%
    b) 9.37%
    c) 14.37%
    d) 15.62%

    Answer: c Difficulty: 2

46. A stock with a beta greater than one has returns that are _____ volatile than the market and a stock with a beta of less than one exhibits returns which are _____ volatile than those of the market portfolio.
    a) more, more
    b) more, less
    c) less, more
    d) less, less

    Answer: b Difficulty: 2

47. You hold a portfolio with the following securities:

Security	Percent of Portfolio	Beta	Return
X Corporation	20%	1.35	14%
Y Corporation	35%	.95	10%
Z Corporation	45%	.75	8%

Compute the expected return and beta for the portfolio.
    a) 10.67%, 1.02
    b) 9.9%, 1.02
    c) 34.4%, .94
    d) 9.9%, .94

    Answer: d Difficulty: 3

48. The prices for the Guns and Hoses Corporation for the first quarter of 1992 are given below. Find the holding period return for February.

Month End	Price
January	$135.28
February	119.40
March	141.57

    a) 18.56%
    b) 13.30%
    c) -11.73%
    d) 8.83%

    Answer: c Difficulty: 2

49. The beta of ABC Co. stock is the slope of:
    a) The security market line.
    b) The characteristic line for a plot of returns on the S&P 500 versus returns on short term Treasury bills.
    c) The arbitrage pricing line.
    d) The characteristic line for a plot of ABC Co. returns against the returns of the market portfolio for the same period.

    Answer: d Difficulty: 2

50. The rate on 6 month T-bills is currently 5%. Andvark Company stock has a beta of 1.69 and a required rate of return of 15.4%. According to CAPM, determine the return on the market portfolio.
    a) 11.15%
    b) 6.15%
    c) 17.07%
    d) 14.11%

    Answer: a Difficulty: 3

51. The return on the market portfolio is currently 13%. Battmobile Corporation stockholders require a rate of return of 21% and the stock has a beta of 3.5. According to CAPM, determine the riskfree rate.
    a) 7%
    b) 14.7%
    c) 9.8%
    d) 24.2%

    Answer: c Difficulty: 3

52. You are thinking of adding one of two investments to an already well diversified portfolio.

Security A   Security B

Expected Return = 12%   Expected Return = 12%
Standard Deviation of   Standard Deviation of
  Returns = 20.9%   Returns = 10.1%
Beta = .8   Beta = 2

If you are a risk averse investor, which one is the better choice?
a) Security A
b) Security B
c) Either security would be acceptable.
d) Cannot be determined with information given.

Answer: a Difficulty: 3

53. The minimum rate of return necessary to attract an investor to purchase or hold a security is referred to as the:
a) Stock's beta
b) Investor's risk premium
c) Investor's required rate of return
d) Risk-free rate

Answer: c Difficulty: 2

54. All of the following are criticisms of the Capital Asset Pricing Model (CAPM) except:
a) Different methods of computing beta can give different results.
b) The accuracy of the model cannot be determined empirically because we cannot determine the "true" market portfolio.
c) It is rather complex and difficult to apply in practice.
d) It is based on the notion that the riskiness of any asset can be represented entirely by its relationship to the market (i.e. all relevant risk can be measured by this one variable).

Answer: c Difficulty: 3

55. Of the following different types of securities, which is typically considered most risky?
a) Long term corporate bonds.
b) Long term government bonds.
c) Common stocks of large companies.
d) U.S. Treasury bills.

Answer: c Difficulty: 2

56. Beginning with an investment in one company's securities, as we add securities of other companies to our portfolio, which type of risk declines?
    a) Systematic risk.
    b) Market risk.
    c) Non-diversifiable risk.
    d) None of the above.

    Answer: d Difficulty: 2

ESSAY

57. You are considering a security with the following possible rates of return:

Probability	Return(%)
0.20	9.6
0.30	12.0
0.30	14.4
0.20	16.8

    a. Calculate the expected rate of return.
    b. Calculate the standard deviation of the returns.

    Answer:

    a. $\bar{R} = (0.2)(9.6)+(0.3)(12.0)+(0.3)(14.4)+(0.2)(16.8) = 13.2$

    b. $\sigma(R) = [(9.6 - 13.2)^2(0.2) + (12 - 13.2)^2(0.3) + (14.4 - 13.2)^2(0.3) + (16.8 - 13.2)^2(0.2)]^{1/2} = 2.459\%$

    Difficulty: 2

58. The return for the market during the next period is expected to be 16 percent; the risk-free rate is 10 percent. Calculate the required rate of return for a stock with a beta of 1.5.

    Answer:

    $K = 10\% + 1.5(16\% - 10\%) = 19\%$

    Difficulty: 2

59. You are considering two bonds. Each bond has a 9 percent coupon rate and is currently selling for $1,000. Bond A matures 2 years from today, while Bond B matures 10 years from today. Assume that the bonds pay interest annually.
    a. What will be the change in market value of each bond if interest rates increase to 10 percent?
    b. You plan to hold one of these bonds (currently selling at $1,000) for exactly 1 year. If you believe interest rates at the end of the year will be 8 percent, which bond should you hold?

    Answer:
    a. $P_A = \$1,000(0.826) + \$90(1.736) = \$982.24$
    Change in market value = -$17.76

    $P_B = \$1,000(0.386) + \$90(6.145) = \$939.05$
    Change in market value = -$60.95

    b. $P_A = \$1,000(0.926) + \$90(0.926) = \$1,009.34$

    $P_B = \$1,000(0.500) + \$90(6.247) = \$1,062.23$

    Hold Bond B, since it is expected to change more in value.
    Difficulty: 2

60. The stock of the Preston Corporation is expected to pay a dividend of $6 during the coming year. Dividends are expected to grow far into the future at 8 percent. Investors have recently evaluated future market return variance to be 0.0016 and the covariance of returns for Preston and the market as 0.00352. Assuming a required market return of 14 percent and a risk-free rate of 6 percent, at what price should the stock of Preston sell?

    Answer:
    $$\text{Beta} = \frac{0.00352}{0.0016} = 2.2$$
    $$K = 0.06 + 2.2(0.14 - 0.06)$$
    $$K = 0.236$$
    $$P = \frac{\$6}{0.236 - 0.08} = \frac{\$6}{0.156} = \$38.46$$
    Difficulty: 3

61. Security A has an expected rate of return of 22 percent and a beta of 2.5. Security B has a beta of 1.20. If the treasury bill rate is 10 percent, what is the expected rate of return for Security B?

Answer:

$R_A = R_F + B_A R_m - R_f)$
$.22 = .10 + 2.5 (R_m - .10)$
$.12 = 2.5 (R_m - .10) = 2.5R_m - .25$
$.37 = 2.5R_m$
$.148 = R_m$
$R_B = R_f + B_B (R_m - R_f)$
$R_B = .10 + 1.20(.148 - .10)$
$R_B = .1576$

Difficulty: 2

62. Last year Ajax Plumbing common stock paid a dividend of $1.50 per share. Its dividends have been growing at a rate of 6 percent per year and are expected to continue forever. The stock has a beta of 0.80. The expected rate of return on the market portfolio is 16 percent and the riskless rate of interest is 9 percent. What is the market price of Ajax Plumbing common stock?

Answer:

$R_A = R_f + B_A (R_m - R_f)$
$R_A = .09 + (.80)(.16 - .09)$
$R_A = .146$

$$P = \frac{(\$1.50)(1 + .06)}{.146 - .06} = \frac{\$1.59}{.086} = \$18.49$$

Difficulty: 3

63. AA & Co. has a beta of .656. If the expected market return is 13.2% and the risk-free rate is 5.7%, what is the appropriate required return of AA & Co. using the CAPM model?

Answer:

Required = Risk-Free + (Market - Risk-Free) x Beta
Rate of   Rate   Return   Rate
Return
        = 5.7% + (13.2% - 5.7%) x 0.656
        = 10.62%

Difficulty: 2

Chapter 9: Capital Budgeting Techniques and Practice

TRUE/FALSE

1. Errors resulting from a capital budgeting decision are not considered major since the consequences of such errors average out over the life of the investment.

   Answer: False Difficulty: 1

2. One drawback of the payback method is having to project a project's cash flow over the asset's entire life.

   Answer: False Difficulty: 1

3. The required rate of return reflects the costs of funds needed to finance a project.

   Answer: True Difficulty: 1

4. The profitability index provides the same decision result as the net present value method.

   Answer: True Difficulty: 1

5. The net present value of a project will increase as the required rate of return is increased.

   Answer: False Difficulty: 2

6. Whenever the internal rate of return on a project equals that project's required rate of return, the net present value equals zero.

   Answer: True Difficulty: 2

7. One of the disadvantages of the payback method is that it ignores cash flows beyond the payback period.

   Answer: True Difficulty: 1

8. The capital rationing problem can be correctly solved by ranking projects according to the profitability index.

   Answer: False Difficulty: 2

9. The capital budgeting decision making process involves measuring the incremental cash flows of an investment proposal and evaluating the attractiveness of these cash flows relative to the project's cost.

   Answer: True Difficulty: 1

10. In general, all discounted cash flow criteria are consistent and will give similar accept-reject decisions.

    Answer: True Difficulty: 1

11. When several sign reversals in the cash flow stream occur, the IRR equation can have more than one positive IRR.

    Answer: True Difficulty: 2

12. Many firms today continue to use the payback method but employ the NPV or IRR methods as secondary decision methods of control for risk.

    Answer: False Difficulty: 1

13. The required rate of return is always the prime rate.

    Answer: False Difficulty: 1

14. The payback period deals with cash flows rather than accounting profits.

    Answer: True Difficulty: 1

15. The net present value method of evaluating a project takes into account the time value of money.

    Answer: True Difficulty: 1

16. If the net present value of a project is zero, then the profitability index should equal one.

    Answer: True Difficulty: 2

17. The internal rate of return will equal the discount rate when the net present value equals zero.

    Answer: True Difficulty: 2

18. If the net present value of a project is positive, the profitability index must be greater than one.

    Answer: True Difficulty: 2

19. It is possible for a project to have more than one internal rate of return if there is more than one sign change in the after-tax cash flows due to the project.

    Answer: True Difficulty: 1

20. The higher the discount rate the more valued is the proposal with the early cash flows.

    Answer: True Difficulty: 2

21. If the project's payback period is greater than or equal to zero, the project should be accepted.

    Answer: False Difficulty: 1

22. The net present value of a project will equal zero whenever the payback period of a project equals the required rate of return.

    Answer: False Difficulty: 1

23. The internal rate of return is the discount rate that equates the present value of the project's future net cash flows with the project's initial outlay.

    Answer: True Difficulty: 1

24. If a project's profitability index is less than 0.0 then the project should be rejected.

    Answer: False Difficulty: 1

25. A single project can only have one NPV, PI, and IRR.

    Answer: False Difficulty: 1

26. If the firm decides to impose a capital constraint on investment projects, the appropriate decision criterion is to select the set of projects that has the highest net present value subject to the capital constraint.

    Answer: True Difficulty: 1

27. The size disparity problem occurs when extremely large mutually exclusive projects are being examined.

    Answer: False Difficulty: 2

28. Capital rationing can occur when profitable projects must be rejected because of shortage of capital.

    Answer: True Difficulty: 1

29. A project's equivalent annual annuity (EAA) is calculated by dividing the project's NPV by the $PVIFA_{i,n}$ where i is the appropriate discount rate and n is the project's life.

    Answer: True Difficulty: 2

30. A project's equivalent annual annuity (EAA) is the annuity cash flow that yields the same present value as the project's NPV.

    Answer: True Difficulty: 2

31. An infinite life replacement chain allows projects of different length lives to be compared.

    Answer: True Difficulty: 2

32. In selecting projects when there is capital rationing, the payback period method should be used.

    Answer: False Difficulty: 2

33. The use of the risk-adjusted discount rate assumes that risk increases over time and that cash flows occurring further in the future should be more severely penalized.

    Answer: True Difficulty: 2

34. If the risk-adjusted discount rate method is used, the value of future cash flows that occur further in the future are more severely adjusted downward than are earlier cash flows.

    Answer: True Difficulty: 2

MULTIPLE CHOICE

35. The net present value always provides the correct decision provided that
    a) cash flows are constant over the asset's life
    b) the required rate of return is greater than the internal rate of return
    c) capital rationing is not imposed
    d) the internal rate of return is positive

    Answer: c Difficulty: 2

36. The net present value method
    a) is consistent with the goal of shareholder wealth maximization
    b) recognizes the time value of money
    c) uses cash flows
    d) all of the above

    Answer: d Difficulty: 1

37. If the internal rate of return is greater than the required rate of return
    a) the present value of all the cash inflows will be less than the initial outlay
    b) the payback will be less than the life of the investment
    c) a and c

    Answer: c Difficulty: 1

38. Arguments against using the net present value and internal rate of return methods include that
    a) they fail to use accounting profits
    b) they require detailed long-term forecasts of the incremental benefits and costs
    c) they fail to consider how the investment project is to be financed
    d) they fail to use the cash flow of the project

    Answer: b Difficulty: 1

39. If the cash flow pattern for a project has two sign reversals, then there can be as many as ____ positive IRR's.
    a) 1
    b) 2
    c) 3
    d) 4

    Answer: b Difficulty: 2

40. A project has an initial outlay of $4,000. It has a single payoff at the end of year 4 of $6,996.46. What is the internal rate of return for the project (round to the nearest %)?
    a) 16%
    b) 13%
    c) 21%
    d) 15%

    Answer: d Difficulty: 2

41. ABC Service can purchase a new assembler for $15,052 that will provide an annual net cash flow of $6,000 per year for five years, after which time the assembler will be sold as junk of $750 per year. Calculate the net present value of the assembler if the required rate of return is 12%. (Round your answer to the nearest $10.)
    a) $1,050
    b) $4,560
    c) $6,600
    d) $7,000

    Answer: d Difficulty: 2

42. Given the following annual net cash flows, determine the internal rate of return to the nearest whole percent of a project with an initial outlay of $1,520.

YEAR	NET CASH FLOW
1	$1,000
2	$1,500
3	$ 500

a) 48%
b) 40%
c) 32%
d) 28%

Answer: a Difficulty: 2

43. A machine costs $1,000, has a 3 year life, and has an estimated salvage value of $100. It will generate after tax annual cash flows (ACF) of $600 a year, starting next year. If your required rate of return for the project is 10%, what is the NPV of this investment? (Round your answer to the nearest $10).
a) $490.00
b) $570.00
c) $900.00
d) -$150.00

Answer: b Difficulty: 2

44. Initial Outlay   Cash Flow in Period

	1	2	3	4
$4,000	$1,546.17	$1,546.17	$1,546.17	$1,546.17

The Internal Rate of Return (to nearest whole percent) is:
a) 10%
b) 18%
c) 20%
d) 16%

Answer: c Difficulty: 2

45. We compute the profitability index of a capital budgeting proposal by
a) multiplying the internal rate of return by the cost of capital
b) dividing the present value of the annual after tax cash flows by the cost of capital
c) dividing the present value of the the annual after tax cash flows by the cash investment in the project
d) multiplying the cash inflow by the internal rate of return

Answer: c Difficulty: 2

46. What is the payback period for a $20,000 project that is expected to return $6,000 for the first two years and $3,000 for years three through five?
    a) 3 1/2
    b) 4 1/2
    c) 4 2/3
    d) 5

    Answer: c Difficulty: 2

47. The advantages of NPV are all of the following except:
    a) it can be used as a rough, screening device to eliminate those projects whose returns do not materialize until later years.
    b) all positive NPVs will increase the value of the firm.
    c) it allows the comparison of benefits and costs in a logical manner.
    d) it recognizes the timing of the benefits resulting from the project.

    Answer: a Difficulty: 2

48. The disadvantage of the IRR method is that:
    a) the IRR deals with cash flows.
    b) the IRR gives equal regard to all returns within a project's life.
    c) the IRR will always give the same project accept/reject decision as the NPV.
    d) the IRR requires long, detailed cash flow forecasts.

    Answer: d Difficulty: 2

49. The internal rate of return is:
    a) The discount rate that makes the NPV positive.
    b) The discount rate that equates the present value of the cash inflows with the present value of the cash outflows.
    c) The discount rate that makes NPV negative and the PI greater than one.
    d) The rate of return that makes the NPV positive.

    Answer: b Difficulty: 2

50. All of the following are criticisms of the payback period criteria except:
    a) Time value of money is not accounted for.
    b) Returns occurring after the payback are ignored.
    c) It deals with accounting profits as opposed to cash flows.
    d) None of the above; they are all criticisms of the payback period criteria.

    Answer: c Difficulty: 2

51. Artie's Soccer Ball Company is considering a project with the following cash flows:

    Initial Outlay = $750,000
    Incremental After Tax Cash Flows from Operations Year 1-4 = $250,000 per year
    Additional after tax Terminal Cash Flow at End of Year 4 = $40,000

    Compute the net present value of this project if the company's discount rate is 12%.
    a) $34,758
    b) $784,758
    c) $9,337
    d) $1,534,758

    Answer: a Difficulty: 3

52. Dieyard Battery Recyclers is considering a project with the following cash flows:

    Initial Outlay = $13,000
    Cash Flows: Year 1 = $5,000
                Year 2 = 3,000
                Year 3 = 9,000

    If the appropriate discount rate is 15%, compute the NPV of this project.
    a) $4,000
    b) -$466
    c) $27,534
    d) $8,891

    Answer: b Difficulty: 3

53. Crawfish Kitchen Inc. is planning to invest in 1 of 3 mutually exclusive projects. Projected cash flows for these ventures are as follows:

Plan A	Plan B	Plan C
Initial	Initial	Initial
Outlay=$3,600	Outlay=$6,000	Outlay=$3,500
Cash Flow:	Cash Flow:	Cash Flow:
Yr 1=$ -0-	Yr 1=$4,000	Yr 1=$2,000
Yr 2= -0-	Yr 2= 3,000	Yr 2= -0-
Yr 3= -0-	Yr 3= 2,000	Yr 3=2,000
Yr 4= -0-	Yr 4= -0-	Yr 4=2,000
Yr 5=$7,000	Yr 5= -0-	Yr 5=2,000

    Which project is the most profitable according to the NPV criteria
    a) Plan A
    b) Plan B
    c) Plan C

    Answer: c Difficulty: 3

54. Your company is considering a project with the following cash flows:
    Initial Outlay = $1,748.80
    Cash Flows Year 1-6 = $500

    Compute the internal rate of return on the project.
    a) 9%
    b) 11%
    c) 18%
    d) 24%

    Answer: c Difficulty: 2

55. For the net present value (NPV) criteria, a project is acceptable if NPV
    is _____, while for the profitability index a project is acceptable
    if PI is _____.
    a) less than zero, greater than the required return
    b) greater than zero, greater than one
    c) greater than one, greater than zero
    d) greater than zero, less than one

    Answer: b Difficulty: 2

56. Compute the payback period for a project with the following cash flows,
    if the company's discount rate is 12%.

    Initial Outlay = $450
    Cash Flows: Year 1 = $325
                Year 2 =   65
                Year 3 = 100
    a) 3.13 yrs.
    b) 2.17 yrs.
    c) 4 yrs.
    d) 2.6 yrs.

    Answer: d Difficulty: 2

57. Consider a project with the following cash flows:

Year	After-tax Accounting Profits	After-tax Cash Flow from Operations
1	$799	$ 750
2	150	1,000
3	200	1,200

Initial outlay = $1,500
Terminal cash flow = 0

Compute the profitability index if the company's discount rate is 10%.
a) 15.8
b) 1.61
c) 1.81
d) .62

Answer: b   Difficulty: 2

58. If the NPV (Net Present Value) of a project is positive, then the project's IRR (Internal Rate of Return) _____ the required rate of return.
a) must be less than
b) must be greater than
c) could be greater or less than
d) Cannot be determined without actual cash flows.

Answer: b   Difficulty: 2

59. You are considering investing in a project with the following year end after tax cash flows:

Year 1: $5,000
Year 2: $3,200
Year 3: $7,800

If the initial outlay for the project is $12,113, compute the project's internal rate of return.
a) 14%
b) 10%
c) 32%
d) 24%

Answer: a   Difficulty: 3

60. Different discounted cash flow evaluation methods may provide conflicting rankings of investment projects when
    a) the size of investment outlays differ
    b) the projects have unequal lives
    c) the timing of the cash flows differ
    d) all of the above

    Answer: d Difficulty: 2

61. Capital rationing may be imposed because
    a) capital market conditions are poor
    b) of management's fear of debt
    c) stockholder control problems prevent issuance of additional stock
    d) all of the above

    Answer: d Difficulty: 2

62. When selecting the best project from a group of mutually exclusive projects you should choose the project with the highest
    a) net present value
    b) internal rate of return
    c) accounting rate of return
    d) a and b

    Answer: a Difficulty: 2

63. If a company decides that it needs to impose capital rationing, which statement is true?
    a) The effect is positive if adverse economic conditions exist.
    b) The effect is positive if there is a shortage of effective managers within the firm to manage the project.
    c) The effect is negative because the process involves rejecting a project with a positive net present value, which in turn fails to maximize shareholders' wealth.
    d) The effect is negative because it results from a manager's fear of risk.

    Answer: c Difficulty: 2

64. You are in charge of one division of Bigfella Conglomerate Inc. Your division is subject to capital rationing. Your division has 4 indivisible projects available, detailed as follows:

Project	Initial Outlay	IRR	NPV
1	2 million	18%	2,500,000
2	1 million	15%	950,000
3	1 million	10%	600,000
4	3 million	9%	2,000,000

If you must select projects subject to a budget constraint of 5 million dollars, which set of projects should be accepted so as to maximize firm value?
a) Projects 1, 2 and 3
b) Project 1 only
c) Projects 1 and 4
d) Projects 2, 3 and 4

Answer: c   Difficulty: 3

65. Your company is considering an investment in one of two mutually exclusive projects. Project one involves a labor intensive production process. Initial outlay for Project 1 is $1,495 with expected after tax cash flows of $500 per year in years 1-5. Project two involves a capital intensive process, requiring an initial outlay of $6,704. After tax cash flows for Project 2 are expected to be $2,000 per year for years 1-5. Your firm's discount rate is 10%. If your company is not subject to capital rationing, which project(s) should you take on based on the basic capital budgeting criteria (NPV and IRR)?
a) Project 1
b) Project 2
c) Projects 1 and 2
d) Neither project is acceptable.

Answer: b   Difficulty: 3

66. The Net Present Value (or NPV) criteria for capital budgeting decisions assumes that expected future cash flows are reinvested at _____, and the Internal Rate of Return (or IRR) criteria assumes that expected future cash flows are reinvested at _____.
a) the firm's discount rate, the internal rate of return
b) the internal rate of return, the internal rate of return
c) the internal rate of return, the firm's discount rate
d) neither criteria assumes reinvestment of future cash flows

Answer: a   Difficulty: 2

67. Your firm is considering investing in one of two mutually exclusive projects. Project A requires an initial outlay of $2,500 with expected future cash flows of $1,150 per year for the next three years. Project B requires an initial outlay of $2,500 with expected future cash flows of $1,577 per year for the next two years. The appropriate discount rate for your firm is 14% and it is not subject to capital rationing. Assuming both projects can be replaced with a similar investment at the end of their respective lives, compute the NPV of the two chain cycle for Project A and three chain cycle for Project B.
    a) $170, $97
    b) $4,472, $3,632
    c) $285, $229
    d) -$528, -$1,368

    Answer: c Difficulty: 3

68. Determine the dollar value of a three year annuity that would produce the same NPV as the following project if the appropriate discount rate is 15%, and initial outflow = 0.

    Initial Outflow = $1,200
    Cash Flow Year 1 = $800
    Cash Flow Year 2 = $500
    Cash Flow Year 3 = $700
    a) $50.38
    b) $146.28
    c) $673.94
    d) $430.82

    Answer: c Difficulty: 2

69. In general, what effect does capital rationing have on firm value?
    a) It increases firm value.
    b) It decreases firm value.
    c) It may increase or decrease firm value.
    d) It has no impact on firm value.

    Answer: b Difficulty: 2

70. Which of the following statements is not true with respect to the effect of inflation on capital budgeting decisions?
    a) All use the same; increased inflation raises investors' required rates of return causing project NPV's to fall.
    b) Depreciation charges on a project increase with inflation meaning a smaller percentage of cash inflows is sheltered.
    c) Salvage value of the project could be higher than expected due to inflation.
    d) Product selling price could be affected more than expenses so that higher than expected inflation could lead to higher cash flows.

    Answer: b Difficulty: 2

ESSAY

71. Rymer Inc. is considering a new assembler which costs $180,000 installed, and has a depreciable life of 5 years. The expected annual after-tax cash flows for the assembler are $60,000 in each of the 5 years and nothing thereafter. Calculate the net present value of the assembler if the required rate of return is 14 percent.

Answer:

Initial Outlay

Cost of assembler $180,000
NPV = $60,000 x 3.433 - $180,000
NPV = $25,980.00

Difficulty: 2

72. Carter Paving plans to purchase a new grader. The one under consideration costs $250,000, and has a depreciable life of 5 years. After-tax cash flows are expected to be $67,124 in each of the 5 years and nothing thereafter. Calculate the internal rate of return for the grader.

Answer:
Initial Outlay

Cost of grader $250,000
Calculate IRR

$250,000 = $67,124 $PVIFA_{IRR\%,\ 5\ yr.}$
   3.725 = $PVIFA_{IRR\%,\ 5\ yr.}$
      IRR = between 10% and 11%

Difficulty: 2

73. Consider the following two projects:

	Initial Outlay	Net Cash Flow Each Period			
		1	2	3	4
Project A	$4,000	$2,003	$2,003	$2,003	$ 2,003
Project B	$4,000				$10,736

a. Calculate the net present value of each of the above projects, assuming a 14 percent discount rate.
b. What is the internal rate of return for each of the above projects?
c. Compare and explain the conflicting rankings of the NPV's and IRR's obtained in parts a and b above.
d. If 14 percent is the required rate of return for these projects, which project is preferred?

Answer:
a. At a discount rate of 14 percent:
$NPV_A = \$2,003(2.914) - \$4,000$
$NPV_A = \$1,836.74$
$NPV_B = \$10,736(.592) - \$4,000$
$NPV_B = \$2,355.71$

b. $IRR_A = 35\%$
$IRR_B = 28\%$

c. Time disparity problem due to implicit reinvestment rate assumption.

d. Pick project B if they are mutually exclusive.
Difficulty: 3

74. Consider two mutually exclusive projects X and Y with identical initial outlays of $90,000 and depreciable lives of 5 years. Project X is expected to produce an after-tax cash flow of $32,787 each year. Project Y is expected to generate a single after-tax net cash flow of $223,880 in year 6. The cost of capital is 15 percent.

    a. Calculate the net present value for each project.
    b. Calculate the IRR for each project.
    c. What problem(s) do you foresee in selecting one of the projects?
    d. What project should be selected?

Answer:
a. $NPV_X = \$32,787 \times 3.352 - \$90,000$
    $NPV_X = \$19,902$
    $NPV_Y = \$223,880 \times .497 - \$90,000$
    $NPV_Y = \$21,268$

b. IRR_X
    $\$90,000 = 32,787 \ PVIFA_{IRR\%, \ 5 \ yr.}$
      $2.745 = PVIFA_{IRR\%, \ 5 \ yr.}$
        $24\% = IRR_X$
    IRR_Y
    $90,000 = 223,880 \ PVIF_{IRR\%, \ 5 \ yr.}$
      $.402 = PVIF_{IRR\%, \ 5 \ yr.}$
      $20\% = IRR_Y$

c. There is a conflict in the rankings of the projects.

Project	NPV(15%)	IRR
X	$19,902	24%
Y	$21,268	20%

d. Select project Y because it has the highest NPV.

Difficulty: 3

75. What is the net present value of a $45,000 project that is expected to have an after-tax cash flow of $14,000 for the first two years, $10,000 for the next two years, and $8,000 for the fifth year? Use a 10% discount rate. Would you accept the project?

Answer:

Year	After-Tax Cash Flow	PVIF at 10%	Present Value
1	$14,000	.909	$ 12,726
2	14,000	.826	11,564
3	10,000	.751	7,510
4	10,000	.683	6,830
	58,000	.621	4,968

Present value of cash flows $ 43,598
Initial outlay 45,000
Net present value $ -1,402

Project should be rejected.

Difficulty: 3

76. Referring to the above problem: if the discount rate was 8%, what would the NPV be? Would you accept or reject the investment?

Answer:

Year	After-Tax Cash Flow	PVIF at 8%	Present Value
1	$14,000	.926	$ 12,964
2	14,000	.857	11,998
3	10,000	.794	7,940
4	10,000	.735	7,350
	58,000	.681	5,448

Present value of cash flows $ 45,700
Initial outlay 45,000
Net present value $ 700

The project is acceptable.

Difficulty: 3

77. Patrick Motors has several investment projects under consideration, all with positive net present values. However, due to a shortage of trained personnel, a limit of $1,250,000 has been placed on the capital budget for this year. Which of the projects listed below should be included in this year's capital budget?

Project	Initial Outlay	NPV
A	$ 250,000	$325,000
B	250,000	350,000
C	1,000,000	700,000
D	375,000	112,500
E	375,000	75,000

Answer:

Project	P.I.
A	2.3
B	2.4
C	1.7
D	1.3
E	1.2

Select combination with highest NPV or PI

Ex. (1) NPV (A + B + D + E) = $862,500
        or PI (A + B + D + E) = 1.69
    (2) NPV (C + B) = $1,050,000
        or PI (C + B) = 1.84

Projects B and C should be selected
Difficulty: 3

78. The Bolster Company is considering two mutually exclusive projects:

Year	Cash Flow A	Cash Flow B
0	-$100,000	-$100,000
1	31,250	0
2	31,250	0
3	31,250	0
4	31,250	0
5	31,250	$200,000

The required rate of return on these projects is 12 percent.

a. What is each project's payback period?
b. What is each project's net present value?
c. What is each project's internal rate of return?
d. Fully explain the results of your analysis. Which project do you prefer?

Answer:

a. $PB_A = \dfrac{\$100,000}{31,250} = 3.2$ years

$PB_B = 5$ years

b. $NPV_A = \$31,250 \times 3.605 - \$100,000 = \$12,656$
$NPV_B = \$200,000 \times .567 - \$100,000 = \$13,400$

c. $\dfrac{IRR}{\$100,000} = \$31,250 \ PVIFA_{IRR\%, \ 5 \ yr.}$

$3.200 = PVIFA_{IRR\%, \ 5 \ yr.}$
$17\% = IRR_A$
$\$100,000 = \$200,000 \ PVIF_{IRR\%, \ 5 \ yr.}$
$.5 = PVIF_{IRR\%, \ 5 \ yr.}$
$15\% = IRR_B$

d. A conflict in rankings has occurred because the timing of the cash flows is different. Project B is preferred at a required rate of return of 12 percent.

Difficulty: 3

79. The Deacon Company is considering two mutually exclusive projects with depreciable lives of 3 and 6 years. The after-tax cash flows for projects S and L are listed below.

Year	Cash Flow S	Cash Flow L
0	-$50,000	-$50,000
1	25,625	16,563
2	25,625	16,563
3	25,625	16,563
4		16,563
5		16,563
6		16,563

The required rate of return on these projects is 15 percent. Which project should be accepted?

Answer:
Calculate net present values

NPV_S = $25,625 x 2.283 - $50,000
NPV_S = $8,502
NPV_L = $16,563 x 3.784 - $50,000
NPV_L = $12,674

Create a replacement chain for S.

NPV_S^* = NPV_S + NPV_S x .658
NPV_S = $8,502 + $8,502 x .658
NPV_S = $14,096

Project S should be accepted.

Difficulty: 3

80. Company K is considering two mutually exclusive projects. The cash flows of the projects are as follows:

Year	Project A	Project B
0	-$2,000	-$2,000
1	$500	
2	$500	
3	$500	
4	$500	
5	$500	
6	$500	
7	$500	$5,650

a. Compute the NPV and IRR for the above two projects, assuming a 13% required rate of return.
b. Discuss the ranking conflict.
c. Which of these two projects should be chosen?

Answer:
a. The conflicting rankings are caused by the differing reinvestment assumptions made by the NPV and IRR decision criteria. The NPV criteria assumes that cash flows over the life of the project can be reinvested at the required rate of return or cost of capital, while the IRR criterion implicitly assumes that the cash flows over the life of the project can be reinvested at the internal rate of return.

b.
$$NPV_A = \frac{\$500}{(1 + 0.13)^t} - \$2,000$$
$$= \$2,211.30 - \$2,000$$
$$= \$211.3$$

$$NPV_B = \frac{\$5,650}{(1 + 0.13)^5} - \$2,000$$
$$= \$2,401.59 - \$2,000$$
$$= \$401.59$$
$$IRR = \$2,000 = \$500\ PVIFA_{IRR\%,\ 7\ yr.}$$

Thus,
$$IRR_A = 16.3\%$$
$$\$2,000 = \$9,000\ PVIF_{IRR\%,\ 7\ yr.}$$

Thus,
$$IRR_B = 15.99\%$$

c. Project B should be taken because it has the largest NPV. The NPV criterion in preferred because it makes the most acceptable assumption for the wealth maximizing firm.

Difficulty: 3

Chapter 10: Cash Flows and Other Topics in Capital Budgeting

TRUE/FALSE

1. Because installment costs of a new asset are a current cash expense, they are excluded from the initial outlay.

   Answer: False Difficulty: 1

2. When an old asset is sold for exactly its depreciated value, the only taxable income is the difference between the initial cost of the machine and the selling price.

   Answer: False Difficulty: 1

3. If the funds for an investment proposal are obtained by issuing bonds, we must consider the interest charges when calculating the net cash flows.

   Answer: False Difficulty: 1

4. The initial outlay involves the immediate cash outflow necessary to purchase the asset and put it in operating order.

   Answer: True Difficulty: 1

5. When replacing an existing asset, the cash inflow associated with the sale of the old asset and any related tax effects must be considered and accounted for in the analysis.

   Answer: True Difficulty: 1

6. In measuring cash flows we are interested only in the incremental or differential after-tax cash flows that are attributed to the investment proposal being evaluated.

   Answer: True Difficulty: 1

7. Cash flows associated with a project's termination generally include the salvage value of the project plus or minus any taxable gains or losses associated with its sale.

   Answer: True Difficulty: 1

8. If the tax rate increases, a project's net present value decreases.

   Answer: True Difficulty: 1

9. If the tax rate increases, a project's payback period increases.

   Answer: T Difficulty: 2

10. The initial outlay of an asset does not include installation costs.

    Answer: False Difficulty: 1

11. Additional cash needed to fill increased working capital requirements should be included in the initial cost of a product when analyzing an investment.

    Answer: T Difficulty: 2

12. Any increase in interest payments caused by a project should be counted in the differential cash flows.

    Answer: F Difficulty: 2

13. In making a capital budgeting decision we only include the incremental cash flows resulting from the investment decision.

    Answer: True Difficulty: 1

14. By examining cash flows, we are correctly able to analyze the timing of the benefits.

    Answer: True Difficulty: 1

15. Any increase in interest payments incurred as a result of issuing bonds to finance the project should be included in the calculation of after-tax cash flows.

    Answer: F Difficulty: 2

16. In order to implement the certainty equivalent approach, we must know the financial manager's preference for bearing risk.

    Answer: T Difficulty: 2

17. The appropriate discount rate to use with the certainty equivalent approach is the project's required rate of return.

    Answer: False Difficulty: 1

18. The certainty equivalent approach compares the internal rate of return to the required rate of return on a similar risky project.

    Answer: False Difficulty: 2

19. The use of risk-adjusted discount rates is based on the concept that investors require a higher rate of return for more risky projects.

    Answer: True Difficulty: 1

20. The risk-adjusted discount rate assumes that distant cash flows have the same risk as near cash flows.

    Answer: F Difficulty: 2

21. One benefit of simulation is that only a simple estimate of each variable included in the simulation is required rather than the probability distribution of each variable.

    Answer: False Difficulty: 1

22. Sensitivity analysis is a benefit of simulation.

    Answer: True Difficulty: 1

23. Since stockholders are able to reduce their exposure to risk by efficiently diversifying their holdings of securities, there is no reason for individual firms to seek diversification of their holdings of assets.

    Answer: F Difficulty: 2

24. If the cash flows of an accepted investment project are positively correlated with the average cash flow of the firm's existing assets, then the company's total exposure to risk can decrease.

    Answer: T Difficulty: 2

25. In spite of varying project risk, as long as proposed investment projects are evaluated at the average cost of capital, the maximization of shareholder wealth will be assured.

    Answer: F Difficulty: 2

26. A typical company will not use the same risk-adjusted discount rate for evaluating both replacement projects and research and development projects.

    Answer: T Difficulty: 2

27. A typical decision rule used in simulation is to accept the project if the probability is sufficiently high that the net present value is positive.

    Answer: T Difficulty: 2

28. Reducing the probability of bankruptcy is a benefit of diversification.

    Answer: T Difficulty: 2

29. In reality, anticipated cash flows are only estimates and are thus uncertain.

    Answer: T Difficulty: 2

30. Risk is defined as an absolute measure of the degree of variability of possible outcomes over time.

    Answer: F Difficulty: 2

31. Financial theory assumes that individuals are risk averse.

    Answer: True Difficulty: 1

32. Using simulation provides the financial manager with a probability distribution of an investment's net present value or internal rate of return.

    Answer: True Difficulty: 1

33. One drawback of simulation is that the resulting decisions are based solely on point estimates rather than on a range of possible outcomes.

    Answer: F Difficulty: 2

34. The certainty equivalent is calculated by dividing the risky (or expected) cash flow by the certain cash flow.

    Answer: False Difficulty: 2

35. The risk-adjusted discount rate makes the implicit assumption that risk becomes greater over time.

    Answer: T Difficulty: 2

36. The less-risky investment is always the more desirable choice.

    Answer: F Difficulty: 2

37. If the required rate of return is not adjusted to compensate for added risk, acceptance of marginal projects can lower the firm's share price.

    Answer: T Difficulty: 2

38. According to the CAPM, systematic risk is the only relevant risk for capital budgeting purposes.

    Answer: T Difficulty: 2

MULTIPLE CHOICE

39. The calculation of differential cash flows over a project's life should include
    a) labor and material saving
    b) additional revenue
    c) interest to bondholders
    d) a and b

    Answer: d Difficulty: 1

40. If the federal income tax rate were increased, the result would be to
    a) decrease the net present value
    b) increase the net present value
    c) increase the payback period
    d) a and c

    Answer: d Difficulty: 2

41. Salvage value would most likely not be considered by
    a) net present value
    b) internal rate of return
    c) payback
    d) a and b

    Answer: c Difficulty: 2

42. Which of the following cash flows are not considered in the calculation of the initial outlay for a capital investment proposal?
    a) increase in accounts receivable
    b) cost of issuing new bonds if the project is financed by a new bond issue
    c) installation costs
    d) none of the above

    Answer: b Difficulty: 2

43. Which of the following is not considered in the calculation of differential cash flows?
    a) depreciation tax shield
    b) repayment of principal if new debt is issued
    c) increased dividend payments if additional common stock is issued
    d) b and c

    Answer: d Difficulty: 2

44. If the federal income tax rate were increased, the impact of the tax increase on "acceptable" investment proposals would be to (ignore the impact of the tax change on the cost of capital)
   a) decrease the net present value
   b) increase the net present value
   c) increase the payback period
   d) a and c

   Answer: d Difficulty: 3

45. Which of the following should be included in the initial outlay?
   a) shipping and installation costs
   b) increased working capital requirements
   c) cost of employee training associated specifically with the asset being evaluated
   d) all of the above

   Answer: d Difficulty: 1

46. Increased depreciation expenses affect tax-related cash flows by
   a) increasing taxable income, thus increasing taxes
   b) decreasing taxable income, thus reducing taxes
   c) decreasing taxable income, with no effect on cash flow since depreciation is a non-cash expense
   d) none of the above

   Answer: b Difficulty: 2

47. Which of the following are included in the terminal cash flow?
   a) the expected salvage value of the asset
   b) any tax payments or receipts associated with the salvage value of the asset
   c) recapture of any working capital increase included in the initial outlay
   d) all of the above

   Answer: d Difficulty: 1

48. A firm purchased an asset with a 5 year life for $90,000, and it cost $10,000 for shipping and installation. According to the current tax laws the initial depreciation value of the asset is
   a) $100,000
   b) $80,000
   c) $95,000
   d) $70,000

   Answer: a Difficulty: 2

49. The initial outlay includes:
    a) working capital requirements
    b) installation fees
    c) shipping fees
    d) all of the above

    Answer: d Difficulty: 1

50. Which of the following is not included in the calculation of the initial outlay for a capital budget.
    a) additional working-capital investments
    b) training expenses
    c) installation
    d) all are included in the initial outlay

    Answer: d Difficulty: 2

51. When terminating a project for capital budgeting purposes, the working capital outlay required at the initiation of the project will
    a) not affect the cash flow.
    b) will decrease the cash flow because it is a historical cost.
    c) will increase the cash flow because it is recaptured.
    d) will decrease the cash flow because it is an outlay.

    Answer: c Difficulty: 2

52. Your company is considering replacing an old steel cutting machine with a new one. Two months ago, you sent the company engineer to a training seminar demonstrating the new machine's operation and efficiency. The $2,500 cost for this training session has already been paid. If the new machine is purchased, it would require $5,000 in installation and modification costs to make it suitable for operation in your factory. The old machine originally cost $50,000 five years ago and is being depreciated by $7,000 per year. The new machine will cost $75,000 before installation and modification. It will be depreciated by $5,000 per year. The old machine can be sold today for $10,000. The marginal tax rate for the firm is 40%. Compute the relevant initial outlay in this capital budgeting decision.
    a) $72,500
    b) $68,000
    c) $70,500
    d) $78,000

    Answer: b Difficulty: 3

53. Brrr Habit Corporation is considering a new product line. The company currently manufactures several lines of snow skiing apparel. The new products, insulated ski shorts, are expected to generate sales of $1 million per year for the next five years. They expect that during this five year period, they will lose about $250,000 in sales on their existing lines of longer ski pants. The new line will require no additional equipment or space in the plant and can be produced in the same manner as the apparel products. The new project will, however, require that the company spend an additional $80,000 per year on insurance in case customers sue for frostbite. Also, a new marketing director would be hired to oversee the line at $45,000 per year in salary and benefits. Because of the different construction of the shorts, an increase in inventory of 3,800 would be required initially. If the marginal tax rate is 30%, compute the incremental after tax cash flows for years 1-5.
a) $434,500 per year
b) $625,000 per year
c) $187,500 per year
d) $437,500 per year

Answer: d Difficulty: 3

54. Al's Fabrication Shop is purchasing a new rivet machine to replace an existing one. The new machine costs $8,000 and will require an additional cost of $1,000 for modification. It will be depreciated using simplified straight line depreciation over five years. The new machine operates much faster than the old machine and with better quality. Consequently, sales are expected to increase by $2,100 per year for the next five years. While it is faster, it is fully automated and will result in increased electricity costs for the firm by $700 per year. It will, however, save about $850 per year in labor costs. The old machine is 20 years old and has already been fully depreciated. If the firm's marginal tax rate is 28%, compute the after tax incremental cash flows for the new machine for years 1 through 5.
a) $2,698
b) $450
c) $2,124
d) $1,620

Answer: c Difficulty: 3

55. Evaluating risky capital investments by means of the risk-adjusted discount rate:
a) assumes that the risk of the project equals the average risk of the firm
b) requires the certainty equivalent of the project to be determined
c) assumes that the riskiness of the project increases through time
d) provides for a higher risk-adjustment net present value for projects with above average risk than would be obtained by discounting cash flows at the marginal cost of capital

Answer: c Difficulty: 3

56. Projects of varying risk can be evaluated by:
    a) identical certainty equivalents
    b) high-risk projects having high certainty equivalents
    c) comparable risk-adjusted net present values
    d) a and b

    Answer: c Difficulty: 2

57. The major difference between the risk-adjusted discount rate and the certainty equivalent method of evaluating capital investments is:
    a) the risk-adjusted discount rate adjusts the expected cash flows downward for risk
    b) the certainty equivalent method adjusts the discount rate down for more risky projects
    c) the certainty equivalent approach requires projects to be discounted at the marginal costs of capital
    d) the risk-adjusted discount rate is larger for projects of greater risk than for projects of lesser risk

    Answer: a Difficulty: 2

58. The financial manager selecting one of two projects of differing risk should:
    a) select the project with the larger risk-adjusted net present value
    b) choose the project with the least relative risk
    c) choose the project with greater return even if that project has greater risk
    d) choose the project with less risk even though that project has less return

    Answer: a Difficulty: 2

59. Advantages of using simulation include:
    a) adjustment for risk in the resulting distribution of net present values
    b) a range of possible outcomes presented
    c) is good only for single period investments since discounting is not possible
    d) graphically displays all possible outcomes of the investment

    Answer: b Difficulty: 2

60. Most individuals are:
    a) risk averse
    b) gamblers
    c) risk neutral
    d) none of the above

    Answer: a Difficulty: 1

61. The certainty equivalent approach is characterized by:
    a) risky expected cash flows being deflated to riskless cash flows
    b) a risk adjusted discount rate being estimated to calculate the present value of the risky cash flows
    c) the decision maker's utility function being used in the analysis
    d) both a and c

    Answer: d Difficulty: 2

62. Certainty equivalent coefficients are defined as:
    a) risky cashflow/certain cash flow
    b) certain cash flow/risky cash flow
    c) certain cash flow/(i+k)/risky cash flow
    d) none of the above

    Answer: b Difficulty: 2

63. What method is used for calculation of the accounting beta?
    a) simulation
    b) regression analysis
    c) sensitivity analysis
    d) both a and c

    Answer: b Difficulty: 2

64. All of the following variables are used in the calculation of the certainty equivalent approach except:
    a) number of possible outcomes
    b) project's expected life
    c) risk-free interest rate
    d) initial cash outlay

    Answer: a Difficulty: 2

65. The certainty equivalent approach uses all the following steps except:
    a) the risk for each outcome is measured
    b) the normal capital budgeting criterion are applied
    c) the riskless cash flows are discounted back to present at the riskless rate of interest
    d) the risk is removed from the cash flows by substituting equivalent certain cash flows for the risky cash flows

    Answer: a Difficulty: 2

66. The simulation approach provides us with:
    a) a single value for the risk-adjusted net present value
    b) an approximation of the systematic risk level
    c) a probability distribution of the project's net present value or internal rate of return
    d) a graphic exposition of the year-by-year sequence of possible outcomes

    Answer: c Difficulty: 2

67. Which of the following is not an important consideration in measuring risk for a capital budgeting project for a well diversified firm?
    a) Systematic risk.
    b) Contribution to firm risk.
    c) Total project risk.
    d) None of the above - all may be important in measuring project risk.

    Answer: c Difficulty: 2

68. The Acu Punct Corporation is considering the purchase of a new machine with an initial outlay of $4,500 and expected cash flows in years 1-4 of $2,200. The certainty equivalent coefficient for each period is .87. The appropriate discount rate for the firm is 12%, and the risk-free rate is 5%. Compute the Net Present Value of this project using the certainty equivalent approach.
    a) $1,314
    b) $2,287
    c) $1,899
    d) $2,872

    Answer: b Difficulty: 3

69. Your firm is considering investing in a new product line. It is considerably more risky than the projects your firm typically invests in. As a result, the appropriate risk adjusted discount rate for this project of 22% is much higher than the discount rate for the firm's current projects of 16%. This new line would require an initial outlay of $20,000 and is expected to produce cash flows of $15,000 per year in years 1 and 2. If the risk free rate of return is 4%, determine the certainty equivalent coefficient applicable to the cash flows in years 1 and 2.
    a) .79 in years 1 and 2
    b) .8525 in year 1, .7267 in year 2
    c) 1.04 in year 1, .5316 in year 2
    d) .6933 in year 1, .8922 in year 2

    Answer: b Difficulty: 3

70. The Uh Uh Cola Company is considering investing in a new type of drink flavored spring water. The project is considered risky relative to the firm's current operations because it targets an entirely different market. The project would require an initial outlay of $15,000 and is expected to generate one cash flow at the end of year 5 of $35,000. The applicable certainty equivalent risk coefficient for this cash flow is .61. The discount rate applicable to projects with the same risk as the firm's current investments is 13%. This project, however, involves more risk than usual. If the risk free rate is 6%, what is the risk adjusted discount rate applicable to this project?
    a) 18%
    b) 17%
    c) 7%
    d) 23%

    Answer: b Difficulty: 3

71. Humungous Corporation is a multidivisional conglomerate. The Food Division is undergoing a capital budgeting analysis and must estimate the divisions beta. This division has a different level of systematic risk than is typical for Humungous Corporation as a whole. The most appropriate method for estimating this beta is _____.
    a) The regression coefficient from a time series regression of Humungous Corporation stock returns on a market index.
    b) To multiply the company' beta by the ratio of the Food Division's total assets/Humungous Corporation total assets.
    c) The regression coefficient from a time series regression of Food Division's net income on the Humungous Corporation's return on assets.
    d) The regression coefficient from a time series regression of Food Division's return on assets on a market index.

    Answer: d Difficulty: 3

72. One method of accounting for systematic risk for a project involves identifying a publicly traded firm that is engaged in the same business as that project and using its required rate of return to evaluate the project. This method is referred to as _____.
    a) the accounting beta method.
    b) the certainty equivalent approach.
    c) the pure play method.
    d) sensitivity analysis.

    Answer: c Difficulty: 2

73. If bankruptcy costs and/or shareholder underdiversification are an issue, what measure of risk is relevant when evaluating project risk in capital budgeting?
    a) Total project risk
    b) Contribution-to-firm risk
    c) Systematic risk
    d) Capital rationing risk

Answer: b Difficulty: 2

ESSAY

74. Bull Gator Industries is considering a new assembly line costing $6,000,000. The assembly line will be fully depreciated by the simplified straight line method over its 5 year depreciable life. Operating costs of the new machine are expected to be $1,100,000 per year. The existing assembly line has 5 years remaining before it will be fully depreciated and has a book value of $3,000,000. If sold today the company would receive $2,400,000 for the existing machine. Annual operating costs on the existing machine are $2,100,000 per year. Bull Gator is in the 46 percent marginal tax bracket and has a required rate of return of 12 percent.

   a. Calculate the net present value of replacing the existing machine
   b. Explain the impact on NPV of the following
   i. Required rate of return increases
  ii. Operating costs of new machine are increased
iii. Existing machine sold for less

Answer:
   a.   Calculate Initial Outlay

Purchase Price	$6,000,000
Sale of old	(2,400,000)
Tax savings from sale	
($3,000,000 - 2,400,000).46	(276,000)
Initial Outlay	$3,324,000

Differential Cash Flow

	Book Profit	Cash Flow
Reduce costs	$1,000,000	$1,000,000
Increased depreciation*	- 600,000	
Net savings (before tax)	$ 400,000	
Less taxes	- 184,000	- 184,000
Net cash flow		$ 816,000

*Depreciation on old machine

$$\frac{\$3,000,000}{5} = \$600,000$$

Depreciation on new machine

$$\frac{\$6,000,000}{5} = \$1,200,000$$

Answer:

> Increase Depreciation=$600,000-$1,200,000=-$600,000
> Calculate NPV
> NPV = $816,000 x 3.605 - $3,324,000
> NPV = -$382,320

b.   i. NPV decreases
      ii. NPV decreases
     iii. NPV decreases

Difficulty: 3

75. AFX Industries purchased some agricultural land at the edge of a large metropolitan area for $200,000 five years ago. In order to have the land classified as agricultural for property tax purposes, the company has been leasing the property to neighboring farmers. The before-tax return from leasing the property is $8,000 per year. This company's corporate tax rate is 46 percent. If the company sells the land for $300,000 today, what is the internal rate of return on this investment?

Answer:
Initial investment at time 0 = $200,000
Differential after-tax cash flows time 1-5 = (1-.46)($8,000)
$$= \$4,320$$

Terminal after-tax cash flow time 5

$$= \$300,000 - (\$300,000 - \$200,000)(.46) = \$254,000$$

$$\$200,000 = \sum_{t=1}^{5} \frac{\$4,320}{(1 + IRR)^t} + \frac{254,000}{(1 + IRR)^5}$$

$$\$200,000 = \$4,320 \text{ PVIFA}_{IRR\%, 5 \text{ yr.}} + \$254,000 \text{ PVIF}_{IRR\% 5 \text{ yr.}}$$
IRR = 6.8675%

Difficulty: 3

76. Determine the internal rate of return on the following projects:
    a. Initial outlay of $35,000 with an after-tax cash flow at the end of the year of $5,836 for seven years
    b. Initial outlay of $350,000 with an after-tax cash flow at the end of the year of $70,000 for seven years
    c. Initial outlay of $3,500 with an after-tax cash flow at the end of the year of $1,500 for three years

Answer:

a. $IO = ACF_t\ PVIF_{IRR\%,\ t\ yr.}$
   $\$35,000 = \$5,836\ PVIF_{IRR\%,\ 7\ yr.}$
   Thus,
   $IRR = 4\%$

b. $\$350,000 = \$70,000\ PVIF_{IRR\%,\ 7\ yr.}$
   Thus,
   $IRR = 9.2\%$

c. $\$3,500 = \$1,500\ PVIF_{IRR\%,\ 3\ yr.}$
   Thus,
   $IRR = 13.7\%$

Difficulty: 2

77. Knoko Systems is considering a capital budgeting project with a life of 5 years that requires an outlay of $90,000. It has cash flows each period as shown in the following distribution.

P(ACF)	ACF
0.10	$ 0
0.20	12,500
0.40	37,500
0.20	43,750
0.10	50,000

    a. Assuming a risk-adjusted required rate of return of 0.20 is appropriate for projects of this level of risk, calculate the risk-adjusted net present value of the project.
    b. Should the project be accepted?

Answer:
a. $\overline{X}$ = (0)(0.10) + ($12,500)(0.20) + ($37,500)(0.40) +
   ($43,750)(0.20) + ($50,000)(0.10)
   = 0 + $2,500 + $15,000 + $8,750 + $5,000
   = $31,250

   NPV = $31,250(2.991) - $90,000
   NPV = $3,469
b. Accept: NPV is positive

Difficulty: 3

78. Armstrong Company has under consideration two mutually exclusive investment projects with the expected cash flows shown below.

Year	Project A	Project B
0	$ -20,000	$ -22,500
1	6,000	10,000
2	6,000	12,000
3	6,000	12,000
4	6,000	12,000
5	6,000	12,000

The following schedule of certainty equivalent coefficients for the net cash flows each year reflect the company's aversion to risk.

Year	Project A	Project B
0	1.00	1.00
1	0.90	0.70
2	0.90	0.50
3	0.90	0.50
4	0.80	0.50
5	0.80	0.40

If the risk-free rate is 6 percent, which project should be selected?

Answer:

Project A

Year	CF	σ_t	CF times σ_t
0	-$20,000	1.00	-$20,000
1	6,000	0.90	5,400
2	6,000	0.90	5,400
3	6,000	0.90	5,400
4	6,000	0.80	4,800
5	6,000	0.80	4,800

$NPV_A = \$5,400(2.673) + \$4,800(1.833)(0.840) - \$20,000$
$NPV_A = \$1,825$

Project B

Year	CF	σ_t	CF times σ_t
0	-$22,500	1.00	-$22,500
1	10,000	0.70	7,000
2	12,000	0.50	6,000
3	12,000	0.50	6,000
4	12,000	0.50	6,000
5	12,000	0.40	4,800

$NPV_B = \$7,000(0.943)+\$6,000(2.673)(0.943)+\$4,800(0.747)-\$22,500$
$NPV_B = \$2,810$
Select Project B
Difficulty: 3

79. The F. Morgan Company must decide whether or not to accept Project X. The cash flows for Project X are given below.

Cash Flows Years 1 - 2

Probability	Outcome
.30	$ 20,000
.40	70,000
.30	100,000

Cash Flows Years 3 - 5

Probability	Outcome
.20	$55,000
.60	70,000
.20	95,000

The certainty equivalent coefficient for each year is given below.

Year	Certainty Equivalent Coefficient
0	1.00
1	.90
2	.80
3	.60
4	.50
5	.40

The cost of the project is $200,000 and the riskless rate of interest is 8 percent. Should F. Morgan Company make this investment?

Answer:

Expected cash flows years 1-2 =
$(.30)(\$20,000)+(.40)(\$70,000)+(.30)(\$100,000) = \$64,000$
Expected cash flows years 3-5 =
$(.20)(\$55,000)+(.60)(\$70,000)+(.20)(\$95,000) = \$72,000$

$NPV = -\$200,000 + (.90)(\$64,000) \, PVIF_{8\%, \, 1 \, yr.}$
$+ (.80)(\$64,000) \quad PVIF_{8\%, \, 2 \, yr.} + (.60)(\$72,000)$
$PVIF_{8\%, \, 3 \, yr.} + (.50)(\$72,000) \quad PVIF_{8\%, \, 4 \, yr.} +$
$(.40)(\$72,000) \, PVIF_{8\%, \, 5 \, yr.}$
$= -\$200,000 + (\$57,600)(.926) + (\$51,200)(.857) +$
$(\$43,200)(.794) + (\$36,000)(.735) + (\$28,800)(.681)$
$= -\$200,000 + \$53,337.60 + \$43,878.40 + \$34,300.80 +$
$\$26,460 + \$19,612.80 = -\$22,410.40$

Difficulty: 3

80. The Slumber Corp. is considering two mutually exclusive mattress assemblers. Both require an initial outlay of $75,000 and will operate for five years. The probability distributions associated with each assembler for years 1 through 5 are given below:

Cash Flow Years 1-5

Assembler A		Assembler B	
Probability	Cash Flow	Probability	Cash Flow
.20	$30,000	.20	$18,000
.60	45,000	.60	54,000
.20	60,000	.20	90,000

Since assembler B is the riskier of the two, management has decided to apply a required rate of return of 18 percent to its evaluation but only a 12 percent required rate of return to assembler A.

a. Determine the expected value of each assembler's cash flows.

b. Determine each assembler's risk-adjusted net present value.

Answer:

a. $$\bar{X} = \sum_{i=1}^{n} x_i \ P(x_i)$$

$$\bar{X}_A = 0.20(\$30,000)+0.60(\$45,000)+0.20(\$60,000) = \$45,000$$
$$\bar{X}_B = 0.20(\$18,000)+0.60(\$54,000)+0.20(\$90,000) = \$54,000$$

b. $$NPV = \sum_{t=1}^{n} \frac{ACF_t}{(1 + i^*)^t} - IO$$

$$NPV_A = \$45,000 \ (3.605) - \$75,000$$
$$= \$87,225$$
$$NPV_B = \$54,000(3.127) - \$75,000$$
$$= \$93,858$$

Difficulty: 3

81. Metro Communication Co. is considering two mutually exclusive projects. The expected values for each project's cash flows are given below.

Year	Project A	Project B
0	$-600,000	$-600,000
1	200,000	400,000
2	400,000	400,000
3	400,000	400,000
4	600,000	600,000
5	600,000	800,000

Metro's management has decided to evaluate these projects using the certainty equivalent method. The certainty equivalent coefficients for each project's cash flows are given below.

Year	Project A	Project B
0	1.00	1.00
1	.95	.90
2	.90	.80
3	.85	.70
4	.80	.60
5	.75	.50

Given that this company's normal required rate of return is 15 percent and the after-tax risk-free rate is 8 percent, which project should be selected?

Answer:
Project A:

Year	(A) Expected Cash Flow	(B) α_t	(A . B) (Expected Cash Flow) X (α_t)	Present Value Factor at 8%	Present Value
0	-$600,000	1.00	-$600,000	1.000	-$600,000
1	200,000	.95	190,000	0.926	175,940
2	400,000	.90	360,000	0.857	308,520
3	400,000	.85	340,000	0.794	269,960
4	600,000	.80	480,000	0.735	352,800
5	600,000	.75	450,000	0.681	306,450
				NPV_A =	$813,670

Project B:

Year	(A) Expected Cash Flow	(B) α_t	(A . B) (Expected Cash Flow) X (α_t)	Present Value Factor at 8%	Present Value
0	-$600,000	1.00	-$600,000	1.000	-$600,000
1	400,000	.90	360,000	0.926	333,360
2	400,000	.80	320,000	0.857	274,240
3	400,000	.70	280,000	0.794	222,320
4	600,000	.60	360,000	0.735	264,600
5	800,000	.50	400,000	0.681	270,400
				NPV_B =	$764,920

Difficulty: 3

82. Dave Company, Inc. is considering purchasing a new grinding machine with a useful life of five years. The initial outlay for the machine is $165,000. The expected cash inflows and certainty equivalents are as follows:

Year	After-tax Expected Cash Flow	Certainty Equivalent
1	15,000	.95
2	35,000	.90
3	70,000	.80
4	90,000	.70
5	70,000	.65

Given that the firm has a 10% required rate of return and the risk-free rate is 5%, what is the NPV?

Answer:

Year	Equivalent Risk-Free Cash Flow	PVIF @ 5%	Present Value
1	$14,250	.952	$ 13,566.00
2	31,500	.907	28,570.50
3	56,000	.864	48,384.00
4	63,000	.823	51,849.00
5	45,500	.784	35,672.00

Present value of cash flows $178,041.50
Initial outlay 165,000.00
Net present value $ 13,041.50

Difficulty: 3

83. Referring to Dave Co. in the prior problem, what will the NPV be if the firm decides instead of the certainty equivalent method to use the risk-adjusted discount rate method of evaluating projects? Dave Co. feels the risk premium for the project is 3%.

Answer:

Year	After-Tax Cash Flow	PVIF @ 13%	Present Value
1	$15,000	.885	$ 13,275
2	35,000	.783	27,405
3	70,000	.693	48,510
4	90,000	.613	55,170
5	70,000	.543	38,010

Present value of cash flows $182,370
Initial outlay 165,000
Net present value $ 17,370

Difficulty: 3

84. April's Stationary and Gift Store is considering two different lines of houseware. The probability distributions of cash flows in each year associated with the two projects are:

Project A		Project B	
Probability	Outcome	Probability	Outcome
.25	$ 4,000	.25	$ 3,000
.50	$ 8,000	.50	$ 6,000
.25	$12,000	.25	$ 9,000

Both projects will require an initial outlay of $13,000 and will have an estimated life of 6 years. Project A is considered a riskier investment and will have to have an adjusted required rate of return of 15%, while Project B's required rate of return is 12%.

a. Determine the expected value of each project
b. Determine each project's risk-adjusted net present value
c. What other factors might be considered when deciding between these two investments?

Answer:

	Project A	Project B
a.	$ 8,000	$ 6,000
b.	$17,275.86	$11,668.44

Difficulty: 3

85. Akin, Gumble Co. is considering a new project that their research division has proposed and have decided to use the certainty equivalent approach to evaluate it. The expected cash flows and the estimated certainty equivalent coefficients associated with this project are as follows:

Year	Expected cash flows	Estimated certainty equivalent coefficients
0	-$95,000	1.00
1	$18,000	.95
2	$28,000	.90
3	$38,000	.85
4	$28,000	.80
5	$18,000	.75

Assuming a risk-free rate of 7%, calculate the NPV.

Answer:

Year	Present Value
1	$15,981
2	22,010
3	26,366
4	17,089
5	9,625
	$91,071

NPV =   ($3,929)

Difficulty: 3

Chapter 11: Cost of Capital

TRUE/FALSE

1. A firm's cost of capital varies with both business risk and financial risk.

   Answer: True Difficulty: 1

2. A firm's cost of capital is the rate of return earned on the most profitable investment opportunity available.

   Answer: False Difficulty: 1

3. The firm financed completely with equity capital has a cost of capital equal to the required return on common stock.

   Answer: True Difficulty: 2

4. The cost of debt is equal to one minus the marginal tax rate times the coupon rate of interest on the firm's outstanding debt.

   Answer: False Difficulty: 1

5. The average cost of capital is the minimum required return that must be earned on additional investment if firm value is to remain unchanged.

   Answer: True Difficulty: 1

6. One of the simplifying assumptions made when computing the weighted cost of capital is constant financial list.

   Answer: True Difficulty: 1

7. Assuming an after-tax cost of preferred stock of 12.0 percent and a corporate tax rate of 40 percent, a firm must earn at least $20 before tax on every $100 invested.

   Answer: True Difficulty: 3

8. Other things equal, management should retain profits only if the company's investments within the firm are at least as attractive as the stockholders' other investment opportunities.

   Answer: True Difficulty: 2

9. The cost of new common stock is generally less than the cost of retained earnings.

   Answer: False Difficulty: 1

10. The firm's best financial structure is determined by finding the capital structure that minimizes the firm's cost of capital.

    Answer: True Difficulty: 2

11. Inflation in the economy causes an increase in the risk premium demanded by investors for any particular source of capital.

    Answer: False Difficulty: 2

12. The best financial structure is determined by finding the debt and equity mix that maximizes the firm's cost of capital.

    Answer: False Difficulty: 2

13. If a firm was to earn exactly its cost of capital, we would expect the price of its common stock to remain unchanged.

    Answer: True Difficulty: 1

14. In determining the cost of financing, management should consider the needs and desires of the creditors and owners of the firm.

    Answer: True Difficulty: 1

15. Investors require higher rates of return to compensate for purchasing power losses resulting from inflation.

    Answer: True Difficulty: 1

16. A security with a reasonably stable price will require a higher required return than a security with an unstable price.

    Answer: False Difficulty: 2

17. The average cost of capital is the appropriate rate to use when evaluating new investments, even though the new investments may be in a higher risk class.

    Answer: False Difficulty: 1

18. If the before-tax cost of debt is 9% and the firm has a 34% marginal tax rate, the after-tax cost of debt is 5.4%.

    Answer: True Difficulty: 1

19. No adjustment is made in the cost of preferred stock for taxes since preferred stock dividends are not tax deductible.

    Answer: True Difficulty: 1

20. The cost of internal common funds is already on an after-tax basis since dividends paid to common stockholders are not tax deductible.

    Answer: True Difficulty: 1

21. Market conditions are reflected by the riskless rate of return, while general economic conditions are reflected by the risk premium.

    Answer: False Difficulty: 1

22. Financial risk is the variability in returns on assets and is affected by the firm's investment decisions.

    Answer: False Difficulty: 1

23. Using the weighted cost of capital as a cutoff rate assumes that the riskiness of the project being evaluated is similar to the riskiness of the company's existing assets.

    Answer: True Difficulty: 2

24. Using the weighted cost of capital as a cutoff rate assumes that future investments will be financed so as to maintain the firm's target degree of financial leverage.

    Answer: True Difficulty: 2

25. Book value weights are often used to calculate a firm's weighted average cost of capital although the preferred set of weights are those that actually reflect the firm's chosen financing mix.

    Answer: True Difficulty: 2

MULTIPLE CHOICE

26. Cost of capital is:
    a) the coupon rate of debt
    b) a hurdle rate set by the board of directors
    c) the rate of return that must be earned on additional investment if firm value is to remain unchanged
    d) the average cost of the firm's assets

    Answer: c Difficulty: 1

27. Components of capital structure may include:
    a) bonds
    b) common stock
    c) preferred stock
    d) all of the above

    Answer: d Difficulty: 1

28. J & B, Inc. has $5 million of debt outstanding with a coupon rate of 12 percent. Currently the yield to maturity on these bonds is 14 percent. If the firm's tax rate is 40 percent, what is cost of debt to J & B?
    a) 12.0 percent
    b) 14.0 percent
    c) 8.4 percent
    d) 5.6 percent

    Answer: c Difficulty: 1

29. The expected dividend is $2.50 for a share of stock priced at $25. What is the cost of retained earnings if the long-term growth in dividends is projected to be 8 percent?
    a) 10.0 percent
    b) 8.0 percent
    c) 25.0 percent
    d) 18.0 percent

    Answer: d Difficulty: 2

30. The average cost associated with each additional dollar of financing for investment projects is:
    a) the incremental return
    b) the marginal cost of capital
    c) risk-free rate
    d) beta

    Answer: b Difficulty: 1

31. A firm's cost of capital is influenced by:
    a) risk-free rate
    b) business risk
    c) financial risk
    d) all of the above

    Answer: d Difficulty: 1

32. The Huang Company has an optimal capital structure of 40 percent debt and 60 percent equity. Additions to retained earnings for the forthcoming year are estimated at $12 million. How large can the capital budget be before common stock must be sold?
    a) $20.0 million
    b) $4.8 million
    c) $8.2 million
    d) $12.0 million

    Answer: a Difficulty: 2

33. Shawhan Supply plans to maintain its optimal capital structure of 30 percent debt, 20 percent preferred stock, and 50 percent common stock far into the future. The required return on each component is; debt--10 percent; preferred stock--11 percent; common stock--18 percent. Assuming a 40 percent marginal tax rate, what after-tax rate of return must Shawhan Supply earn on its investments if the value of the firm is to remain unchanged?
    a) 18.0 percent
    b) 13.0 percent
    c) 10.0 percent
    d) 14.2 percent

    Answer: b Difficulty: 2

34. Scott Mfg. has five possible investment projects for the coming year. They are:

Project	Investment (million)	IRR
A	$ 6	20%
B	$12	16%
C	$ 6	15%
D	$ 8	14%
E	$ 4	9%

    Scott's weighted marginal cost of capital schedule is 12 percent for up to $24 million of investment; beyond $24 million the weighted cost of capital is 13 percent. The optimal capital budget is:
    a) $18 million
    b) $24 million
    c) $32 million
    d) $6 million

    Answer: c Difficulty: 2

35. The cost of preferred stock is equal to:
    a) the preferred stock dividend divided by market price
    b) the preferred stock dividend divided by its par value
    c) (1 - tax rate) times the preferred stock dividend divided by net price
    d) preferred stock dividend divided by the net market price

    Answer: d Difficulty: 2

36. In general, the most expensive source of capital is:
    a) preferred stock
    b) new common stock
    c) debt
    d) retained earnings

    Answer: b Difficulty: 2

37. The XYZ Company is planning a $50 million expansion. The expansion is to be financed by selling $20 million in new debt and $30 million in new common stock. The before-tax required rate of return on debt is 9 percent and the required rate of return on equity is 14 percent. If the company is in the 40 percent tax bracket, what is the firm's cost of capital?
    a) 14.0
    b) 9.0
    c) 10.6
    d) 11.5

    Answer: c Difficulty: 2

38. The cost of external equity capital is greater than the cost of retained earnings because of:
    a) flotation costs on new equity
    b) capital gains tax on new equity
    c) both a and b
    d) the costs are the same

    Answer: a Difficulty: 2

39. Bender and Co. is issuing a $1,000 par value bond that pays 9% interest annually. Investors are expected to pay $918 for the 10-year bond. Bender will have to pay $33 per bond in flotation costs. What is the cost of debt if the firm is in the 34% tax bracket?
    a) 8.23%
    b) 9.01%
    c) 9.23%
    d) 11.95%

    Answer: a Difficulty: 2

40. All the following variables are used in computing the cost of debt except:
    a) maturity value of the debt
    b) market price of the debt
    c) number of years to maturity
    d) risk-free rate

    Answer: d Difficulty: 2

41. Which problem listed is not associated with the corresponding method of measuring the common stockholder's required rate of return?
    a) Estimation of the expected growth rate of future dividends: The dividend-growth model
    b) Determination of the expectations in the minds of investors: The CAPM approach
    c) The estimates of the risk premium involve subjectivity: The risk-premium approach
    d) All of the above are correct

    Answer: d Difficulty: 2

42. Armadillo Mfg. Co. has a target capital structure of 50% debt 50% equity. They are planning to invest in a project which will necessitate raising new capital. New debt will be issued at a before tax yield of 12%, with a coupon rate of 10%. The equity will be provided by internally generated funds. No new outside equity will be issued. If the required rate of return on the firm's stock is 15% and its marginal tax rate is 40%, compute the firm's cost of capital.
    a) 13.5%
    b) 12.5%
    c) 7.2%
    d) 11.1%

    Answer: d Difficulty: 3

43. As financial manager for ABZ Corporation you are trying to determine the appropriate cost of capital for the firm. The firm is considering an investment which will require an initial outlay of $100,000. The firm can issue bonds at a price of $940.82 which have a coupon rate of 8% on 10 years to maturity and a face value of $1,000. The underwriter would charge flotation costs, however, of $5 per bond. The company can issue new equity at a before tax cost of 16%. It has $75,000 of internal equity availablefor investment projects at this time. The required rate of return on the company's stock is 14% and its marginal tax rate is 34%. If the company wishes to maintain its current capital structure of 60% debt and 40% equity, what is the appropriate cost of capital to use for this project's capital budgeting analysis?
    a) 14%
    b) 8.77%
    c) 9.16%
    d) 10%

    Answer: c Difficulty: 3

44. Verigreen Lawn Care products just paid a dividend of $1.85. This dividend is expected to grow at a constant rate of 3% per year, so the next expected dividend is $1.90. The stock price is currently $12.50. New stock can be sold at this price subject to flotation costs of 15%. The company's marginal tax rate is 40%. Compute the cost of internal (retained earnings) and the cost of external equity (new common stock).
    a) 0, 17.8%
    b) 15.2%, 17.8%
    c) 18.2%, 20.9%
    d) 18.2%, 16.21%

    Answer: c Difficulty: 3

45. Your company is considering an investment in a project which would require an initial outlay of $300,000 and produce expected cash flows in years 1-5 of $87,385 per year. You have determined that the current after-tax cost of the firm's capital (required rate of return) for each source of financing is as follows:

Cost of Debt   8%
Cost of Preferred Stock 12%
Cost of Common Stock   16%

Long term debt currently makes up 20% of the capital structure, preferred stock 10%, and common stock 70%. What is the net present value of this project?
a) -$13,876
b) $0
c) $287,692
d) $1,568

Answer: b   Difficulty: 3

46. Risk arising from the variability in return on assets is referred to as _____ risk.
a) Financial
b) Business
c) Marketability
d) Cost of capital

Answer: b   Difficulty: 2

47. Dublin International Corporation's marginal tax rate is 40%. It can issue 3 year bonds with a coupon rate of 8.5% and par value of $1,000. The bonds can be sold now at a price of $938.90 each. The underwriters will charge $23 per bond in flotation costs. Determine the appropriate after tax cost of debt for Dublin International to use in a capital budgeting analysis.
a) 4.5%
b) 5.2%
c) 6.0%
d) 7.2%

Answer: d   Difficulty: 2

48. XYZ Corporation is trying to determine the appropriate cost of preferred stock to use in determining the firm's cost of capital. This firm's preferred stock is currently selling for $36.00, and pays a perpetual annual dividend of $2.60 per share. Underwriters of a new issue of preferred stock would charge $6 per share in flotation costs. The firm's tax rate is 30%. Compute the cost of new preferred stock for XYZ.
    a) 7.2%
    b) 6.2%
    c) 8.7%
    d) 16.7%

    Answer: c Difficulty: 2

49. Sonderson Corporation is undertaking a capital budgeting analysis. The firm's beta is 1.5. The rate on 6 month t-bills is 5%, and the return on the S&P 500 index is 12%. The firm can issue external equity with flotation costs of 14%. What is the appropriate cost for retained earnings in determining the firm's cost of capital?
    a) 0
    b) 15.5%
    c) 17.7%
    d) 10.5%

    Answer: b Difficulty: 2

50. Given the following information on S & G Inc. capital structure, compute the company's weighted average cost of capital.

Type of Capital	Percent of Capital Structure	Before Tax Component Cost
Bonds	40%	7.5%
Preferred Stock	5%	11%
Common Stock (Internal Only)	55%	15%

The company's marginal tax rate is 40%.
    a) 13.3%
    b) 7.1%
    c) 10.6%
    d) 10%

    Answer: c Difficulty: 2

51. Mars Car Company has a capital structure made up of 40% debt and 60% equity and a tax rate of 30%. A new issue of bonds maturing in 20 years can be issued with a coupon of 9% at a price of $1,098.18 with no flotation costs. The firm has no internal equity available for investment at this time, but can issue new common stock at a price of $45. The next expected dividend on the stock is $2.70. The dividend for Mars Co. is expected to grow at a constant annual rate of 5% per year indefinitely. Flotation costs on new equity will be $7.00 per share. The company has the following investment projects available:

Project	Initial Outlay	IRR
1	$100,000	10%
2	$ 10,000	8.5%
3	$ 50,000	12.5%

Which of the above projects should the company take on?

a) Project 3 only
b) Projects 1 and 2
c) Projects 1 and 3
d) Projects 1, 2 and 3

Answer: c Difficulty: 3

52. In capital budgeting analysis, when computing the weighted average cost of capital, the CAPM approach is typically used to find the component cost of which type of capital?
a) Debt
b) Preferred stock
c) Internal equity
d) External equity

Answer: c Difficulty: 2

ESSAY

53. Vipsu Corporation plans to issue 10-year bonds with a par value of $1,000 that will pay $55 every six months. The net amount of capital to the firm from the sale of each bond is $840.68. If Vipsu is in the 25 percent tax bracket, what is the after-tax cost of debt?

Answer:
Find the present value factors that equate

$$\$840.67 = \$55 \ (PVIFA, \ 20, \ \frac{r}{2}) + \$1,000 \ (PVIF, \ 20, \ \frac{r}{2})$$

$$r = 0.14$$

$$k_d = .14 \ (1-0.25) = .105 = 10.5\%$$

Difficulty: 2

54. Moore Financing Corporation has preferred stock in its capital structure paying a dividend of $3.75 and selling for $25.00. If the marginal-tax rate for Moore is 34 percent, what is the after-tax cost of preferred financing?

Answer:

After-tax cost of preferred financing $= \dfrac{\$3.75}{\$25.00} = .15$

Difficulty: 2

55. Hoak Company's common stock is currently selling for $50. Last year's dividend was $1.83 per share. Investors expect dividends to grow at an annual rate of 9 percent into the future.

a. What is the cost of internal common equity?
b. Selling new common stock is expected to decrease the price of the stock by $5.00. What is the cost of new common stock?

Answer:

a. $K_r = \dfrac{\$1.83(1.09)}{\$50} + 0.09 = 0.13$

b. $K_s = \dfrac{\$1.83(1.09)}{\$50 - \$5} + 0.09 = 0.134$

Difficulty: 2

56. Taylor Service has a capital structure consisting of 40 percent debt and 60 percent common equity. Assuming the capital structure is optimal, what amount of total investment can be financed by a $54 million addition to retained earnings?

Answer:

$\dfrac{\$54 \text{ million}}{0.6} = \$90 \text{ million}$

Difficulty: 2

57. Last year Gator Getters, Inc. had $50 million in total assets. Management desires to increase its plant and equipment during the coming year by $12 million. The company plans to finance 40 percent of the expansion with debt and the remaining 60 percent with equity capital. Bond financing will be at a 9 percent rate and will be sold at its par value. Common stock is currently selling for $50 per share, and flotation costs for new common stock will amount to $5 per share. The expected dividend next year for Gator is $2.50. Furthermore, dividends are expected to grow at a 6 percent rate far into the future. The marginal corporate tax rate is 34 percent. Internal funding available from additions to retained earnings is $4,000,000.

a. What amount of new common stock must be sold if the existing capital structure is to be maintained?

b. Calculate the weighted marginal cost of capital at an investment level of $12 million.

Answer:

a.
$12 million x 0.6 =	$8.2 million
Less additions to R/E	4.0 million
New common stock	$3.2 million

b. $K_d = 9(1 - .34) = 5.94\%$

$K_{nc} = \dfrac{\$2.50}{\$45} + 0.06$

$K_{nc} = 11.5\%$

$K_o = 0.4 \times 5.94\% + 0.6 \times 11.5\%$

$K_o = 9.28\%$

Difficulty: 3

58. The common stock for Grapevine Plumbing Company currently sells for $40 per share. If a new issue is sold the flotation cost is estimated to be $7 per share. The company had earnings of $2.00 per share four years ago. Next year the company expects to have earnings of $3.22 per share. The company maintains a constant dividend payout ratio of 40 percent. Earnings per share are anticipated to grow at the same rate in the future. The firm's marginal tax rate is 30 percent. Calculate the cost of internal equity capital and external equity capital.

Answer:
$$\$3.22 = \$2.00(FVIF_{g,5})$$

$$1.61 = (FVIF_{g,5})$$
growth rate in earnings = growth rate in dividends = .10

$$K_c = \frac{(\$3.22)(.40)}{\$40} + .10 = .1322$$

$$K_{nc} = \frac{(\$3.22)(.40)}{(\$40 - \$7)} + .10 = .1390$$

Difficulty: 3

59. A company is going to issue a $1,000 par value bond which pays 8% in annual interest. The company expects investors to pay $910 for the 20-year bond. The expected flotation cost per bond is $42. What is the firm's cost of debt in this example? (Assume a 34% tax rate.)

Answer:

$$\$868 = \sum_{t=1}^{20} \frac{80}{(1 + Kd)^t} + \frac{1000}{(1 + Kd)^{20}}$$

$$K_d = 9.5\% \ (1-.34) = 6.3\%$$
Difficulty: 3

60. Toto and Associates' preferred stock is selling for $19.20 a share. The firm nets $18.40 after issuance costs. The stock pays an annual dividend of $2.21 per share. What is the cost of preferred stock to the company.

Answer:
$$K_p = \frac{\$2.21}{\$18.40} = 12\%$$
Difficulty: 2

61. Sutter Corporation's common stock is selling for $16.80 a share. Last year Sutter paid a dividend of $.80. Investors are expecting Sutter's dividends to grow at an annual rate of 5% per year. What is the cost of internal equity?

    Answer:
    K_c = (D1/Po) + 6

        = [$80(1.05)/16.80] + .05

        = 10%

    Difficulty: 2

62. Gibson Industries is issuing a $1,000 par value bond with an 8% annual interest coupon rate and matures in 11 years. Investors are willing to pay $972, and flotation costs will be 9%. Gibson is in the 34% tax bracket. What will be the after-tax cost of debt of the bond?

    Answer:

    After-tax cost of debt = 9.76%(1-.34)

    After-tax cost of debt = 6.44%
    Difficulty: 2

63. The preferred stock of Wells Co. sells for $17 and pays a $1.75 dividend. The net price of the stock after issuance costs is $15.30. What is the cost of capital for preferred stock?

    Answer:
    Cost of preferred stock = 1.75/15.30

    Cost of preferred stock = 11.44%
    Difficulty: 2

64. Caribe's common stock sells for $41, and dividends paid last year were $1.18. Flotation costs on issuing stock will be 12% of the market price. The dividends and earnings per share are predicted to have a 10% growth rate. What is the cost of internal equity for Caribe?

    Answer:
    Cost of internal equity = ((1.18(1 + .10))/41) + .10

    Cost of internal equity = 13.17%
    Difficulty: 2

65. Combs, Inc. is issuing new common stock at a market price of $22. Dividends last year were $1.15 per share and are expected to grow at a rate of 7%. Flotation costs will be 5% of the market price. What is Combs cost of external equity?

Answer:
Cost of internal equity = ((1.15(1 + .07)))/(22 − (22(.05))) + .07

Cost of equity   = (1.23/20.9) + .07

Cost of equity   = 12.89%

Difficulty: 2

Chapter 12:   Determining the Financing Mix

TRUE/FALSE

1. Financial risk refers to the relative dispersion of a firm's earnings before interest and taxes.

   Answer: False Difficulty: 1

2. Operating leverage means financing a portion of a firm's earnings per share with debt.

   Answer: False Difficulty: 1

3. Financial leverage increases the variability of a firm's earnings per share.

   Answer: True Difficulty: 1

4. Break even analysis utilizes known relationships to equate quantities of input to the quantities of output.

   Answer: False Difficulty: 1

5. As the volume of production increases the fixed cost-per unit of the product decreases.

   Answer: True Difficulty: 1

6. A decrease in the level of production results in decreased variable cost per unit.

   Answer: False Difficulty: 1

7. If sales increase by 20 percent, the break even model assumes that total variable costs will increase by 30 percent.

   Answer: False Difficulty: 1

8. The break-even model expresses the volume of output as a unit quantity.

   Answer: True Difficulty: 1

9. The break-even model assumes that selling price per unit and fixed cost per unit of output are constant over the relevant range of output.

   Answer: False Difficulty: 1

10. If the cost estimates used in a break even analysis make allowances for non-cash expenses, a firm's production and sales levels do not have to be as great to cover the cash costs of production.

    Answer: True Difficulty: 2

11. Operating leverage is measured as the responsiveness of the firm's earnings before interest and taxes relative to fluctuations in sales.

    Answer: True Difficulty: 2

12. If a firm's production process has fixed costs, the degree of operating leverage will decrease as sales exceed the break even point.

    Answer: True Difficulty: 2

13. If a firm utilizes debt financing and experiences a 10 percent drop in earnings before interest and taxes, the resulting decrease in earnings per share will be greater than 10 percent.

    Answer: True Difficulty: 2

14. Business risk refers to the relative dispersion of the firm's earnings available to common stockholders.

    Answer: False Difficulty: 2

15. In the long run all costs are variable.

    Answer: True Difficulty: 2

16. If fixed costs are $120,000, price per unit is $8, and variable cost per unit is $5, the break even point is 40,000 units.

    Answer: True Difficulty: 1

17. Break even analysis assumes a quadratic relationship between variable costs and the number of units produced.

    Answer: False Difficulty: 1

18. The break even point on an accounting profit basis is equal to or less than the break even point on a cash basis.

    Answer: False Difficulty: 2

19. Break even analysis assumes that a multiproduct firm maintains a constant production and sales mix.

    Answer: True Difficulty: 2

20. When calculating the degree of financial leverage for a firm with preferred stock in its financial structure, the preferred stock dividends must be adjusted to a before-tax basis.

    Answer: True Difficulty: 2

21. Dispersion in operating income causes business risk.

    Answer: False Difficulty: 2

22. The asset structure affects the level and variability of the firm's net operating income (EBIT).

    Answer: True Difficulty: 2

23. The financial structure affects the level and variability of the firm's net operating income (EBIT).

    Answer: False Difficulty: 2

24. Financial leverage means financing a portion of the firm's assets with securities bearing a fixed rate of return in hopes of increasing the stockholder's ultimate return.

    Answer: True Difficulty: 2

25. Operating leverage refers to the incurrence of fixed operating costs in the firm's income stream.

    Answer: True Difficulty: 2

26. The break even quantity of output is the quantity in units which results in a level of EBIT just equal to the cost of debt and preferred stock.

    Answer: False Difficulty: 2

27. Fixed costs vary directly with production output.

    Answer: False Difficulty: 1

28. A potential use of break even analysis is in labor contract negotiations.

    Answer: True Difficulty: 2

29. Over a particular range of output, fixed costs remain unchanged.

    Answer: True Difficulty: 2

30. Unit contribution margin is the difference between the unit selling price and unit variable cost.

    Answer: True Difficulty: 2

31. If unit sales price is $12, unit variable cost is $8, and fixed cost is $1,000,000, the break even point is 125,000 units.

   Answer: False Difficulty: 2

32. If the degree of operating leverage is 4 times, we would expect an increase in EBIT of 1 percent for a 4 percent increase in sales.

   Answer: False Difficulty: 2

33. The greater the degree of operating leverage, the greater is the sensitivity of EPS to change in EBIT.

   Answer: False Difficulty: 2

34. If the degree of financial leverage is 1.25 times, we would expect an increase in EBIT of 4 percent to result in a 5 percent increase in EPS.

   Answer: True Difficulty: 2

35. The degree of combined leverage is the percentage change in sales divided by the percentage change in EPS.

   Answer: False Difficulty: 2

36. If the degree of operating leverage is 2 times, and the degree of financial leverage is 1.5 times, then if sales increase by 10 percent we will expect EPS to increase by 30 percent.

   Answer: True Difficulty: 2

37. Depreciation is considered a fixed cost.

   Answer: True Difficulty: 2

38. Operating leverage is more controllable by management than financial leverage.

   Answer: False Difficulty: 2

39. The contribution margin is the difference between unit variable cost and unit fixed cost.

   Answer: False Difficulty: 2

40. Fixed operating costs do not include charges incurred from the firm's use of debt financing.

   Answer: True Difficulty: 2

41. The degree of operating leverage measure can "work" only in the positive direction.

    Answer: False Difficulty: 2

42. Dispersion in operating income causes business risk.

    Answer: False Difficulty: 2

43. The more fixed-charge securities the firm employs in its financial structure, the greater its degree of financial leverage.

    Answer: True Difficulty: 2

44. Financial risk is a direct result of the firm's financing decision.

    Answer: True Difficulty: 2

45. The cost-volume-profit relationship in a break-even analysis is presumed linear over the entire range of output.

    Answer: True Difficulty: 2

46. The break-even quantity of output is the annual fixed costs divided by the unit contribution margin.

    Answer: True Difficulty: 1

47. Financial structure includes long- and short-term sources of funds.

    Answer: True Difficulty: 1

48. Capital structure management strives to increase the expected earnings per share of the firm.

    Answer: False Difficulty: 2

49. According to the dependence hypothesis of debt financing, the cost of common equity is constant regardless of the debt financing level.

    Answer: True Difficulty: 2

50. An increase in financial leverage will increase EBIT.

    Answer: False Difficulty: 2

51. Because preferred stock dividends are not tax deductible, they are not a source of financial leverage.

    Answer: False Difficulty: 2

52. The objective of capital structure management is to maximize the market value of the firm's equity.

    Answer: True Difficulty: 2

53. Capital costs, like other costs, potentially reduce the size of the cash dividend that can be paid.

    Answer: True Difficulty: 2

54. The independence hypothesis suggests that the total market value of the firm's outstanding securities is <u>unaffected</u> by its capital structure.

    Answer: True Difficulty: 2

55. According to the independence hypothesis, earnings and dividends are expected to fall as financial leverage increases.

    Answer: False Difficulty: 2

56. The major implication of the independence hypothesis is that one capital structure is as good as any other.

    Answer: True Difficulty: 2

57. The independence hypothesis is also called the net-income approach to valuation.

    Answer: False Difficulty: 2

58. The independence hypothesis suggests that the cost of equity decreases as financial leverage increases.

    Answer: False Difficulty: 2

59. Other things the same, the use of debt financing reduces the firm's total tax bill resulting in a higher total market value.

    Answer: True Difficulty: 2

60. Even before bankruptcy costs become detrimental, tax shield effects exert a downward pressure on the price of the firm's common stock.

    Answer: False Difficulty: 2

61. One benefit from using fixed cost securities is the reduced variability in the earnings per share stream.

    Answer: False Difficulty: 2

62. An EBIT-EPS analysis allows the decision maker to visualize the impact of different financing plans on EPS over a range of EBIT levels.

Answer: True Difficulty: 2

63. Because there are no fixed financing costs, a common stock plan line in an EBIT-EPS analysis chart will have a steeper slope than will a bond-plan line.

Answer: False Difficulty: 2

64. One danger of EBIT-EPS analysis is that it ignores the implicit cost of debt financing.

Answer: True Difficulty: 2

65. Debt capacity is the maximum proportion of debt that the firm can include in its capital structure without increasing its tax liability.

Answer: False Difficulty: 2

66. Based on the results of a study reviewed in the text, the single most important influence on target debt ratios is the advice of investment bankers.

Answer: False Difficulty: 2

67. When a firm's capital structure is all common equity, the cost of common equity is equal to the weighted cost of capital.

Answer: True Difficulty: 1

68. The implicit cost of debt takes into consideration the change in the cost of common equity brought on by using additional debt.

Answer: True Difficulty: 2

69. The tax shield on interest is calculated by multiplying the interest rate paid on debt by the principal amount of the debt and the firm's marginal tax rate.

Answer: True Difficulty: 2

70. The EBIT-EPS indifference point, sometimes called the break-even point, identifies the optimal range of financial leverage regardless of the financing plan chosen by the financial manager.

Answer: False Difficulty: 2

71. Debt capacity is the minimum proportion of debt the firm can include in its capital structure and still maintain its lowest composite cost of capital.

    Answer: False Difficulty: 2

72. Capital structure is the mix of the long-term sources of funds used by the firm.

    Answer: True Difficulty: 1

73. Agency costs tend to occur in business organizations when ownership and management control are confined to the same individuals.

    Answer: False Difficulty: 1

74. Comparative leverage ratio analysis does not involve the use of industry norms.

    Answer: False Difficulty: 2

MULTIPLE CHOICE

75. A firm's business risk is influenced by:
    a) the competitive position of the firm within the industry
    b) demand characteristics of the firm's products
    c) the operating cost structure of the firm
    d) all of the above

    Answer: d Difficulty: 1

76. The break even model enables the manager of the firm to:
    a) calculate the minimum price of common stock for certain situations
    b) set appropriate equilibrium thresholds
    c) determine the quantity of output that must be sold to cover all operating costs
    d) determine the optimal amount of debt financing to use

    Answer: c Difficulty: 1

77. Fixed costs include all of the following except:
    a) administrative sales
    b) property taxes
    c) sales commissions
    d) insurance

    Answer: c Difficulty: 1

78. Which of the following is not an example of variable costs?
    a) packaging
    b) depreciation
    c) direct labor
    d) freight costs on products

    Answer: b Difficulty: 1

79. A plant may remain operating when sales are depressed.
    a) if the selling price per unit exceeds the variable cost per unit
    b) to help the local economy
    c) in an effort to cover at least some of the variable cost
    d) unless variable costs are zero when production is zero

    Answer: a Difficulty: 2

80. An example of a semivariable or semifixed cost is:
    a) rent
    b) salaries paid production foremen
    c) energy costs associated with production
    d) direct labor

    Answer: b Difficulty: 2

81. Noncash expenses include:
    a) depreciation expenses
    b) salaries of administrative personnel
    c) foremen's salaries
    d) packaging expenses

    Answer: a Difficulty: 1

82. A firm that uses large amounts of debt financing in an industry characterized by a high degree of business risk would have _____ earnings per share fluctuations resulting from changes in levels of sales.
    a) no
    b) constant
    c) large
    d) small

    Answer: c Difficulty: 2

83. Financial leverage means financing some of a firm's assets with:
    a) money market instruments
    b) preferred stock
    c) corporate bonds
    d) all of the above

    Answer: d Difficulty: 2

84. Potential applications of the break even model include:
    a) replacement for time-adjusted capital budgeting techniques
    b) pricing policy
    c) optimizing the cash-marketable securities position of a firm
    d) all of the above

    Answer: b Difficulty: 2

85. Break even analysis can be useful in:
    a) capital expenditure analysis
    b) bond refunding decisions
    c) rights offering decisions
    d) all of the above

    Answer: a Difficulty: 1

86. An analytical income statement:
    a) can be easily calculated from a corporation's annual report
    b) emphasizes the relationship between fixed and variable costs
    c) assumes that the company produces only one product
    d) assumes that the company does not alter its degree of financial leverage

    Answer: b Difficulty: 2

87. Which costs should be excluded when calculating the degree of operating leverage?
    a) depreciation
    b) administrative expenses
    c) real estate taxes
    d) none of the above

    Answer: d Difficulty: 2

88. Break even analysis is limited to:
    a) linear cost-volume-profit relationships
    b) fixed production and sales mixes
    c) both a and b
    d) none of the above

    Answer: b Difficulty: 2

89. Fixed operating costs do not include:
    a) interest changes
    b) rent
    c) depreciation
    d) all of the above

    Answer: a Difficulty: 1

90. The degree of operating leverage is defined as:
    a) $\dfrac{\% \text{ change in EBIT}}{\% \text{ change in Variable Cost}}$

    b) $\dfrac{\% \text{ change in EBIT}}{\% \text{ change in Sales}}$

    c) $\dfrac{\% \text{ change in Sales}}{\% \text{ change in EBIT}}$

    d) $\dfrac{\% \text{ change in EBIT}}{\% \text{ change in contribution margin}}$

    Answer: b Difficulty: 2

91. The degree of operating leverage applies only to:
    a) positive changes in sales
    b) negative changes in sales
    c) positive or negative changes in sales
    d) positive changes in sales and EBIT

    Answer: c Difficulty: 2

92. In general, as the level of sales rises above the break even point, the degree of operating leverage:
    a) increases
    b) decreases
    c) remains constant
    d) a or b

    Answer: b Difficulty: 1

TABLE A

Average selling price per unit	$16.00
Variable cost per unit	$11.00
Units sold	200,000
Fixed costs	$800,000
Interest expense	$ 50,000

93. Based on the data contained in Table A, what is the break even point in units produced and sold?
    a) $18,182
    b) $50,000
    c) $150,000
    d) $160,000

    Answer: d Difficulty: 2

94. Based on the data contained in Table A, what is the contribution margin?
    a) 1.18 times
    b) 1.25 times
    c) 4.00 times
    d) 16.00 times
    e) 5.00 times

    Answer: e Difficulty: 2

95. Based on the data contained in Table A, what is the contribution margin?
    a) $5.00
    b) $4.00
    c) $27.00
    d) none of the above

    Answer: a Difficulty: 2

96. Based on the data contained in Table A, what is the degree of financial leverage?
    a) 4.00 times
    b) 2.00 times
    c) 1.50 times
    d) 1.33 times

    Answer: d Difficulty: 2

97. Based on the data contained in Table A, what is the degree of combined leverage?
    a) 1.58
    b) 6.67
    c) 1.87
    d) 2.75

    Answer: b Difficulty: 2

98. Financing a portion of a firm's assets with securities bearing a fixed rate of return in hopes of increasing the return to stockholders refers to:
    a) business risk
    b) financial leverage
    c) operating leverage
    d) all of the above

    Answer: b Difficulty: 2

99. A high degree of variability in a firm's earnings before interest and taxes relates to:
    a) business risk
    b) financial risk
    c) financial leverage
    d) operating leverage

    Answer: a Difficulty: 2

100. Which type of risk is a direct result of a firm's financing decision?
    a) business risk
    b) financial risk
    c) systematic risk
    d) risk aversion

    Answer: b Difficulty: 2

101. Break-even analysis can be used in
    a) pricing policy decisions
    b) financing decisions
    c) labor contract negotiations
    d) all of the above

    Answer: d Difficulty: 2

102. Tom's Trashbin Inc. has fixed costs of $225,000. Tom's trashbins sell for $45 and have a unit variable cost of $20. What is Tom's break-even point in units?
    a) 8,500
    b) 8,750
    c) 9,000
    d) 9,200

    Answer: c Difficulty: 2

103. Due to a technical breakthrough, the fixed costs for a firm drop by 25%. Prior to this breakthrough, fixed costs were $100,000 and unit contribution margin was and remains at $5.00. The new amount of break-even units will be:
    a) 20,000
    b) 25,000
    c) 15,000
    d) 5,000

    Answer: c Difficulty: 3

104. The degree of financial leverage is found by dividing:
   a) $\dfrac{\% \text{ change in EPS}}{\% \text{ change in EBIT}}$

   b) $\dfrac{\% \text{ change in EBIT}}{\% \text{ change in EPS}}$

   c) $\dfrac{\% \text{ change in EBIT}}{\% \text{ change in sales}}$

   d) $\dfrac{\% \text{ change in EPS}}{\% \text{ change in sales}}$

   Answer: a Difficulty: 2

105. Operating leverage refers to:
   a) financing a portion of the firm's assets with securities bearing a fixed rate of return
   b) the additional chance of insolvency borne by the common shareholder
   c) the incurrence of fixed operating costs in the firm's income stream
   d) none of the above

   Answer: c Difficulty: 2

106. Which one of the following is not a limitation of break-even analysis?
   a) Cost-volume-profit relationship is assumed to be linear
   b) The total revenue curve (sales curve) is presumed to increase linearly with the volume of output
   c) The break-even chart and the break-even computations are static forms of analysis
   d) Break-even analysis assumes a constant capital structure

   Answer: d Difficulty: 2

107. The break-even quantity of output results in an EBIT level:
   a) equal to the fixed costs
   b) equal to the contribution margin
   c) equal to zero
   d) dependent upon the sales level

   Answer: c Difficulty: 2

108. The break-even point in sales dollars is convenient if:
   a) the firm sells a large amount of one product
   b) the firm deals with more than one product
   c) both a and b
   d) none of the above

   Answer: b Difficulty: 2

109. The inclusion of bankruptcy risk in firm valuation:
    a) acknowledges that a firm has an upper limit to debt financing
    b) provides a rationale for a saucer-shaped cost of capital curve
    c) is ignored in BOTH the net-operating-income and net-income of cost of capital
    d) all of the above

    Answer: d Difficulty: 2

110. One component of a firm's financial structure which is not a component of its capital structure is:
    a) preferred stock
    b) mortgage bonds
    c) accounts payable
    d) retained earnings

    Answer: c Difficulty: 2

111. According to the moderate view of capital costs and financial leverage, as the use of debt financing increases:
    a) the cost of capital continuously decreases
    b) the cost of capital remains constant
    c) the cost of capital continuously increases
    d) there is an optimal level of debt financing

    Answer: d Difficulty: 2

112. Financial leverage is distinct from operating leverage since it accounts for:
    a) use of debt and preferred stock
    b) variability in fixed operating costs
    c) variability in sales
    d) none of the above

    Answer: a Difficulty: 2

113. Fluctuations in EBIT result in:
    a) fluctuations in EPS which may be larger or smaller as financial leverage increases
    b) smaller fluctuations in EPS, the greater the degree of financial leverage
    c) greater fluctuations in EPS, the greater the degree of financial leverage
    d) equal fluctuations in EPS, the greater the degree of financial leverage

    Answer: c Difficulty: 3

114. When using an EPS-EBIT chart to evaluate a pure debt financing and pure equity financing plan:
    a) the debt financing plan line will graph with a steeper slope than the equity financing plan line
    b) the debt financing plan line will have a lower level of EBIT at EPS = 0
    c) the line of the two financing plans will intersect on the EBIT axis
    d) the slope of the equity financing plan line will be steeper than the debt financing plan line below the intersection of the two lines

    Answer: a Difficulty: 3

115. When deciding upon how much debt financing to employ, most practitioners would cite which of the following as the most important influence on the level of the debt ratio?
    a) providing a borrowing reserve
    b) maintaining desired bond rating
    c) ability to adequately meet financing charges
    d) exploiting advantages of financial leverage

    Answer: c Difficulty: 3

116. The moderate view of capital structure management assumes:
    a) no corporate income taxes
    b) cost of equity remains constant with an increase in financial leverage
    c) firms may fail
    d) both b and c

    Answer: c Difficulty: 2

117. The moderate view of capital structure management says that the cost of capital curve is:
    a) a straight line
    b) V-shaped
    c) S-shaped
    d) none of the above

    Answer: d Difficulty: 2

118. The single most important factor that should influence a firm's financing mix is:
    a) their industry's average debt ratio
    b) the cost of debt capital
    c) the cost of equity capital
    d) the probability distribution of the firm's EBIT

    Answer: d Difficulty: 2

119. The primary weakness of EBIT-EPS analysis is that:
    a) it ignores the implicit cost of debt financing
    b) it double counts the cost of debt financing
    c) it applies only to firms with large amounts of debt in their capital structure
    d) none of the above

    Answer: a Difficulty: 3

120. Which two ratios would be most helpful in managing a firm's capital structure?
    a) balance sheet leverage ratios and profitability ratios
    b) balance sheet ratios and coverage ratios
    c) coverage ratios and liquidity ratios
    d) coverage ratios and profitability ratios

    Answer: b Difficulty: 2

121. A sinking fund is:
    a) a cash reserve used for speculative investment
    b) a cash reserve used to repurchase equity in the case of a hostile takeover
    c) a cash reserve used for the early retirement of the principal amount of a bond issue
    d) a cash reserve used to pay for the executives' vacation to small tropical islands

    Answer: c Difficulty: 2

122. Optimal capital structure is:
    a) the mix of permanent sources of funds used by the firm in a manner that will maximize the company's common stock price.
    b) the mix of all items that appear on the right-hand side of the company's balance sheet.
    c) the mix of funds that will minimize the firm's composite cost of capital
    d) a and c above

    Answer: d Difficulty: 2

123. Optimal capital structure is:
    a) the explicit cost of debt
    b) the implicit cost of debt
    c) the change in the cost of equity caused by the issuance of the debt
    d) all of the above

    Answer: d Difficulty: 2

124. Basic tools of capital-structure management include:
   a) EBIT-EPS analysis
   b) comparative leverage ratios
   c) capital budgeting techniques
   d) both a and b

   Answer: d Difficulty: 2

125. The EBIT-EPS indifference point:
   a) identifies the EBIT level at which the EPS will be the same regardless of the financing plan
   b) identifies the point at which the analysis can use EBIT and EPS interchangeably
   c) identifies the level of earnings at which the management is indifferent about the payments of dividends
   d) none of the above

   Answer: a Difficulty: 2

126. In equation form, the relationship between financial and capital structure can be expressed by:

   financial structure-_____=capital structure
   a) equity
   b) current liabilities
   c) long-term debt
   d) none of the above

   Answer: b Difficulty: 2

ESSAY

127. The Basic Sports Company produces graphite surf-casting fishing rods. The average selling price for one of their rods is $132. The variable cost per unit is $80. Basic Sports has average fixed costs per year of $90,000.

   a. What is the break-even point in units for Basic Sports?
   b. What is the break-even point in dollar sales?
   c. What would be the profit or loss associated with the production and sale of (1) 2,000 rods, (2) 10,000 rods?
   d. Determine the degree of operating leverage for the two levels of production and sales given in part (c) above.

Answer:

a. $Q_{B1} = \dfrac{\$90,000}{\$132 - \$80} = 1,731$

b. $S = 1,731 \times 132 = \$228,492$

c. (1)
$$
\begin{array}{rl}
2,000 \times \$132 = & \$264,000 \\
-2,000 \times \$80 = & -\ 160,000 \\
& -\ \underline{90,000} \\
\text{Profit} & \$14,000
\end{array}
$$

    (2)
$$
\begin{array}{rl}
10,000 \times \$132 = & \$1,320,000 \\
-10,000 \times \$80 = & -\ 800,000 \\
& -\ \underline{90,000} \\
\text{Profit} & \$430,000
\end{array}
$$

d. (1) $\text{DOL } (2,000) = \dfrac{2,000(\$132 - \$80)}{2,000\ (\$132 - \$80) - \$90,000} = 7.43$

    (2) $\text{DOL}(10,000) = \dfrac{10,000(\$132 - \$80)}{10,000(\$132 - \$80) - \$90,000} = 1.21$

Difficulty: 2

128. As the financial manager for a manufacturing firm, you have constructed the following partial pro forma income statement for the next fiscal year.

Sales	$11,200,000
Variable costs	5,600,000
Revenue before fixed costs	5,600,000
Fixed costs	2,400,000
EBIT	3,200,000
Interest expenses	1,600,000
Earnings before taxes	1,600,000
Taxes (40%)	640,000
Net income	$960,000

a. What is the degree of operating leverage at this level of output?
b. What is the degree of financial leverage?
c. What is the degree of combined leverage?
d. What is the break-even point in sales dollars for the firm?
e. If the average unit cost is $8, what is the break even point in units?

221

Answer:

a. $DOL = \dfrac{5,600,000}{3,200,000} = 1.75$

b. $DFL = \dfrac{3,200,000}{3,200,000 - 1,600,000} = 2.00$

c. $CL = 1.75 \times 2.00 = 3.50$

d. $S^* = \dfrac{2,400,000}{1 - 0.5} = \$4,800,000$

e.   600,000 units

Difficulty: 2

129. Rodney Racket, Inc. produces a high quality racketball racket. At a production and sales level of 75,000 rackets, the firm is characterized as follows:

Return on operating assets = 12%
Operating asset turnover   = 4 times
Operating assets   = $1,000,000
Degree of operating leverage = 6 times

What is the break-even point in units for the firm?

Answer:

Return on operating assets = $0.12 = \dfrac{EBIT}{100,000,000}$

EBIT = $120,000

Operating asset turnover = $4 = \dfrac{Sales}{100,000,000}$

Sales = $4,000,000

$DOL\ (75,000) = 6 = \dfrac{\text{Revenue before fixed costs}}{120,000}$

Revenue before fixed costs = $720,000
Variable cost = $4,000,000 - $720,000 = $3,280,000
Variable cost per unit = $3,280,000/75,000 = $43.73
Fixed cost = $720,000 - $120,000 = $600,000
Price = $\dfrac{\$4,000,000}{75,000} = \$53.33$

$BE = \dfrac{\$600,000}{\$53.33 - 43.73} = \dfrac{600,000}{9.60} = 62,500 \text{ units}$

Difficulty: 2

130. The Clearwater Aquarium Company will produce 66,000 ten-gallon aquariums next year. Variable costs are 40 percent of sales while fixed costs total $133,200. At what price must each aquarium be sold for Clearwater to obtain an EBIT of $114,000?

Answer:

$66,000P - (.40)(66,000)P-\$133,200 = \$114,000$
$66,000P - 26,400P-\$133,200 = \$114,000$
$39,600P = \$247,200$
$P = \$6.24$

Difficulty: 3

131. Positronic Products manufactures three lines of heavy equipment for electrical, chemical, and atomic research. Each of the three lines constitutes a third of the total sales of Positronic. The contribution margin ratio is 10 percent for the electrical line, 25 percent for the chemical line, and 65 percent for the atomic research line. Total sales have been forecast at $24,000,000 for the next year, while total fixed costs are expected to be $5,500,000.

a. Prepare a table showing (1) sales, (2) total variable costs, and (3) the total contribution margin associated with each product line.
b. At the given sales mix, what is the break even point in dollars?

Answer:

a.

	Sales	Variable costs	Contribution margin
Electrical	$8,000,000	$7,200,000	$ 800,000
Chemical	8,000,000	6,000,000	2,000,000
Atomic	8,000,000	2,800,000	5,200,000

b. $S* = \dfrac{\$5,500,000}{1 - \dfrac{7,200,000 + 6,000,000 + 2,800,000}{24,000,000}} = \dfrac{5,000,000}{1 - 0.67}$

$= \dfrac{5,500,000}{0.331} = \$16,666,667$

Difficulty: 3

132. APM, Inc. has a break even sales level of $5,000,000 and has fixed costs of $2,000,000 per year. The selling price per unit is $50. What is the variable cost per unit?

Answer:
S–VC = f
$5,000,000 – VC = $2,000,000
VC = $3,000,000

Number of units sold $= \dfrac{\$5,000,000}{\$50} = 100,000$ units

Variable cost per unit $= \dfrac{\$3,000,000}{100,000} = \$30$

Difficulty: 3

133. For a sales level of $3,000,000, BCD Company has a DOL of 2.00 and a DCL of 3.00. The company's contribution margin from sales is 60 percent. What are the company's fixed costs and interest expense?

Answer:
$$DOL = \dfrac{\text{revenue before fixed costs}}{EBIT}$$

$$2.00 = \dfrac{(\$3,000,000)(.60)}{(\$3,000,000)(.60) - F}$$

2.00 ($1,800,000) – 2F = $1,800,000
– 2F = –$1,800,000
F = $900,000

DCL = DOL x DFL

$DFL = \dfrac{DCL}{DOL} = \dfrac{3.00}{2.00} = 1.50$

$DFL = \dfrac{EBIT}{EBIT - I}$

$1.50 = \dfrac{\$900,000}{\$900,000 - I}$

(1.50)($900,000 – I) = $900,000
–1.50 I = –$450,000

$I = \dfrac{\$450,000}{1.5} = \$300,000$

Difficulty: 3

134. DXZ, Inc. currently produces one product which sells for $250 per unit. The company's fixed costs are $75,000 per year; variable costs are $205 per unit. A salesman has offered to sell the company a new piece of equipment which will increase fixed costs to $100,000. The salesman claims that the company's break-even point will not be altered if the company purchases this equipment. What will be the company's new variable cost per unit?

Answer:

$$\text{Current break even point} = \frac{\$75,000}{(\$250 - \$205)} = 1,667 \text{ units}$$

$$\frac{\$100,000}{(\$250 - VC)} = 1,667 \text{ units}$$

$$
\begin{aligned}
1,667\,(\$250 - VC) &= \$100,000 \\
\$416,750 - 1,667\,VC &= \$100,000 \\
-1,667\,VC &= -\$316,750 \\
VC &= \$1904
\end{aligned}
$$

Difficulty: 3

135. The following is an analytical income statement for The Swill & Spoon, a fine dining establishment.

Sales	$ 150,000
Variable costs	90,000
Revenue before fixed costs	$ 60,000
Fixed costs	35,000
EBIT	$ 25,000
Interest expense	$ 10,000
Earnings before taxes	$ 15,000
Taxes (.34)	5,100
Net income	$9,900

a. Calculate the degree of operating leverage at this output level.
b. Calculate the degree of financial leverage at this level of EBIT.
c. What is the degree of combined leverage?

Answer:

a. $DOL_{\$150,000} = \$60,000/\$25,000 = 2.4 \text{ times}$
b. $DFL_{\$25,000} = \$25,000/(\$25,000 - \$10,000) = 1.67 \text{ times}$
c. $DCL_{\$150,000} = 2.4 \times 1.67 = 4.01 \text{ times}$

Difficulty: 3

136. Stan's Cans, Inc. expects to earn $150,000 next year after taxes on sales of $2,200,000. Stan's manufactures only one size of garbage can and is located in the small, but beautiful, town of Mount Dora, Florida. Stan sells his cans for $8 apiece and they have a variable cost of $2.40 apiece. Stan's tax rate is currently 34%.

    a. What are the firm's expected fixed costs for next year?
    b. What is the break-even point in units?

Answer:

    a.

$$([P \times Q] - [(V \times Q) + F])(1 - T) = \$150,000$$
$$(2,200,000 - 660,000 - F)(.66) = \$150,000$$
$$(1,540,000 - F)(.66) = \$150,000$$
$$866,400 = .66F$$
$$F = 1,312,727$$

    b. $$Q = \frac{\$1,312,727}{\$8 - \$2.40} = 234,416 \text{ units}$$

Difficulty: 3

137. The Western Boot Company will produce 94,000 pairs of boots next year. Variable costs are 35 percent of sales, while fixed costs total $223,000. At what price must each pair of boots be sold for Western to obtain an EBIT of $1,391,500?

Answer:

$$94,000P - (0.35)(94,000)P - 223,000 = 1,391,500$$
$$94,000P - 32,900P - 223,000 = 1,391,500$$
$$61,100P = 1,614,500$$
$$P = \$26.42$$

Difficulty: 3

138. Bob's Donuts, Inc., expects to earn $44,000 next year after taxes on sales of $250,000. Bob's bakes only one type of specialty donut and is located in the small, but beautiful town of Oviedo, Florida. Bob sells his donuts for $.75 a piece, and they have a variable cost of $.25 a piece. Bob's tax rate is currently 34 percent.

   a. What are the firm's expected fixed costs for next year?
   b. What is the break-even point in units?

   Answer:

   a. $([P \times Q] - [V \times Q] + F) (1 - T) = 60,500$
       $(250,000 - 83,333 - F) (0.66) = 60,500$
       $(166,667 - F) (0.66) = 60,500$
       $49,500 = 0.66F$
       $\qquad F = 75,000$

   b. $Q = \dfrac{75,000}{\$0.75 - 0.25} = 150,000$ donuts

   Difficulty: 3

139. The Knight Corporation projects that next year its fixed costs will total $240,000. Its only product sells for $34 per unit, of which $18 is a variable cost. The management of Knight is considering the purchase of a new machine that will lower the variable cost per unit to $14. The new machine, however, will add to fixed costs through an increase in depreciation expense. How large can the addition to fixed costs be in order to keep the firm's break-even point in units produced and sold unchanged?

   Answer:

   Step 1
   Compute the percent level of break-even output:
   $$Q_B = \frac{F}{P - V} = \frac{240,000}{34 - 18} = \frac{240,000}{16} = 15,000 \text{ units}$$

   Step 2
   Compute the new level of fixed cost at the break-even output:
   $F + (14) (15,000) = 34 (15,000)$
   $\qquad F + 210,000 = 510,000$
   $\qquad\qquad F = 300,000$

   Step 3
   Compute the addition to fixed costs
   $300,000 - $240,000 = $60,000$ addition
   Difficulty: 3

140. Alpha Accessories, Inc., produces three different lines of automobile accessories. The product lines are numbered. The firm's sales mix and contribution margin ratios appear in the chart below.

Product Line	% of Total Sales	Contribution Margin Ratio
1	20	42%
2	25	31%
3	55	20%

Forecasted sales for the coming year are $1,500,000. The firm's fixed costs are $250,000.

a. Prepare a table showing sales, total variable costs, and the total contribution margin(dollars) associated with each line.
b. What is the aggregate contribution margin ratio indicative of this mix?
c. What is the break-even point in dollars for this particular sales mix?

Answer:

a.
Product	1	2	3	TOTAL
Sales	300,000	375,000	825,000	1,500,000
VC*	174,000	258,000	660,000	1,092,750
Contribution Margins	126,000	116,250	165,000	407,250

b.
Contribution Margin Ratio	42%	31%	20%	27.15%

c.
$$S^* = \frac{FC}{1 - \frac{VC}{S}} = 250,000/0.2715$$

$$S^* = \$920,810$$

Difficulty: 3

141. Roberts, Inc. is trying to decide how best to finance a proposed $10,000,000 capital investment. Under Plan I, the project will be financed entirely with long-term 9 percent bonds. The firm currently has no debt or preferred stock. Under Plan II, common stock will be sold to net the firm $20 a share; presently, 1,000,000 shares are outstanding. The corporate tax rate for Roberts is 40 percent.

    a. Calculate the indifference level of EBIT associated with the two financing plans.
    b. Prepare an EBIT-EPS analysis chart, showing the intersection of the two financing plan lines.
    c. Which financing plan would you expect to cause the greatest change in EPS relative to a change in EBIT? Why?
    d. If EBIT is expected to be $3.1 million, which plan will result in a higher EPS?

Answer:

    a.
$$\frac{(EBIT)(1 - 0.4)}{1,500,000} = \frac{(EBIT - \$900,000)(1 - 0.4)}{1,000,000}$$

$$EBIT = \$2,700,000$$

    b. GRAPH SHOULD BE DRAWN BY STUDENT

    c. The bond plan will magnify changes in EPS since it increases financial leverage.
    d. Since $3.1 million EBIT is above the indifference point of $2.7 million, the bond plan will give a higher EPS.

Difficulty: 3

142. Young Enterprises is financed entirely with 3 million shares of common stock selling for $20 a share. Capital of $4 million is needed for this year's capital budget. Additional funds can be raised with new stock (ignore dilution) or with 13 percent 10-year bonds. Young's tax rate is 40 percent.

    a. Calculate the financing plan's EBIT indifference point.
    b. The expected level of EBIT is $10,320,000 with a standard deviation of $2,000,000. What is the probability that EBIT will be above the indifference point?
    c. Does the "indifference point" calculated in question (a) above truly represent a point where stockholders are indifferent between stock and debt financing? Explain your answer.

229

Answer:

a. $$\frac{(EBIT - 0)(1 - 0.4)}{3,200,000} = \frac{(EBIT - 520,000)(1 - 0.4)}{3,000,000}$$
$$EBIT = \$8,320,000$$

b. $Z = \dfrac{8.32 - 10.32}{2} = 1.00$ to the left of the mean

$P(EBIT \geq \$8.32 \text{ million}) = 1 - 0.16 = 0.84$

c. No. Financial risk is ignored.

Difficulty: 3

143. The MAX Corporation is planning a $4,000,000 expansion this year. The expansion can be financed by issuing either common stock or bonds. The new common stock can be sold for $60 per share. The bonds can be issued with a 12 percent coupon rate. The firm's existing shares of preferred stock pay dividends of $2.00 per share. The company's corporate income tax rate is 46 percent. The company's balance sheet prior to expansion is as follows:

MAX Corporation

Current Assets	$ 2,000,000
Fixed Assets	8,000,000
Total Assets	$10,000,000
Current Liabilities	$ 1,500,000
Bonds:	
(8%, $1,000 par value)	1,000,000
(10%, $1,000 par value)	4,000,000
Preferred Stock:	
($100 par value)	500,000
Common Stock:	
($2 par value)	700,000
Retained Earnings	2,300,000
Total Liabilities and Equity	$10,000,000

a. Calculate the indifference level of EBIT between the two plans.
b. If EBIT is expected to be $3 million, which plan will result in higher EPS?

Answer:

a.

EPS: Stock Plan	EPS: Bond Plan

$$\frac{(EBIT-\$48,000)(1-.46)-10,000}{(350,000+66,667)} \qquad \frac{(EBIT-\$960,000)(1-.46)-10,000}{(350,000)}$$

$$\frac{(EBIT)(.54)-\$259,200-10,000}{(416,667)} \qquad \frac{(EBIT)(.54)-\$518,400-10,000}{(350,000)}$$

$$(350,000)[EBIT(.54)-\$269,200] = (416,667)[EBIT(.54)-\$528,400]$$
$$(189,000)EBIT-\$94,220,000,000 = (225,000)EBIT-\$220,000,000,000$$
$$(36,000)EBIT = \$125,780,000,000$$
$$EBIT = \$3,493,889$$

b. EPS: Stock Plan
$$\frac{(\$3,000,000-\$480,000)(1-.46) - \$10,000}{(350,000 + 66,667)} \quad \frac{\$1,350,800}{416,667} = \$3.24$$

EPS: Bond Plan
$$\frac{(\$3,000,000 - \$960,000)(1-.46) - \$10,000}{350,000} \quad \frac{\$1,091,600}{350,000} = \$3.12$$

Stock plan has higher EPS.

Difficulty: 3

144. Sunshine Candy Company's capital structure for the past year of operation is shown below.

First mortgage bonds at 12%	$2,000,000
Debentures at 15%	1,500,000
Common stock (1,000,000 shares)	5,000,000
Retained earnings	500,000
TOTAL	$9,000,000

The federal tax rate is 50 percent. Sunshine Candy Company, home-based in Orlando, wants to raise an additional $1,000,000 to open new facilities in Tampa and Miami. The firm can accomplish this via two alternatives: (1) It can sell a new issue of 20-year debentures with 16 percent interest; or (2) 20,000 new shares of common stock can be sold to the public to net the candy company $50 per share. A recent study, performed by an outside consulting organization, projected Sunshine Candy Company's long-term EBIT level at approximately $6,800,000. Find the indifference level of EBIT (with regard to earnings per share) between the suggested financing plans.

Answer:

$$\frac{[EBIT - 465,000]\ (0.5)}{1,020,000} = \frac{[EBIT - 625,000]\ (.05)}{1,000,000}$$

$$\frac{0.5\ EBIT - 232,500}{102} = \frac{0.5\ EBIT - 312,500}{100}$$

50 EBIT - 23,250,000 = 51 EBIT - 31,875,000

EBIT = $8,625,000 indifference level

Difficulty: 3

145. Long Lodging, Inc., is financed entirely with $5 million shares of common stock selling for $25 a share. Capital of $7 million is needed for this year's capital budget. Additional funds can be raised with new stock (ignore dilution) or with 12 percent 10-year bonds. Long Lodging's tax rate is 45 percent.

a. Calculate the financing plan's EBIT indifference point.
b. The expected level of EBIT is $18,840,000 with a standard deviation of $3,000,000. What is the probability that EBIT will be above the indifference point?

Answer:

a. $$\frac{(EBIT - 0)\ (1-0.45)}{5,280,000} = \frac{(EBIT - 840,000)(1 - 0.45)}{5,000,000}$$

$$\frac{0.55\ EBIT}{525} = \frac{0.55\ EBIT - 462,000}{500}$$

275 EBIT = 290.4 EBIT - 243,936,000

15.4 EBIT = 243,936,000

EBIT = $15,840,000 indifference level

b.
$$Z = \frac{15.84 - 18.84}{3} = 1.00 \text{ to the left of the mean}$$

P (EBIT > $15.84 million) = 1 - 0.16 = 0.84

Difficulty: 3

Chapter 13:   Dividend Policy

1. Dividends per share divided by earnings per share equal the dividend retention date.

   Answer: False Difficulty: 1

2. The residual theory of dividends connects a firm's dividend policy and its level of capital investments.

   Answer: True Difficulty: 1

3. We typically expect to find rapidly growing firms to have high payout ratios.

   Answer: False Difficulty: 1

4. A firm's payout is calculated as the ratio of interest payments to EBIT.

   Answer: False Difficulty: 1

5. Under the ideal conditions of perfect capital markets, dividend policy has no effect upon share price.

   Answer: True Difficulty: 1

6. Dividend policy takes on greater importance, the more perfect are the market conditions.

   Answer: False Difficulty: 1

7. If a firm was to unexpectedly omit payment of its quarterly dividend, that firm's stock price would probably drop.

   Answer: True Difficulty: 1

8. A stock dividend increases a firm's retained earnings.

   Answer: False Difficulty: 1

9. As long as a firm has a positive level of retained earnings, it can pay a dividend.

   Answer: False Difficulty: 1

10. Other things equal, in imperfect markets a firm that maintains a stable dividend will have a lower required rate of return on its equity.

    Answer: True Difficulty: 2

11. After a stock split of 2:1, each investor will have one half of the percentage ownership in the firm that he had before the split.

    Answer: False Difficulty: 1

12. If a company in a perfect capital market decreased its dividend per share, an investor would be forced to sell his common stock at a depressed price.

    Answer: False Difficulty: 1

13. Other things equal, individuals in high income tax brackets should have a preference for firms that retain their earnings rather than pay dividends.

    Answer: True Difficulty: 2

14. The ex-dividend date occurs prior to the declaration date.

    Answer: False Difficulty: 2

15. A firm's dividend policy includes information pertaining to the firm's payout ratio and its stability.

    Answer: True Difficulty: 1

16. Security markets are considered to be perfect when firms can issue securities at no cost and the investor incurs no brokerage commissions.

    Answer: True Difficulty: 2

17. By virtue of its nature, dividend policy is inherently a wealth-creating activity for the firm's owners.

    Answer: False Difficulty: 1

18. The existence of taxes can directly affect a common shareholder's preference for capital gains or dividend income.

    Answer: True Difficulty: 1

19. When an unexpected change in dividend policy develops, investors may attach informational content to the events.

    Answer: True Difficulty: 2

20. When Firm X makes the decision to pay dividends, they also make the decision not to reinvest the cash in the firm.

    Answer: True Difficulty: 1

21. The residual dividend theory suggests that dividends should be paid to stockholders first and then what is left can be reinvested by the firm.

    Answer: False Difficulty: 1

22. The residual dividend theory implies that dividend policy by itself has no direct influence on the market price of common equity.

    Answer: True Difficulty: 2

23. A stable dividend policy generally leads to a lower required rate of return, on the part of the investor, when compared to similar stocks with erratic fluctuations in dividends.

    Answer: True Difficulty: 1

24. In a perfect market, investors are only concerned with total returns and are not concerned whether it is in capital gains or dividend income.

    Answer: True Difficulty: 2

25. Increasing a firm's dividend reduces the stock's risk.

    Answer: False Difficulty: 2

26. When considering taxes, most investors prefer capital gains over dividend income.

    Answer: False Difficulty: 2

27. Conceptually, stock dividends and stock splits may be expected to increase the shareholder's value.

    Answer: False Difficulty: 2

MULTIPLE CHOICE

28. A large number of investment projects this year with positive NPV's will likely result in:
    a) lower taxes in the future
    b) the par value of the firm's stock increasing
    c) future dividends probably increasing
    d) future dividends probably decreasing

    Answer: c Difficulty: 1

29. The difference between the capital gains tax rate and the income tax rate is an incentive for:
    a) firms never to split their stock
    b) firms to declare more stock dividends
    c) firms to pay more earnings as dividends
    d) firms to retain more earnings

    Answer: d Difficulty: 2

30. Flotation costs:
    a) include the fees paid to the investment bankers, lawyers, and accountants involved in selling a new security issue
    b) encourage firms to pay large dividends
    c) are encountered whenever a firm fails to pay a dividend
    d) are incurred when investors fail to cash their dividend check

    Answer: a Difficulty: 1

31. According to the perfect markets approach to dividend policy:
    a) other things equal, the greater the payout ratio, the greater the share price of the firm
    b) the price of a share of stock is invariant to dividend policy
    c) the firm should retain earnings so stockholders will receive a capital gain
    d) the firm should pay a dividend only after current equity financing needs have been met

    Answer: b Difficulty: 1

32. According to the residual theory of dividends:
    a) dividends are a residual after investment financing needs have been met
    b) earnings remaining after payment of preferred stock dividends should be paid to common stockholders
    c) dividend payments are a constant percentage of earnings per share
    d) a dividend is the residual above the payout ratio

    Answer: a Difficulty: 2

33. The ex-dividend date is _____ the holder of record date.
    a) 5 days before
    b) 2 weeks before
    c) 4 days before
    d) 3 days after

    Answer: c Difficulty: 2

34. Dividends generally:
    a) are paid as a fixed percentage of earnings
    b) fluctuate more than earnings
    c) are guaranteed by the SEC
    d) are more stable than earnings

    Answer: d Difficulty: 2

35. All of the following may influence a firm's dividend payment except:
    a) investment opportunities
    b) investor transaction costs
    c) common stock par value
    d) flotation costs

    Answer: c Difficulty: 2

36. A stock dividend:
    a) decreases the par value of the stock and increases the number of shares
    b) reduces the pro rata number of shares to each stockholder
    c) increases retained earnings by the total market value of stock dividends
    d) none of the above

    Answer: d Difficulty: 2

37. Stock splits:
    a) increase the number of shares to stockholders
    b) decrease the common stock account by the amount of the split
    c) reduce retained earnings
    d) increase the total wealth of stockholders

    Answer: a Difficulty: 2

38. In perfect capital markets there:
    a) is no informational content assigned to a particular dividend policy
    b) are no income taxes
    c) are no flotation costs
    d) all of the above

    Answer: d Difficulty: 2

39. Which of the following are not subject to income taxes?
    a) commercial banks
    b) manufacturing corporations
    c) pension funds
    d) both a and c

    Answer: c Difficulty: 2

40. Which of the following dividend policies will cause dividends per share to fluctuate the most?
    a) constant dividend payout ratio
    b) stable dollar dividend
    c) small, low, regular dividend plus a year-end extra
    d) no difference between the various dividend policies

    Answer: a Difficulty: 3

41. For accounting purposes a stock split has been defined as a stock dividend exceeding:
    a) 25 percent
    b) 35 percent
    c) 50 percent
    d) 66 2/3 percent

    Answer: a Difficulty: 3

42. Some key determinants of dividend policy are:
    a) legal restrictions
    b) liquidity position
    c) earnings predictability
    d) all of the above

    Answer: d Difficulty: 2

43. A firm that maintains a "stable dollar dividend per share" will generally not increase the dividend unless:
    a) a stock split occurs
    b) the firm merges with another profitable firm
    c) the firm is sure that a higher dividend level can be maintained
    d) the P/E ratio increases steadily over the past 5 years

    Answer: c Difficulty: 3

44. A justification for stable dividends could be:
    a) satisfaction of guaranteed current income
    b) satisfaction for stockholders informational needs
    c) existence of legal listing
    d) all of the above

    Answer: d Difficulty: 2

45. The final approval of a dividend payment comes from:
    a) the controller
    b) the president of the company
    c) the board of directors
    d) It is a joint decision requiring approval from all of the above.

    Answer: c Difficulty: 2

46. The only definite result from a stock dividend or a stock split is:
    a) an increase in the P/E ratio
    b) an increase in the common stock's market value
    c) an increase in the number of shares outstanding
    d) cannot be determined from the above

    Answer: c Difficulty: 2

47. Dividend policy is influenced by:
    a) a company's investment opportunities
    b) a firm's capital structure mix
    c) a company's availability of internally generated funds
    d) a and c
    e) a, b, and c

    Answer: e Difficulty: 2

48. The _____ designates the date on which the stock transfer books are closed in regard to a dividend payment.
    a) declaration date
    b) ex-dividend date
    c) date of record
    d) payment date

    Answer: c Difficulty: 2

49. All of the following conclusions on the importance of a dividend policy are true except:
    a) As a firm's investment opportunities increase, the dividend payout ratio should decrease.
    b) The firm's expected earning power and the riskiness of these earnings are more important to the investor than the dividend policy.
    c) Dividends may influence stock price by the investor's desire to minimize and/or defer taxes and from the role of dividends in minimizing agency costs.
    d) In order to avoid surprising investors, management should anticipate financing needs for the short-term, but not for the long term.

    Answer: d Difficulty: 3

50. The problem with the constant dividend payout ratio is:
    a) Investors may come to expect a specified amount.
    b) The dollar amount of the dividend fluctuates from year-to-year.
    c) Management is reluctant to cut the dividend even if there are low profits that year.
    d) All of the above are possible problems.

    Answer: b Difficulty: 3

51. All of the following are rationales given for a stock dividend or split except:
    a) The price will not fall proportionately to the share increase.
    b) An optimum price range does not exist.
    c) There is positive informational content associated with the announcement.
    d) Conservation of corporate cash.

    Answer: b Difficulty: 3

52. All of the following are methods available to a corporation who desires to repurchase stock except:
    a) offering to employees who own an interest in the firm.
    b) open market.
    c) tender offer to all existing stockholders.
    d) offer to one or more major stockholders on a negotiated basis.

    Answer: a Difficulty: 2

ESSAY

53. Pettry, Inc. expects earnings per share this year to be $5.25. If earnings per share grow at an average annual rate of 10 percent and if Pettry pays 60 percent of its earnings as dividends, what will the expected dividend per share be in 10 years?

    Answer:
    $5.25 \ (1 + 0.10)^{10} = 13.62 =$ Earnings per share in 10 years

    $13.62 \times 0.6 = $8.17 =$ Expected dividends per share
    Difficulty: 1

54. Klone Enterprises maintains a capital structure of 40 percent debt and 60 percent equity. If additions to retained earnings for the coming year are expected to be $36 million, how large can the capital budget be? Assume the existing capital structure is to be maintained.

    Answer:

    $36,000,000/0.6 = $60,000,000$
    Difficulty: 1

55. The Clysdale Corporation has an optimal capital structure consisting of 40 percent debt and 60 percent equity. The marginal cost of capital is calculated to be 14 percent. Total earnings available to common stockholders for the coming year total $1,200,000. Investment opportunities are:

Project	Investment	IRR(%)
A	$1,200,000	21
B	100,000	19
C	600,000	15
D	200,000	13

a. According to the residual dividend theory, what should the firm's total dividend payment be?
b. If the firm paid a total dividend of $480,000, and restricted equity financing to internally generated funds, which projects should be selected? Assume the marginal cost of capital is constant.

Answer:

a. Select projects A, B, C for an investment of $1,900,000
$1,900,000 x .4 = $760,000 debt
$1,900,000 x .6 = $1,140,000 common equity
Dividend payment $1,200,000 - $1,140,000 = $60,000

b. $1,200,000 - $480,000 = $720,000 for investment. Choose project A only.

Difficulty: 2

56. XYZ has 400,000 shares of common stock outstanding, a P/E ratio of 8, and $500,000 available for common stockholders. The board of directors has just voted a 3:2 stock split.

a. If you had 100 shares of stock before the split, how many shares will you have after the split?
b. What was the total value of your investment in XYZ stock before the split?
c. What should be the total value of your investment in XYZ stock after the split?
d. In view of your answers to (b) and (c) above, why would a firm's management want to have a stock split?

Answer:

a. Number of shares after split = 3/2 x 100 = 150

b. Earnings per share before split = $\frac{\$500,0000}{400,000}$ = $1.25

Price per share before split = 8 x $1.25 = $10
Total value of investment = $10 x 100 = $1,000

c. Total number of shares after split = $3(\frac{400,000}{2})$ = 600,000

Earnings per share after split = $\frac{\$500,000}{600,000}$ = $.8333

Price per share after split = 8 x $.833 = $6.67
Total value of investment after split = $6.67 x 150 = $1,000

d. (1) Stock splits are believed to have favorable information content. Splits are often associated with growth companies.
(2) Splits can conserve corporate cash if the firm has cash flow problems or needs additional funds for attractive investment opportunities.

Difficulty: 3

57. Coppell Timber Company had total earnings last year of $5,000,000, but expects total earnings to drop to $4,750,000 this year because of a slump in the housing industry. There are currently 1,000,000 shares of common stock outstanding. The company has $4,000,000 worth of investments to undertake this year. The company finances 40 percent of its investments with debt and 60 percent with equity capital. The company paid $3.00 per share in dividends last year.

a. If the company follows a pure residual dividend policy, how large a dividend will each shareholder receive this year?
b. If the company maintains a constant dividend payout ratio each year, how large a dividend will each shareholder receive this year?
c. If the company follows a constant dollar dividend policy, how large a dividend will each shareholder receive this year?

Answer:
a. Equity financing for new investments =
$4,000,000(.60) = $2,400,000
Residual dividends = $4,750,000 - $2,400,000
= $2,350,000
Dividends per share =
$$\frac{\$2,350,000}{1,000,000} = \$2.35$$

b. Dividends = ($3.00)(1,000,000) = $3,000,000

Dividend payout ratio = $\frac{\$3,000,000}{\$5,000,000}$ = .60

Dividends this year = (.60)($4,750,000) = $2,850,000

Dividends per share = $\frac{\$2,850,000}{1,000,000}$ = $2.85

c. Dividends per share = $3.00
Difficulty: 2

58. Noblesville Auto Supply Company's stock is trading ex-dividend at $5.00 per share. The company just paid a 10 percent stock dividend. The P/E ratio for the stock is ten. What was the price of the stock prior to trading ex-dividend?

Answer:

Earnings per share after stock dividend = $\frac{\$5.00}{10.00}$ = $.50

Earnings per share after stock dividend =

$$\left[\frac{\text{earnings per share before stock dividend}}{(1.10)}\right]$$
($.50) (1.10) = $.55 - earnings per share before stock dividend

Stock price prior to stock dividend = (10) ($.5) = $ 5.50
Difficulty: 2

59. The equity section of the TMW Corporation balance sheet is shown below. The company's common stock is currently trading at $20 per share. Reconstruct the equity section of the balance sheet assuming:
    a. a 2 for 1 stock split
    b. a five percent stock dividend.

                     TMW Corporation
                      Balance Sheet
    Common Stock:
     Par Value (4,000,000 shares; $2 par value) $ 8,000,000
     Paid in Capital   22,000,000
     Retained earnings   40,000,000

    Answer:

    a. Common stock
       Par Value (8,000,000 shares; $1 par value $ 8,000,000
       Paid in Capital   22,000,000
       Retained earnings   40,000,000
    b. Common Stock:
       Par Value (4,200,000 shares; $2 par value $ 8,400,000[b]
       Paid in Capital   25,600,000[c]
       Retained Earnings   36,000,000[a]

    [a]Market value of stock dividend =   ($20)(4,000,000)(.05) = $4,000,000

    Retained earnings = $40,000,000 – $4,000,000 = $36,000,000

    [b]Par value = $8,000,000 + ($2.00)(200,000) = $8,400,000

    [c]Paid in Capital = $22,000,000 + $4,000,000 + $400,000 = $25,600,000

    Difficulty: 3

60. Ernest T. Bass Frozen Frog Legs, Inc. has found three acceptable investment opportunities. The three projects require a total of $3 million in financing. It is the company's policy to finance its investments by using 35% debt and 65% common equity. The firm has generated $2.2 million dollars from its operations that could be used to finance the common equity portion of its investments.

    a. What portion of the new investments will be financed by common equity and what portion by debt?
    b. According to the residual dividend theory, how much would be paid out in dividends?

    Answer:

    a. Common equity = .65 x $3 million = $1,950,000
       Debt = .35 x $3 million = $1,050,000

    b. Dividends = $2,200,000 – $1,950,000 = $250,000
    Difficulty: 3

61. Ted Tech Inc. is offering a 10% stock dividend. The firm currently has 200,000 shares outstanding and after-tax profits of $800,000. The current price of the stock is $48.

    a. Calculate the new earnings per share.
    b. What is the original price/earnings multiple?
    c. Providing that the price/earnings multiple stays the same, what will the new stock price be after the stock dividend?

Answer:

    a. EPS = $800,000/200,000 (1.10)
       EPS = $3.636

    b. price/earnings multiple = $48/$4 = 12

    c. 12 x $3.636 = $43.63

Difficulty: 3

62. If flotation costs for a common stock issue are 18%, how large will a stock issue have to be so that the firm will net $8 million? If the market price of the common stock is $132, how many shares must be issued?

Answer:
a. $8,000,000 = x−.18x
   $8,000,000 = x(1−.18)
   x   = $8,000,000/.82
   x   = $9,756,097

b. x   = $9,756,097/$132
   x   = 73,910

Difficulty: 3

63. Outpost has 2 million shares of common stock outstanding; net income is $300,000; the P/E ratio is 9; and management is considering an 18% stock dividend. What will be the expected effect on the price of the common stock? If an investor owns 300 shares in the company, how does this change his total value? Explain.

Answer:
a.
Before dividend

Shares outstanding	2,000,000	
Net income	$300,000	
EPS	$0.15	
Price/Earnings	9	
Current price	$ 1.35	= $0.15 x 9
Investor's shares	300	
Value before dividend	$ 405.00	= $1.35 x 300 shares

After dividend
Shares outstanding	2,360,000	= 2,000,000 x (1 + 0.18)
New EPS	$0.127	
New price	$1.144	= $0.127 x 9
Investor's shares	354	= 300 x 1.18
Value after dividend	$ 405.00	= 354 x $1.144
Change	$ 0.00	= $405(before)
		$405 (after)

The total value of the investors' holdings does not change because the price of the stock reacted fully to the increase in the shares outstanding.

Difficulty: 3

64. Kelly owns 10,000 shares in McCormick Spices which currently has 500,000 shares outstanding. The stock sells for $86 on the open market. McCormick's management has decided on a two-for-one split.

   a. Will Kelly's financial position alter after the split, assuming that the stocks will fall proportionately?
   b. Assuming only a 35% fall on each stock, what will be Kelly's value after the split?

   Answer:

   Trevor Corporation - Stock Split
   Market price $ 86.00
   Split multiple   2
   Shares outstanding   500,000

   a.
   Investor's shares =   10,000
   Position before split $860,000   = 10,000 shares x $86 per share
   Price after split $ 43.00   = $86/2
   Your shares after split   20,000   = 10,000 x 2
   Position after split $860,000   = 20,000 shares x $43 per share
   Net gain $ 0

   b.
   Price fall   0.35
   Price after split $ 55.90   = $86.00(1-.35)
   Position after split $1,118,000   = 20,000 shares x $55.90 per share
   Net gain $ 258,000   = $1,118,000-$860,000
   Difficulty: 3

65. Trevor Co.'s future earnings for the next four years are predicted below. Assuming there are 500,000 shares outstanding, what will the yearly dividend per share be if the dividend policy is:

   a. a constant payout ratio of 40%
   b. stable dollar dividend targeted at 40% of the average earnings over the four-year period
   c. small, regular dividend of $0.75 plus a year-end extra of 40% of profits exceeding $1,000,000

   Trevor & Co.
   1    $ 900,000
   2   1,200,000
   3   850,000
   4   1,350,000

Answer:

a.

.40(900,000)/500,000	=	$0.72
.40(1,200,000)/500,000	=	0.96
.40(850,000)/500,000	=	0.68
.40(1,350,000)/500,000	=	1.08

b.   .40(1,075,000)   = $430,000/500,000 $0.86

c.

Year 1	$0.75	=	$0.75
Year 2	0.75 + 0.16	=	0.91
Year 3	0.75	=	0.75
Year 4	0.75 + 0.28	=	1.03

Difficulty: 3

Chapter 14:   Introduction to Working-Capital Management

1. Management of a firm's liquidity involves management of the firm's investment in current assets as well as its mix of long-term capital.

   Answer: False Difficulty: 1

2. The hedging principle involves matching the cash flow from an asset with the cash flow requirements of the financing used.

   Answer: True Difficulty: 1

3. The firm's total investment in current assets should be financed with temporary sources of financing.

   Answer: False Difficulty: 1

4. Working capital refers to investment in current assets, while net working capital is the difference between current assets and current liabilities.

   Answer: True Difficulty: 1

5. A firm increases the risks of insolvency by keeping relatively large amounts of money tied up in marketable securities.

   Answer: False Difficulty: 1

6. The use of short-term debt provides flexibility in financing since the firm is only paying interest when it is actually using the borrowed funds.

   Answer: True Difficulty: 1

7. A company with an aggressive net working-capital plan would finance all permanent assets with short-term debt.

   Answer: True Difficulty: 1

8. Notes payable is a spontaneous source of financing.

   Answer: False Difficulty: 1

9. A company decreases the risk of insolvency by financing long-term assets with short-term debt.

   Answer: False Difficulty: 1

10. As a means of increasing its liquidity, the firm may choose to invest additional funds in cash and/or marketable securities.

    Answer: True Difficulty: 1

11. There is a risk-return tradeoff involved in managing a firm's liquidity.

    Answer: True Difficulty: 1

12. One advantage of long-term liabilities is their flexibility; it is easy to get out of long-term obligations.

    Answer: False Difficulty: 1

13. Trade credit is a source of spontaneous financing.

    Answer: True Difficulty: 1

14. Under the hedging principle, the cash needed to repay the loan will be generated by the sale of the excess inventory.

    Answer: True Difficulty: 2

15. Commercial paper is an example of spontaneous financing because it is generated by the day-to-day operations.

    Answer: False Difficulty: 2

16. Sources of financing repaid in six months to one year are usually categorized as intermediate term.

    Answer: False Difficulty: 2

17. Major sources of secured credit include commercial banks, finance companies, and factors.

    Answer: True Difficulty: 2

18. Secured funds may take the form of trade credit, bank loans, or commercial paper.

    Answer: False Difficulty: 2

19. The cost of trade credit varies directly with the size of the cash discount and inversely with the length of time between the end of the discount period and the final due date.

    Answer: True Difficulty: 2

20. The continual practice of stretching on trade credit is potentially a very useful source of short-term credit for the firm.

    Answer: False Difficulty: 2

21. The effective cost to the borrower of an unsecured bank loan is increased if a compensating balance is required.

    Answer: True Difficulty: 1

22. Commercial banks often require that a firm "clean up" all short-term loans for some period of time to insure that working-capital needs are not being financed with short-term bank credit.

    Answer: False Difficulty: 2

23. A major risk in using commercial paper for short-term financing is the inflexible repayment schedule.

    Answer: True Difficulty: 1

24. The amount that can be obtained on an inventory loan depends on both the marketability and perishability of the items in the inventory.

    Answer: True Difficulty: 1

25. When the accounts receivable of a firm have been factored, bad debt losses remain the responsibility of the borrowing firm and must be made good.

    Answer: False Difficulty: 2

26. Under terms of a field warehouse financing agreement, the collateral inventories are physically separated from the borrower's other inventories but remain under the borrower's control.

    Answer: False Difficulty: 2

27. The cost of a terminal warehouse agreement is usually lower than the cost for a field warehouse financing agreement.

    Answer: False Difficulty: 2

28. A commercial bank loan which must be repaid in two years is considered long-term financing.

    Answer: False Difficulty: 1

29. Trade credit appears on a company's balance sheet as accounts payable.

    Answer: True Difficulty: 2

30. Equipment is frequently used as collateral for short-term loans.

    Answer: False   Difficulty: 2

31. A revolving credit agreement is a legally binding agreement between a borrower and lender.

    Answer: True   Difficulty: 2

32. Issuers of commercial paper usually maintain lines of credit with banks to back up their short-term financing needs.

    Answer: True   Difficulty: 2

33. The primary sources of collateral for secured loans are accounts receivable and inventory.

    Answer: True   Difficulty: 2

34. The cost of trade credit varies directly with the size of the cash discount and inversely with the length of time between the end of the discount period and the final due date.

    Answer: True   Difficulty: 2

35. Accounts receivable and inventories can be used as collateral to secure a loan.

    Answer: True   Difficulty: 2

36. Commercial paper is an unsecured form of credit.

    Answer: True   Difficulty: 1

37. Trade credit is considered one of the most inflexible sources of financing available to a firm.

    Answer: False   Difficulty: 1

38. In a chattel mortgage, specific items of inventory are identified in the security agreement.

    Answer: True   Difficulty: 2

MULTIPLE CHOICE

39. Current assets would usually not include
    a) plant and equipment
    b) marketable securities
    c) accounts receivable
    d) inventories

    Answer: a Difficulty: 1

40. Which of the following is not true regarding the use of short-term debt?
    a) It must be rolled over more often than long-term debt.
    b) There is uncertainty connected with interest costs on short-term debt from year to year.
    c) The firm is subjected to greater liquidity risk when using short-term credit.
    d) Interest rates are usually higher on short-term debt.

    Answer: d Difficulty: 2

41. Spontaneous sources of financing include
    a) marketable securities
    b) wages payable
    c) accounts receivable
    d) all of the above

    Answer: b Difficulty: 1

42. Permanent sources of financing include all but
    a) corporate bonds
    b) common stock
    c) preferred stock
    d) commercial paper

    Answer: d Difficulty: 1

43. According to the hedging principle, plant and equipment should be financed with
    a) commercial paper
    b) long-term funds
    c) short-term bank loans
    d) none of the above

    Answer: b Difficulty: 1

44. A toy manufacturer following the hedging principle will generally finance seasonal inventory build-up prior to the Christmas season with
    a) short-term debt
    b) selling equipment
    c) trade credit
    d) a and c

Answer: d Difficulty: 1

45. Which of the following is a disadvantage of the use of current liabilities to finance assets?
    a) greater risk of illiquidity
    b) less flexibility
    c) higher interest costs
    d) both a and c

Answer: a Difficulty: 1

46. Which of the following is an advantage of the use of current liabilities to finance assets?
    a) less risk of illiquidity
    b) more flexibility
    c) lower interest costs
    d) both b and c

Answer: d Difficulty: 1

47. With regard to the hedging principle, which of the following assets should be financed with permanent sources of financing?

    I. Minimum level of accounts receivable required year round
    II. Machinery
    III. Minimum level of cash required for year round operations
    IV. Expansion of inventory to meet seasonal demands
    a) II only
    b) IV only
    c) II and IV
    d) I, II, and III

Answer: d Difficulty: 2

48. With regard to the hedging principle, which of the following would be an appropriate method to finance a minimum level of cash required for year round operations?
    a) short-term notes payable
    b) 10 year bonds
    c) all common stock
    d) both b and c

Answer: d Difficulty: 2

49. Which of the following is a spontaneous source of financing?

    I. long-term debt
    II. preferred stock
   III. trade credit
    IV. accrued interest
a) I only
b) II only
c) I and II
d) III and IV

Answer: d Difficulty: 2

50. With regard to the hedging principle, which of the following assets should be financed with permanent sources of financing?
a) cannot be determined
b) inventories
c) accounts receivable
d) cash

Answer: a Difficulty: 2

51. With regard to the hedging principle, which of the following assets should be financed with current liabilities?
a) minimum level of cash required for year round operations
b) expansion of accounts receivable to meet seasonal demand
c) machinery
d) both a and b

Answer: b Difficulty: 2

52. Trade credit is an example of which of the following sources of financing?
a) spontaneous
b) temporary
c) permanent
d) both a and b

Answer: a Difficulty: 2

53. Which of the following is a spontaneous source of financing?

    I. accounts payable
    II. wages and salaries payable
   III. accrued interest
    IV. inventories
a) I only
b) I and II
c) I and IV
d) I, II, and III

Answer: d Difficulty: 2

54. Which of the following actions would improve a firm's liquidity?
    a) selling stock and reducing accounts payable
    b) selling bonds and increasing cash
    c) buying bonds
    d) both a and b

Answer: d Difficulty: 3

55. Which of the following actions would decrease a firm's liquidity?
    a) buying bonds
    b) selling bonds and increasing inventories
    c) selling bonds and reducing accounts payable
    d) both b and c

Answer: a Difficulty: 3

56. Which of the following actions would improve a firm's liquidity?
    a) reducing cash and increasing inventories
    b) buying bonds
    c) selling bonds and allowing accounts receivable to increase
    d) buying machinery

Answer: c Difficulty: 3

57. Which of the following actions would decrease a firm's liquidity?
    a) selling stocks and reducing accounts payable
    b) selling machinery and using proceeds to retire bonds
    c) reducing accounts receivable and buying bonds
    d) selling bonds and holding proceeds in cash account

Answer: c Difficulty: 3

58. Which of the following are true?
    a) Permanent asset needs are matched exactly with spontaneous plus permanent sources of financing.
    b) Temporary current assets are financed with temporary sources of financing.
    c) both a and b
    d) neither a nor b

Answer: c Difficulty: 2

59. A firm following an aggressive financing policy is:
    a) not subject to any increased risks regarding cash shortfall
    b) subject to increased risks of a cash shortfall
    c) subject to a negligible increased risk of a cash shortfall
    d) none of the above

Answer: b Difficulty: 2

60. The hedging approach:
    a) can be used to guide decisions regarding the appropriate use of short-term credit
    b) is only theoretically valid
    c) is useful only for analyzing working capital
    d) none of the above

    Answer: a Difficulty: 2

61. In general the greater a firm's reliance upon short-term debt or current liabilities:
    a) the lower will be its liquidity
    b) the greater will be its liquidity
    c) liquidity will remain constant
    d) there will be no effect on liquidity

    Answer: a Difficulty: 2

62. Advantages of financing with current liabilities are:
    a) flexibility in financing
    b) reduced interest rates
    c) both a and b
    d) neither a nor b

    Answer: c Difficulty: 2

63. If a firm relies on short-term debt or current liabilities in financing its asset investments, and all other things remain the same, what can be said about the firm's liquidity?
    a) The firm will be relatively more liquid.
    b) The firm will be relatively less liquid.
    c) The liquidity of the firm will be unchanged.
    d) No firm would do such a dumb thing.

    Answer: b Difficulty: 2

64. A firm might use current liabilities versus long-term debt for financing because:
    a) it reduces the chances of illiquidity.
    b) generally it is less costly than long-term debt.
    c) it offers greater flexibility.
    d) a and b
    e) b and c

    Answer: e Difficulty: 2

65. Total assets must equal the sum of which sources of financing:
    a) spontaneous
    b) temporary
    c) permanent
    d) b and c
    e) a, b, and c

    Answer: e Difficulty: 2

66. Which of the following is most likely to be a temporary source of financing?
    a) commercial paper
    b) preferred stock
    c) long-term debt
    d) all of the above

    Answer: a Difficulty: 2

67. Which of the following is not consistent with the "hedging principle"?
    a) The time pattern of a financial liability should be set to match the time pattern of the cash flows generated by the asset being financed.
    b) A seasonal expansion should be financed with either a spontaneous or temporary source of financing.
    c) An example of spontaneous financing is a short-term bank note.
    d) Preferred stock is an example of a permanent source of financing.

    Answer: c Difficulty: 3

68. The correct equation for calculating the cost of short-term credit is:
    a) rate = interest/(principal x time)
    b) rate = (principal x time)/interest
    c) rate = principal/(time x interest)
    d) rate = principal x interest x time

    Answer: a Difficulty: 2

69. The primary source(s) of collateral for secured funds is (are):
    a) accounts receivable
    b) inventories
    c) a and b
    d) commercial paper

    Answer: c Difficulty: 2

70. Which of the following is not an advantage of trade credit?
    a) The amount of extended credit expands and contracts with the needs of the firm
    b) The cost of foregoing the discount is less than the prime rate.
    c) Generally no formal agreements are involved in the extension of trade credit.
    d) none of the above

    Answer: b Difficulty: 2

71. Which of the following statements regarding a line of credit is true?
    a) The purpose for which the money is being borrowed must be stated by the borrower.
    b) A line of credit agreement usually fixes the interest rate that will be applied to any extensions of credit.
    c) A line of credit agreement is a legal commitment on the part of the bank to provide the stated credit.
    d) Such agreements usually cover the borrower's fiscal year.

    Answer: d Difficulty: 3

72. Which item would constitute poor collateral for an inventory loan?
    a) lumber
    b) vegetables
    c) grain
    d) chemicals

    Answer: b Difficulty: 2

73. The inventory loan arrangement in which all of the borrower's inventories are used as collateral is termed a:
    a) terminal warehouse agreement
    b) floating lien agreement
    c) chattel mortgage agreement
    d) field warehouse financial agreement

    Answer: b Difficulty: 3

74. A chattel mortgage:
    a) is a relatively inexpensive form of credit
    b) is an agreement where all items in an inventory are subject to the lien
    c) allows the borrower to retain title to the inventory
    d) allows the borrower full control over the inventory

    Answer: c Difficulty: 3

75. Advantages of using commercial paper for short-term credit include:
    a) the ability of some firms to obtain large amounts of credit
    b) a readily available source of credit for most firms
    c) a lower interest rate than bank rates
    d) a and c

    Answer: d Difficulty: 2

76. The prime rate of interest is:
    a) the rate the bank charges its most credit-worthy borrowers
    b) the rate the bank charges for money it borrows from the Federal Reserve Board
    c) the rate the bank charges its average borrower
    d) the rate the bank charges on home mortgages

    Answer: a Difficulty: 2

77. Terminal warehouse agreements:
    a) are particularly useful where large bulky items are used as collateral
    b) give the lender a lien against all inventories while only removing representative items
    c) remove control of the inventory from the borrower
    d) are less costly than field warehouse agreements

    Answer: c Difficulty: 2

78. Under a field warehouse financing agreement:
    a) collateral inventories are physically separated from other inventories of the borrower
    b) collateral inventories are placed under the control of a third party
    c) a warehouse receipt is issued which may or may not be negotiable
    d) all of the above

    Answer: d Difficulty: 2

79. A company which foregoes the discount when credit terms are 4/15 net 70 is essentially borrowing money from his supplier for an additional:
    a) 15 days
    b) 55 days
    c) 70 days
    d) 85 days

    Answer: b Difficulty: 2

80. A company purchased 20 tractors for a total of $200,000. The credit terms are 3/15 net 30. If the company does not take the discount, how much money is the company implicitly borrowing from his supplier?
   a) $200,000
   b) $196,000
   c) $197,000
   d) none of the above

   Answer: d Difficulty: 2

81. Which of the following loans provide the least amount of security to the lender?
   a) chattel mortgage
   b) factoring
   c) floating lien
   d) terminal warehouse agreement

   Answer: c Difficulty: 2

82. Which of the following businesses might obtain secured inventory loans with chattel mortgages?
   a) automobile dealers
   b) department stores
   c) clothing stores
   d) none of the above

   Answer: a Difficulty: 2

83. What factor(s) should we consider when selecting a source of short-term credit?
   a) effective cost of availability
   b) liquidity and profitability
   c) historical trend analysis
   d) none of the above

   Answer: a Difficulty: 2

84. Which of the following is not a source of unsecured short-term credit?
   a) trade credit
   b) a line of credit
   c) floating lien
   d) commercial paper

   Answer: c Difficulty: 2

85. Once a cash discount period has passed:
   a) one should pay immediately
   b) there is no reason to pay before the final due date
   c) one should pay after the final due date
   d) cannot be determined from the information

   Answer: b Difficulty: 2

86. Unsecured short-term credit is characterized by:
    a) one year or less maturity
    b) costs, depending on the credit worthiness of the borrower and the economy
    c) both a and b
    d) none of the above

    Answer: c Difficulty: 2

87. The Stant Shoe Company established a line of credit with a local bank. The maximum amount that can be borrowed under the terms of the agreement is $100,000 at an annual rate of 12 percent. A compensating balance averaging 10 percent of the amount borrowed is required. Prior to the agreement, Stant had no deposit with the bank. Shortly after signing the agreement, Stant needed $50,000 to pay off a note that was due. It borrowed the $50,000 from the bank by drawing on the line of credit. What is the effective annual cost of credit?
    a) 13.2%
    b) 13.3%
    c) 13.6%
    d) cannot be determined with available information

    Answer: b Difficulty: 2

88. Smith enterprises has a line of credit with Fidelity National Bank that allows Smith to borrow up to $350,000 at an interest rate of 15 percent. However, Smith must keep a compensating balance of 10 percent of any amount borrowed on deposit at Fidelity. Smith does not normally keep a cash balance account with Fidelity. What is the effective annual cost of credit (round to nearest .1 percent)?
    a) 17.7%
    b) 17.5%
    c) 15.9%
    d) cannot be determined with available information

    Answer: a Difficulty: 2

89. Georgia Peaches Corporation (GPC) has a line of credit with Trust Company Bank that allows GPC to borrow up to $300,000 at an annual interest rate of 11 percent. However, GPC must keep a compensating balance of 20 percent of any amount borrowed on deposit at the Trust Company. GPC does not normally have a cash balance account with the Trust Company. What is the effective annual cost of credit?
    a) 13.75%
    b) 13.20%
    c) 14.15%
    d) cannot be determined with available information

    Answer: a Difficulty: 2

90. Which of the following is an unsecured short-term bank loan made for a specific purpose?
    a) trade credit
    b) line of credit
    c) revolving credit agreement
    d) transaction loan

    Answer: d Difficulty: 2

91. The Stoney River Pennant Company uses commercial paper to satisfy part of its short-term financing requirements. Next week, it intends to sell $50 million in 180 day maturity paper on which it expects to have to pay discounted interest at an annual rate of 19 percent per annum. In addition, Stoney River expects to incur a cost of approximately $100,000 in dealer placement fees and other expenses of issuing the paper. What is the effective annual cost of credit to Stoney River (round to the nearest .1 percent)?
    a) 14.0%
    b) 19.0%
    c) 21.5%
    d) 18.65%

    Answer: c Difficulty: 3

92. The Dorle Manufacturing Company is going to issue 180 day commercial paper to raise $40 million. It anticipates a discounted interest rate of 13 percent, and dealer placement costs of approximately $60,000. What is the effective annual cost of credit to Dorle (round to the nearest .01 percent)?
    a) 14.25%
    b) 13.47%
    c) 13.90%
    d) 13.02%

    Answer: a Difficulty: 3

93. The effective annual cost of not taking advantage of the 3/10, net 30 terms offered by a supplier is (hint: use $1.00 as the invoice amount and a 360-day year):
    a) 55.7%
    b) 45.4%
    c) 32.3%
    d) 40.5%

    Answer: a Difficulty: 3

94. Atlas Tire Irons, Inc. is considering borrowing $5,000 for a 90-day period. The firm will repay the $5,000 principal amount plus $150 in interest. What is the effective annual rate of interest? Use a 360-day year.
   a) 7%
   b) 12%
   c) 15%
   d) 25%

   Answer: b Difficulty: 3

95. Which of the following apply to commercial paper?

   I. It usually has a maturity of 6 months or less.
   II. It generally carries an interest rate of slightly less than prime.
   III. It is secured by a firm's assets.
   a) I only
   b) II only
   c) III only
   d) I and II
   e) I and III

   Answer: d Difficulty: 2

96. A floating lien, chattel mortgage, or terminal warehouse receipt have which of the following in common?
   a) They all pledge accounts receivables as security.
   b) They have nothing in common.
   c) They are all unsecured forms of financing.
   d) They all use inventory to secure a loan.

   Answer: d Difficulty: 2

97. The primary advantage that pledging accounts receivable provides is:
   a) the flexibility it gives to the borrower
   b) that the financial institution bears the risk of collection
   c) the low cost as compared with other sources of short-term financing
   d) that the financial institution services the accounts

   Answer: a Difficulty: 2

98. The terminal warehouse agreement differs from the field warehouse agreement in that:
   a) The cost of the terminal warehouse agreement is lower due to the lower degree of risk.
   b) The borrower of the field warehouse agreement can sell the collateral without the consent of the lender.
   c) The warehouse procedure differs for both agreements.
   d) The terminal agreement transports the collateral to a public warehouse.

   Answer: d Difficulty: 3

ESSAY

99. Calculate the effective cost of the following trade credit terms if the discount is foregone and payment is made on the net due date.

   a. 2/15 net 30
   b. 2/15 net 45
   c. 2/15 net 60

   Answer:

   a. $\dfrac{\$0.02}{\$0.98} \times \dfrac{1}{(15/360)} = .4898$

   b. $\dfrac{\$0.02}{\$0.98} \times \dfrac{1}{(30/360)} = .2449$

   c. $\dfrac{\$0.02}{\$0.98} \times \dfrac{1}{(45/360)} = .1663$

   The cost of foregoing trade credit decreases as the length of time between the end of the discount period and the end of the net due period increases.

   Difficulty: 2

100. The U.R. Bloom Corporation established a line of credit with a local bank. The maximum amount that can be borrowed under the terms of the agreement is $125,000 at a rate of 14 percent. A compensating balance averaging 10 percent of the loan is required. Prior to the agreement, URB had maintained an account at the bank averaging $10,000. Any additional funds needed for the compensating balance will also have to be borrowed at the 14 percent rate. If the firm needs $100,000 for 6 months, what is the annual cost of the loan?

   Answer:

   $\text{Borrowed Funds} = \dfrac{\$100,000}{0.9} - \$10,000$

   $\text{Borrowed Funds} = \$101,111$

   $\text{Rate} = \dfrac{\$101,111 \times (.14/2)}{\$100,000} \times \dfrac{1}{(180/360)}$

   $\text{Rate} = .1416 \text{ per year}$

   Difficulty: 2

101. Maximus, Inc. is planning to issue $2,000,000 in 270-day maturity notes carrying a rate of 16 percent per annum. Due to the size of this firm, its commercial paper will be placed at a cost of $8,000. What is the effective cost of credit to Maximus?

Answer:
$$\text{Rate} = \frac{\$240,000 + \$8,000}{\$2,000,000 - \$8,000 - \$240,000} \times \frac{1}{(270/360)} = .1887$$

Difficulty: 2

102. The Smith Corporation is a maker of fine stereo components and presently has finished goods inventories of $750,000. They need a short-term bank loan of $500,000 for three months. The bank has proposed two different financing arrangements. The first is a floating lien arrangement at a rate of 16 percent. The second proposal is for a terminal warehouse arrangement at 13 percent. Under the latter proposal, Smith will pay $3,000 a month plus round trip shipping expense of $4,000. Which source of credit should be selected by the Smith Corporation? Explain.

Answer:
Floating lien arrangement:
Annual rate = 0.1600
Terminal warehouse arrangement:

$$\text{Annual Rate} = \frac{\$16,250 + \$9,000 + \$4,000}{\$500,000} \times \frac{1}{(90/360)} = 0.2340$$

The additional expenses of the terminal warehouse arrangement make it more expensive than the floating lien arrangement.

Difficulty: 3

103. Rainbow Records is a producer and distributor of specialty recordings. It sells directly to large retail firms on terms of net 90 and has average monthly sales of $150,000. It has recently decided to pledge all of its accounts receivable to its bank. The bank advances up to 60 percent of the face value of these receivables at a rate of 2 percent over the prime rate, while charging 2 percent on all receivables pledged for processing to cover billing and collection services. Prior to this arrangement RR was spending $25,000 a year on its credit department. The prime rate is 15 percent.

a. What is the average level of accounts receivable?
b. What is the effective cost of using this short-term credit for one year?

Answer:
a. 3 x $150,000 = $450,000

b. $\text{Rate} = \dfrac{\$45,900 + \$36,000 - \$25,000}{270,000} \times \dfrac{1}{(360/360)} = 0.2107$

Annual interest expense = 0.17 x 0.60 x $450,000 = $45,900
Difficulty: 3

104. The effective interest rate on short-term loans from Bank A is 16 percent per year. Bank B claims that their interest rate is only 14.5 percent per year. However, Bank B charges interest on a discount basis. Which bank is charging the lowest effective rate of interest on a one-year loan?

Answer:
Effective cost of loan from Bank A = .1600

Effective cost of loan from Bank B = $\dfrac{.145}{1-.145}$ = .1696

Bank A is charging the lowest effective rate of interest.
Difficulty: 3

105. AAC, Inc. is planning to issue $5,000,000 in 180-day maturity notes earning a rate of 12 percent per annum. The company expects to incur costs of approximately $20,000 in dealer placement fees and other expenses of issuing the commercial paper. The company plans to back up their commercial paper offering with a line of credit from a bank for $5,000,000. The compensating balance requirement is 10 percent of the line of credit. The company normally maintains $450,000 in its accounts with the bank. What is the effective cost of the commercial paper offering?

Answer:
Additional funds tied up with compensating balance requirements equal:
$(.10)($5,000,000) - $450,000 = $50,000$

Interest on commercial paper=$(.12)$ $($5,000,000)$ $\left[\dfrac{180}{360}\right] = $300,000$

$$\text{Effect rate=}\left[\frac{\$300,000}{\$5,000,000=\$20,000-\$300,000-\$50,000}\right] \times \frac{1}{1/2}$$

$$= \frac{\$300,000}{\$4,630,000} \times 2 = .1296$$

Difficulty: 3

106. Your company needs to pay $10,000 for the overhaul of five trucks. A bank offers you a loan at 18 percent per annum with a compensating balance requirement of 15 percent of the loan amount. You plan to borrow the money for 9 months and currently do not have any account with this bank. What is the effective cost of the loan?

Answer:

$(.85)(\text{loan amount}) = $10,000$

Loan amount $= \dfrac{\$10,000}{.85} = \$11,765$
Interest on loan $= (.18)($11,765) $(\dfrac{9}{12}) = $1,588$

$$\text{Rate} = \frac{\$1,588}{\$10,000} \times \frac{1}{(9/12)} = .2117$$

Difficulty: 3

107. Staplers Inc. has a $400,000 line of credit with a local bank. The bank requires a compensating balance of 10% of the loan and extends credit to Staplers at 1/2% over the current prime rate. Staplers needs the use of $100,000 for the three-month period. They currently have no deposits with the lending bank.

    a. What will the effective annual cost of this credit be? (Assume a 360-day year and a 10-1/2% prime rate.)
    b. Using the above information, what would be the effective interest rate if the firm discounted the interest on the loan?

    Answer:
    a. Loan amount to cover compensating balance
       $.90B = 100,000$
       $B = 111,111$
       Interest paid on the $111,111:
       $111,111 \times .11 \times 1/4 = 3055.56$
       Effective annual cost:

       $$Rate = \frac{3055.56}{100,000} \times \frac{1}{90/360} = 12.22\%$$

    b. $$Rate = \frac{3055.56}{100,000 - 3055.56} \times \frac{1}{90/360} = 12.6\%$$

    Difficulty: 3

108. Dazzly Diamond Corp. called for credit at the Home Alone Bank of Paris, TX. The terms included a $35,000 maximum loan with interest of 1 percent over prime, and the agreement also requires a 15% compensating balance throughout the year. The prime rate is currently 12 percent.

    a. If Dazzly Diamond Corp. maintains a balance in its account of $5,250 to $6,000, what is the effective cost of credit through the line-of-credit agreement where the maximum amount of the loan is used?
    b. Recompute the effective cost of credit to Dazzly Diamond if it will have to borrow the compensating balance and the maximum amount possible under the agreement.

Answer:

```
35,000
x 0.13
_____
$4,550
```

$379/month -- interest
$5,250 -- compensating balance

a. RATE $= \dfrac{\$4,550}{\$35,000}$ x $\dfrac{1}{360/360}$ = 0.13 or 13%

b. RATE $= \dfrac{\$4,550}{\$29750}$ x $\dfrac{1}{360/360}$ = 0.1529 or 15.29%

Interest expense for the loan is

($35,000) (0.13) $\dfrac{360}{360}$ = $4,550

However, the firm gets the use of only .85 x $35,000 = $29,750.

Difficulty: 3

109. Quincy Fathows & Co. plans to issue commercial paper for the first time in its 85-year history. The firm plans to issue $400,000 in 120-day maturity notes. The paper will carry a 13% quarterly compounded rate with discounted interest and will cost Quincy Fathows $8,000 in advance to issue.

    a. What is the effective cost of credit to Quincy Fathows?
    b. What other factors should the firm consider in analyzing whether or not to issue the commercial paper?

Answer:

a. RATE $= \dfrac{\text{interest}}{\text{principal}}$ x $\dfrac{1}{\text{time}}$

RATE $= \dfrac{\$17,333^* + \$8,000}{\$400,000 - \$8,000 - \$17,333}$ x $\dfrac{1}{120/360}$ = .203 = 20.3%

*Interest = 0.13 x $400,000 x 1/3

b. The risk involved with the issue of commercial paper should be considered. This risk relates to the fact that the commercial paper market is highly impersonal and denies even the most credit worthy borrower any flexibility in terms of when repayment is made. In addition, commercial paper is a viable source of credit to only the most credit worthy borrowers. Thus, it may simply not be available to the firm.

Difficulty: 3

110. Richenstein Enterprises is in the business of selling dishwashers. The firm needs $192,000 to finance an anticipated expansion in receivables due to increased sales. Richenstein's credit terms are net 40, and its average monthly credit sales are $180,000. In general, the firm's customers pay within the credit period; thus, the firm's average accounts receivable balance is $240,000.

The comptroller of Richenstein Enterprises, Mr. Gee, approached their bank for the needed capital, placing the accounts receivable as collateral. The bank offered to make the loan at a rate of 2 percent over prime plus a 1 percent processing charge on all receivables pledged. The bank agreed to loan up to 80 percent of the face value of the receivables pledged.

a. Estimate the cost of the receivables loan to Richenstein where the firm borrows the $192,000. The prime rate is currently 13%.

b. Gee also requested a line of credit for $192,000 from the bank. The bank agreed to grant the necessary line of credit at a rate of 4% over prime and required a 12% compensating balance Gee currently maintains an average demand deposit of $40,000. Estimate the cost of the line of credit to Richenstein

c. Which source of credit should Richenstein Enterprises select?

Answer:

a. $$\text{RATE} = \frac{\$28,800^* + \$21,600^{**}}{\$192,000} \times \frac{1}{360/360} = .2625 \text{ or } 26.25\%$$

* ($240,000 x 0.15 x .8) = $28,800
** ($180,000 x .01 x 12) = $21,600

b. $192,000 x .12 = $23,040 (compensating balance)
Since Richenstein maintains a balance of $40,000 normally with the bank, the compensating balance requirement will not increase the effective cost of credit.

$$\frac{\$32,640}{\$192,000} \times \frac{1}{360/360} = 0.17 \text{ or } 17\%$$

Interest = $192,000 x .17 = $32,640.

c. Choose the line of credit since the effective interest is considerably lower. Note, however, that the pledging arrangement may involve credit services to Richenstein which would reduce Richenstein's credit department expense. If this were the case then these savings would reduce the effective cost of that financing arrangement.

Difficulty: 3

111. Bonneau Sunglass Co. is considering the factoring of its receivables. The firm has credit sales of $500,000 per month and has an average receivables balance of $1,000,000 with 60-day credit terms. The factor has offered to extend credit equal to 85% of the receivables factored less interest on the loan at a rate of 2% per month. The 15% difference in the advance and face value of all receivables factored consists of a 2% factoring fee plus a 13% reserve, which the factor maintains. In addition, if Bonneau decides to factor its receivables, it will sell them all, so that it can reduce its credit department costs by $2,000 a month.

a. What is the cost of borrowing the maximum amount of credit available to Bonneau through the factoring agreement?

b. What considerations other than cost should be accounted for by Bonneau in determining whether or not to enter the factoring agreement?

Answer:

a. Maximum advance
Face value of receivables
(2 months credit sales) $1,000,000
Less: factoring fee (2%)   (20,000)
Reserve (13%)
Interest (2% per month for 60 days   *(34,000)
Loan advance (less discount interest $ 816,000
*Interest is calculated on the 85 percent of the factored accounts that can be borrowed, (.85 x $1,000,000 x .02 x 2 months) = $34,000 or ($1,000,000 - $20,000 - $130,000) x .02 x 2 months) = $34,000.
Thus, the effective cost of credit to Bonneau's is calculated as follows:

$$\text{RATE} = \frac{\$34,000 + \$20,000 - \$4,000**}{\$816,000} \times \frac{1}{(60/360)} = .3676 \text{ or } 36.76\%$$

**Credit department savings for 60 days equals 2 x $2,000.
Calculated on an annual basis, the cost of credit would be:

$$\text{RATE} = \frac{\$204,000 + \$120,000 - \$24,000}{\$816,000} \times \frac{1}{360/360} = .3676 \text{ or } 36.76\%$$

where
interest = .02 x $850,000 x 12 = $204,000
factoring fee = .02 x $500,000 x 12 = $120,000
credit department savings= 12 x $2,000 = $24,000
b. Of particular concern here is the presence of any "stigma" associated with factoring. In some industries, factoring simply is not used unless the firm's financial condition is critical.
This would appear to be the case here, given the relatively high effective rate of interest on borrowing.

Difficulty: 3

Chapter 15: Liquid Asset Management

1. Near cash assets consist of marketable securities and accounts receivable.

   Answer: False Difficulty: 1

2. Motives for holding stocks of cash include transaction, precautionary, and speculative.

   Answer: True Difficulty: 1

3. Some firms hold large stocks of cash because their access to additional cash is limited.

   Answer: True Difficulty: 1

4. Because they operate within a highly uncertain environment, utilities hold a large percentage of their total assets in cash.

   Answer: False Difficulty: 1

5. Firms like to hold large stocks of cash since the risk of becoming insolvent is minimized.

   Answer: False Difficulty: 1

6. One way to alleviate uncertainty surrounding inflows and outflows of cash is to construct a cash budget.

   Answer: False Difficulty: 1

7. A lock box system is useful in reducing mail float.

   Answer: True Difficulty: 1

8. Use of concentration banking centralizes the firms' stock of cash.

   Answer: True Difficulty: 1

9. One of the benefits of an automated depository transfer check system is the elimination of mail float.

   Answer: True Difficulty: 1

10. The most economical method used to transfer a relatively small amount of funds quickly is by wire transfer.

    Answer: False Difficulty: 1

11. A zero balance account permits divisions to disburse funds while maintaining centralized control of several bank accounts.

    Answer: True Difficulty: 1

12. Capability of paying through drafts, zero balance accounts, and remote disbursing all help to decrease disbursement float.

    Answer: False Difficulty: 1

13. The funds needed to satisfy the precautionary motive are entirely held in cash.

    Answer: False Difficulty: 1

14. The most important motive for holding liquid assets for a typical company is usually the speculative motive.

    Answer: False Difficulty: 1

15. The Treasury Department has criticized the practice of remote disbursing.

    Answer: False Difficulty: 2

16. A financial manager should be willing to assume greater financial risk in the marketable securities portfolio so long as the expected return is commensurate with the risk.

    Answer: True Difficulty: 1

17. Other things being equal, the longer the maturity of a financial asset, the greater the interest rate risk associated with the asset.

    Answer: True Difficulty: 1

18. T-bills, Treasury bonds and federal agency securities are all guaranteed by the "full faith and credit" of the United States and are therefore default free.

    Answer: False Difficulty: 1

19. A banker's acceptance is a draft drawn on a specific bank by an exporter in order to obtain payment for goods that he has shipped to a customer who maintains an account with that specific bank.

    Answer: True Difficulty: 1

20. One of the drawbacks of including bankers' acceptances in a marketable securities portfolio is the lack of a good secondary market.

    Answer: False Difficulty: 2

21. A negotiable certificate of deposit is a marketable receipt for funds deposited in a bank for a period of one to 18 months.

    Answer: True Difficulty: 2

22. Although CDs are slightly more risky than Treasury Bills, the yield is usually slightly less.

    Answer: False Difficulty: 2

23. Commercial paper is a short-term, unsecured, promissory note.

    Answer: True Difficulty: 1

24. One of the attractive features of commercial paper is an active secondary market.

    Answer: False Difficulty: 2

25. Repurchase agreements effectively protect the purchaser against market fluctuations during the contract period.

    Answer: True Difficulty: 2

26. Yields on various financial instruments tend to be positively correlated over time.

    Answer: True Difficulty: 1

27. The interest earned on U.S. Treasury bills is subject to state and local income taxes.

    Answer: False Difficulty: 2

28. The maturity of commercial paper is usually from 3 to 360 days.

    Answer: False Difficulty: 1

29. The minimum denomination of U.S. Treasury bills is $10,000.

    Answer: True Difficulty: 1

30. Six-month U.S. Treasury bills are auctioned every week.

    Answer: True Difficulty: 1

31. Marketable securities are near-cash assets because they can be converted into cash quickly.

    Answer: True Difficulty: 1

32. The industry in which a firm operates has relatively little effect on the relative amounts of transaction cash held.

    Answer: False Difficulty: 1

33. Speculative cash balances are held to take advantage of uncertain, profit-making opportunities.

    Answer: True Difficulty: 1

34. A treasury bill is a near-cash asset.

    Answer: True Difficulty: 1

35. With a preauthorized check system, the customer of the firm no longer writes his/her own check.

    Answer: True Difficulty: 1

36. Zero balance accounts reduce disbursing float.

    Answer: False Difficulty: 2

37. Payable-through drafts look like checks but are not drawn on a bank.

    Answer: True Difficulty: 2

38. The main purpose of using a payable-through draft system is to gain effective control over field payments.

    Answer: True Difficulty: 2

39. Commercial paper can be described as a short-term corporate IOU.

    Answer: True Difficulty: 1

40. A security is considered liquid if it can be sold, regardless of the time it takes to make the sale.

    Answer: False Difficulty: 1

41. If revenues can be forecast to fall within a tight range of outcomes, then the ratio of cash and near cash to total assets will be greater for the firm than if the prospective cash inflows might be expected to vary over a wide range.

    Answer: False Difficulty: 2

42. The most important reasons firms hold cash balances are the transaction and speculative motives.

    Answer: False Difficulty: 1

43. Lock-box arrangements yield benefits for all companies regardless of the size of sales or customer remittance checks.

    Answer: False Difficulty: 1

44. The main purpose of using a payable-through draft system is to provide for effective control over field payments.

    Answer: True Difficulty: 1

45. Marketable securities are only those security investments the firm can convert into cash balances within one year.

    Answer: False Difficulty: 1

46. Both depository transfer checks and wire transfers are used in conjunction with what is known as concentration banking.

    Answer: True Difficulty: 1

47. Zero balance accounts permit centralized control over cash outflows while maintaining divisional disbursing authority.

    Answer: True Difficulty: 1

48. Accounts receivable is an asset representing sales made on credit.

    Answer: True Difficulty: 1

49. For many industries accounts receivable comprise as much as 25 percent of total assets.

    Answer: True Difficulty: 2

50. Accounts receivable variables under control of the financial manager include level of credit sales, terms of credit sales, and quality of credit customers.

    Answer: False Difficulty: 2

51. If upon examination of a firm's existing credit policy it is discovered that bad debt losses have increased for certain credit groups, it does not follow that extension of credit to those groups should be withheld.

Answer: True Difficulty: 2

52. Carrying inventory reduces the costs associated with periodic bad debt losses.

Answer: False Difficulty: 1

53. The EOQ model calculates the size of the firm's inventory given its expected usage, carrying costs, and ordering costs.

Answer: True Difficulty: 1

54. In the EOQ model the optimal ordering quantity is the quantity for which the sum of the costs of ordering and carrying inventory is minimized.

Answer: True Difficulty: 2

55. Non-uniform demand can be accomplished in the EOQ model by allowing for non-uniform ordering costs.

Answer: False Difficulty: 2

56. Terms of sale are frequently changed by the financial manager in order to increase sales.

Answer: False Difficulty: 1

57. One method used to monitor the collections of accounts receivable is aging.

Answer: True Difficulty: 1

58. Anticipatory buying occurs because of an anticipated decrease in interest rates.

Answer: False Difficulty: 1

59. Efficient collection of accounts receivable helps to determine both the profitability and the liquidity of the firm.

Answer: True Difficulty: 1

60. The nature of a company's business is an important factor in determining the level of credit sales.

Answer: True Difficulty: 1

61. Because poor credit-worthy customers may cause bad debt losses, credit sales to them should not be allowed.

    Answer: False Difficulty: 2

62. As inflation pushes interest rates up, the cost of carrying inventory rises.

    Answer: True Difficulty: 1

63. Determination of safety stock involves a tradeoff between the risk of a stock-out and increased costs of carrying additional inventory.

    Answer: True Difficulty: 2

64. In terms of trade credit, default costs vary <u>indirectly</u> with the quality of the customer.

    Answer: True Difficulty: 1

65. In the EOQ model, the carrying cost on inventory should include the required rate of an investment in inventory.

    Answer: True Difficulty: 2

66. The EOQ model assumes constant demand and constant unit price.

    Answer: True Difficulty: 2

67. The just-in-time inventory control system is just a new approach to the EOQ model which tries to produce the lowest average inventory possible.

    Answer: True Difficulty: 2

68. The decision to forego the discount available for those customers who pay early has an advantage as well as a disadvantage.

    Answer: True Difficulty: 2

69. According to the Altman model, multiple discriminant analysis indicates that those applicants with a Z score below 3.7 have a significant probability of filing for bankruptcy.

    Answer: False Difficulty: 2

70. The purpose of maintaining a raw materials inventory is to integrate the purchasing and production functions.

    Answer: False Difficulty: 2

71. The assumption of instantaneous delivery and independent orders are dealt with by the inclusion of a safety stock.

    Answer: False Difficulty: 2

MULTIPLE CHOICE

72. Cash inflows come from:
    a) purchase of marketable securities
    b) purchase of fixed assets
    c) credit sales
    d) cash sales

    Answer: d Difficulty: 1

73. John Maynard Keynes segmented a firm's demand for cash into the following motives:
    a) risk, investment, and liquidity
    b) transaction, speculative and precautionary
    c) transaction, liquidity, and speculative
    d) transaction, speculative, and risky

    Answer: b Difficulty: 1

74. A construction firm that accumulates cash in anticipation of a significant drop in lumber costs is an example of the _____ motive for holding cash.
    a) transaction
    b) speculative
    c) hedging
    d) none of the above

    Answer: b Difficulty: 1

75. One would expect to find a relatively low level of liquid assets in which industry?
    a) retail trade
    b) services
    c) utilities
    d) construction

    Answer: c Difficulty: 2

76. A company is technically insolvent when:
    a) cash outflows in a given period are greater than cash inflows.
    b) earnings before interest payments are less than the interest payments
    c) it lacks the necessary liquidity to promptly pay its current debt obligations
    d) current ratio is less than 1.0

    Answer: c Difficulty: 3

77. Transit float is caused by:
    a) the time necessary for a deposited check to clear the banking system and become usable funds to the company
    b) the time funds are not available, through the company's bank account, until its payment check has cleared the banking system
    c) the elapsed time from the moment a customer mails his remittance check until the firm begins to process it
    d) the time required for the firm to process remittance checks

    Answer: a Difficulty: 3

78. Assume that liquid funds can be invested to yield 12 percent. If annual remittance checks total $2 billion, what is it worth for the firm to reduce float by 1 day?
    a) $658,000
    b) $24,000,000
    c) $1,000,000
    d) $54,833

    Answer: a Difficulty: 3

79. The benefits of a lock-box arrangement include
    a) elimination of clerical functions
    b) early knowledge of dishonored checks
    c) increased working cash
    d) all of the above

    Answer: d Difficulty: 2

80. Benefits of a PAC system of collection include
    a) reduced billing and postage costs
    b) predictable cash flows
    c) reduced mail and processing float
    d) all of the above

    Answer: d Difficulty: 2

81. Concentration banks
    a) receive surplus balances from multiple bank accounts in different geographic areas of the country
    b) use depository transfer checks for transferring funds from outlying banks
    c) eliminate mail float entirely by using PAC's to transfer funds
    d) a and b

    Answer: d Difficulty: 2

82. Improvements in the management of disbursements include
    a) FPC (field payment control)
    b) automated depository transfer checks
    c) zero balance accounts
    d) disbursed float

    Answer: c Difficulty: 2

83. The PAC system is used often by
    a) automobile dealers
    b) insurance companies
    c) jewelers
    d) appliance stores

    Answer: b Difficulty: 2

84. Payable through drafts
    a) provide for effective control over field payments
    b) are not legal instruments
    c) cannot be cleared through the banking system
    d) all of the above

    Answer: a Difficulty: 2

85. A lock-box system reduces
    a) mail float
    b) transit float
    c) disbursing float
    d) a and b

    Answer: d Difficulty: 2

86. The fastest method of transferring funds between banks is
    a) payable through drafts
    b) automated depository transfer checks
    c) pre-authorized checks
    d) none of the above

    Answer: d Difficulty: 2

87. The financial manager should include the following security in a
    portfolio of marketable securities:
    a) high-grade shares of common stock
    b) long-term shares of common stock
    c) high-quality preferred stock
    d) high-grade commercial paper

    Answer: d Difficulty: 2

88. Given that short-term interest rates typically fluctuate more than long-term rates, interest rate risk is least for
    a) treasury bills
    b) common stock
    c) long-term government bonds
    d) medium-term corporate bonds

    Answer: a Difficulty: 2

89. Federal agency securities
    a) are guaranteed by the U.S. government
    b) include stock of the Federal Reserve Board
    c) all have a denomination or face value of $10,000
    d) have a yield greater than treasury securities of identical maturity

    Answer: d Difficulty: 2

90. Money market funds
    a) are one of the oldest forms of mutual funds
    b) typically invest in a diversified portfolio of short-term, high-grade debt instruments
    c) are generally very profitable but fail to provide liquidity to the small investor
    d) typically sell shares to the public in $5,000 denominations

    Answer: b Difficulty: 2

91. What type of float can be reduced with a lock-box arrangement?
    a) mail
    b) processing
    c) transit
    d) all of the above

    Answer: d Difficulty: 2

92. A company trying to optimize the use of float will try to
    a) increase its disbursing float
    b) decrease its disbursing float
    c) decrease processing float
    d) both a and c

    Answer: d Difficulty: 2

93. Which of the following can be used by a company to increase its disbursing float?
    a) remote disbursing
    b) wire transfer
    c) depository transfer checks
    d) payable through draft

    Answer: a Difficulty: 2

94. Which of the following can be used to decrease a firm's processing float?
    a) lock-box arrangement
    b) preauthorized checks
    c) wire transfer
    d) zero balance account

    Answer: b Difficulty: 2

95. The time necessary for a deposited check to clear through the commercial banking system causes which of the following types of floats?
    a) mail
    b) processing
    c) transit
    d) disbursing

    Answer: c Difficulty: 2

96. The Stone Duck Manufacturing Company is considering the use of a lock-box collection system. Stone Duck's average check receipt is $150. The company invests excess cash in money market certificates and receives an average of 8% annual interest. The lock-box system will speed up Stone Duck's collections by 2.5 days. What is the maximum per check processing cost that Stone Duck should be willing to pay for the lock-box system (round to the nearest $.001)?
    a) $ .083
    b) $ .30
    c) $4.8
    d) $ .03

    Answer: a Difficulty: 3

97. The Decorative Imitation Flamingo Manufacturing Company (DIFCO) processes an estimated 50,000 checks per year from its customers. Total revenues collected by check is $10,000,000. the average float time until the funds are credited to DIFCO's checking account is 8 days. For an extra cost of $ .09/check, DIFCO's bank will install a lock-box system that will reduce float time from 8 days to 5 days. If DIFCO earns 8% on its checking account, how much per check will DIFCO make if it uses the lock-box system (round to the nearest $ .001)?
    a) $ .133
    b) $ .222
    c) $ .047
    d) $ .043

    Answer: d Difficulty: 3

98. The Stonely Manufacturing Company will collect an estimated $4,000,000 next year; and it will receive an estimated 10,000 checks. Stonely's bank has offered to set up a lock-box system that will reduce float time by 2.5 days. The cost of the system will be $ .222 per check. What is the minimum annual interest rate on its cash balance that Stonely should receive before it would be willing to adopt the lock-box system (round to the nearest .1%)?
    a) 20%
    b) 8%
    c) 8.9%
    d) 9.8%

    Answer: b Difficulty: 3

99. Compare the risk of a 90 day unsecured promissory note issued by Southwest Airlines to a 20 year U.S. Government Treasury Bond.
    a) The Treasury Bond has a lower financial risk, but a higher interest rate risk.
    b) The Treasury Bond has a lower financial risk and a lower interest rate risk.
    c) The Treasury Bond has a lower interest rate risk, but higher financial risk.
    d) The Treasury Bond has a higher interest rate risk, and a higher financial risk.

    Answer: a Difficulty: 3

100. Which of the following has the highest interest rate risk?
    a) a 20 year U.S. Treasury Bond
    b) Bendix Corporation 6 month commercial paper
    c) a six month money market certificate at a federally issued bank
    d) a Southwest Airlines bond maturing in 4 years

    Answer: a Difficulty: 3

101. Which of the following has the least interest rate risk?
    a) a six month unsecured promissory note from International Harvester
    b) an eight year investment certificate from a federally insured bank
    c) a 15 year U.S. Treasury bond
    d) an AT&T bond maturing in 15 years

    Answer: a Difficulty: 3

102. If you compare the yield of a municipal bond with that of a treasury bond, what is the equivalent before-tax yield of a municipal bond yielding 5% per year for an investor in the 44% tax bracket (round to nearest .1%)?
    a) 7.6%
    b) 6.1%
    c) 8.9%
    d) 11.4%

    Answer: b Difficulty: 2

103. Which of the following are short-term, unsecured promissory notes sold by large businesses?
    a) negotiable certificates of deposit
    b) repurchase agreements
    c) money market mutual funds
    d) commercial paper

    Answer: d Difficulty: 2

104. Which of the following are characteristics of repurchase agreements?

    I. Agreements are written for very short periods of time.
    II. Agreements are generally written for 6 months or more.
    III. U.S. government issues are often sold and then repurchased.
    IV. The agreements are usually executed in sizes of $500,000 or less.
    a) I
    b) II and III
    c) II, III, and IV
    d) I and III

    Answer: d Difficulty: 3

105. Which of the following is the least liquid?
    a) U.S. Treasury bills
    b) commercial paper
    c) money market mutual funds
    d) federal agency securities

    Answer: b Difficulty: 2

106. Which of the following affects the precautionary motive for holding cash?
    a) the cash flow predictability
    b) the firm's access to external funds
    c) both a and b
    d) none of the above

    Answer: c Difficulty: 2

107. The financial manager is concerned with:
    a) striking a balance between holding too much and too little cash
    b) maintaining high levels of profitability
    c) minimizing the chance of insolvency
    d) all of the above

    Answer: d Difficulty: 2

108. The annual value of one day of float reduction is:
    a) (sales per day) x (assumed yield)
    b) (sales per year) x (assumed yield) x (days' float reduction)
    c) (sales per unit) x (assumed yield)
    d) none of the above

    Answer: b Difficulty: 2

109. A managerial benefit of a lock-box arrangement is:
    a) better audit control of the documents received
    b) elimination of clerical functions
    c) less chance of losing documents
    d) all of the above

    Answer: d Difficulty: 2

110. A PAC:
    a) is the same as a draft
    b) is created only with the payer's legal authorization
    c) is ineffective and rarely used
    d) none of the above

    Answer: b Difficulty: 2

111. A company that has an unpredictable cash flow, and is holding cash
    because of things that might happen due to this uncertainty, is holding
    a larger minimum cash balance due to which type of motive?
    a) transaction
    b) precautionary
    c) speculative
    d) common sense

    Answer: b Difficulty: 2

112. Funds that are available in a company's bank account until its payment
    check has cleared refers to:
    a) mail float
    b) processing float
    c) transit float
    d) disbursing float

    Answer: d Difficulty: 2

113. Bill's Fly-By-Night Inc. recently wrote a check to Doug's Fraud
    Insurance Inc. The funds will remain in Bill's bank account until its
    payment check clears. This refers to:
    a) mail float
    b) processing float
    c) transit float
    d) disbursing float

    Answer: d Difficulty: 2

114. The objective(s) of a preauthorized check system is(are) to reduce:
    a) mail float
    b) processing float
    c) disbursing float
    d) a and b
    e) b and c

    Answer: d Difficulty: 2

115. A way of managing a firm's cash disbursements would be through:
    a) zero balance accounts
    b) payable-through drafts
    c) remote disbursing
    d) all of the above

    Answer: d Difficulty: 2

116. Firms use remote disbursements to:
    a) decrease mail float
    b) increase disbursing float
    c) decrease disbursing float
    d) increase processing float

    Answer: b Difficulty: 2

117. Banker's acceptances are:
    a) not "issued" in specialized denominations
    b) fully taxable at the federal, state, and local levels
    c) are sold on a discount basis and payable to the bearer
    d) All of the above

    Answer: d Difficulty: 2

118. In order to select a proper marketable securities mix, the financial manager should evaluate:
    a) financial and interest rate risk
    b) liquidity and taxability
    c) yields among different financial assets
    d) a and b only
    e) all of the above

    Answer: e Difficulty: 2

119. The benefits of a lock-box arrangement include:
    a) increased working cash
    b) early knowledge of dishonored checks
    c) a and b
    d) a and b, but these increase the clerical functions that have to be performed by the firm

    Answer: c Difficulty: 2

120. The benefits of a lock-box arrangement include:
    a) financial risk
    b) operating leverage
    c) interest rate risk
    d) liquidity

    Answer: b Difficulty: 2

121. Which of the following are government-sponsored corporations that have been created to effect lending programs of the United States government?

       I. the Federal National Mortgage Association (FNMA)
      II. the Federal Home Loan Banks (FHLB)
     III. the Federal Land Banks
      IV. the Federal Deposit Insurance Corporation (FDIC)
    a) I and II
    b) IV only
    c) I, IIi, and III
    d) all of the above

    Answer: c Difficulty: 3

122. What is a "CD"?
    a) a negotiable certificate of deposit
    b) a corporate controlled disbursement account
    c) a commercial demand deposit
    d) a certified disbursement

    Answer: a Difficulty: 2

123. A firm's credit and collection policies usually include:
    a) terms of sale, quality of customers, and collection of credit sales
    b) average collection period, dollar value of aged receivables, and terms of sale
    c) terms of sale and collection of credit sales
    d) terms of sale, level of credit sales, and collection of credit sales

    Answer: a Difficulty: 2

124. An aging schedule of accounts receivable aids the financial manager in determining:
    a) the amount of receivables that are past due
    b) the average age of the customers
    c) the receivables turnover
    d) the average length of the discount period

    Answer: a Difficulty: 2

125. A trade credit discount such as 2/10 net 30 means:
    a) a 2 percent penalty is due after 30 days
    b) a 10 percent discount for cash on delivery and a 2 percent discount for payment within 30 days
    c) a 2 percent discount for payment within 10 days, and a 2 percent penalty if payment is made after 30 days
    d) a 2 percent discount if payment is made within 10 days, otherwise, the total amount is due in 30 days.

    Answer: d Difficulty: 2

126. If a firm with credit terms of 1/10 net 30 were to change its terms to 3/10 net 30, the result would probably be:
    a) increased bank loans
    b) increased accounts receivable turnover
    c) an increase in the average level of accounts receivable
    d) a decrease in accounts payable

    Answer: b Difficulty: 2

127. The purpose of carrying inventory is to:
    a) make different production processes more dependent on sales
    b) make sales more independent of the production process
    c) have collateral for loans
    d) improve the current ratio

    Answer: b Difficulty: 2

128. Of the following EOQ model assumptions, the most limiting is:
    a) uniform demand
    b) constant unit price
    c) constant ordering costs
    d) independent orders

    Answer: a Difficulty: 2

129. The economic ordering quantity for inventory where S is total demand over the planning period in units, O is ordering costs per order, C is carrying costs per unit, and Q is inventory order size in units is:
    a) $Q^* = (S/2)^2$
    b) $Q^* = \left[\dfrac{OC}{2S}\right]^2$
    c) $Q^* = \dfrac{\sqrt{2SO}}{C}$
    d) $Q^* = \dfrac{\sqrt{2OC}}{S}$

    Answer: c Difficulty: 2

130. In the basic model the optimal inventory level is the point at which:
   a) total cost is minimized
   b) total revenue is maximized
   c) carrying costs are minimized
   d) ordering costs are minimized

   Answer: a Difficulty: 2

131. The problems of uncertainty associated with both delivery time and product demand:
   a) decrease the usefulness of the basic EOQ model
   b) result in higher carrying costs
   c) result in the need for safety stocks
   d) b and c

   Answer: d Difficulty: 2

132. If the variables in the EOQ inventory model are defined as: S = total units demanded during the planning period, O = ordering costs per order, C = carrying costs per unit and Q = inventory order size in units, then the average level of inventory which a company should have during the planning period is:
   a) 2/3 Q
   b) 1/2 Q
   c) SO/C
   d) none of the above

   Answer: b Difficulty: 3

133. Determine the effective annualized cost of foregoing the trade discount on terms 3/10 net 90 (round to nearest .1%).
   a) 12.4%
   b) 13.5%
   c) 12.0%
   d) 13.9%

   Answer: d Difficulty: 2

134. Determine the effective annualized cost of foregoing the trade discount on terms 2/10 net 45 (round to nearest .01%).
   a) 21.0%
   b) 16.3%
   c) 16.0%
   d) 20.6%

   Answer: a Difficulty: 2

135. Sterling Clips Inc. estimates that it will sell 10,000 porcelain clips next year. Because porcelain clips are so easily damaged, the average per unit carrying cost of the clips is $10. The per order cost of ordering is $250. Assume that Sterling wants a safety stock of 200 clips. If Sterling reorders the clips based on the economic order quantity, what is Sterling's average inventory of porcelain clips (round to the nearest 100 clips)?
    a) 350
    b) 450
    c) 550
    d) 600

    Answer: c Difficulty: 3

136. Dorning Shade Company will use an estimated 50,000 gumbands in its manufacturing process next year. The carrying cost of gumband inventory is $.04 per unit and the cost of reordering gumbands is $50 per order. What is Dorning Shade's economic ordering quantity for gumbands (round to the nearest 100 gumbands)?
    a) 11,200
    b) 10,200
    c) 10,700
    d) 12,100

    Answer: a Difficulty: 3

137. Stern Corporation uses semi-hex joints in its manufacturing process. If Stern's total demand for the joints for next year is estimated to be 15,000 units, and if the cost per order is $80, what is Stern's economic order quantity of semi-hex joints? Assume that carrying costs for semi-hex joints are $.51 per unit and round off to the nearest 100 units.
    a) 1,500
    b) 1,700
    c) 2,000
    d) 2,200

    Answer: d Difficulty: 3

138. The Steady Fork Company will use an estimated 4,000 wheel assemblies in its manufacturing process next year. The carrying cost of the wheel assembly inventory is $.60 per wheel and the ordering cost per order is $20. What is SteadyFork's economic ordering quantity of wheel assemblies (round to the nearest unit)?
    a) 15
    b) 365
    c) 417
    d) 516

    Answer: d Difficulty: 3

139. How do interest rates affect the optimal order quantity Q*?
    a) As interest rates increase, Q* decreases.
    b) As interest rates decrease, Q* decreases.
    c) As interest rates increase, Q* increases until it reaches a maximum, after which any further increase in interest causes a decline in Q*.
    d) none of the above

    Answer: a Difficulty: 3

140. Which of the following is generally under the control of the financial manager?
    a) the percentage of credit sales to total sales
    b) the actual level of sales
    c) the credit policies
    d) a and b

    Answer: c Difficulty: 2

141. Which of the following are categories of inventory?
    a) raw materials
    b) work-in-progress
    c) finished goods
    d) a, b, and c
    e) a and c

    Answer: d Difficulty: 2

142. In the EOQ model, carrying costs of inventory include:
    a) the required rate of return on inventory
    b) wages for warehouse workers
    c) costs associated with inventory shrinkage
    d) b and c
    e) all of the above

    Answer: d Difficulty: 2

143. Credit and collection policies affect all of the following except:
    a) level of sales
    b) length of time before credit sales are collected
    c) terms of sales
    d) pricing policies

    Answer: b Difficulty: 2

144. Which of the following might occur when a firm increases its collection efforts:
    a) an increase in inventory costs
    b) an increase in bad debts
    c) an increase in sales
    d) a decline in accounts payable
    e) an increase in the average collection period

    Answer: b Difficulty: 2

145. Modification of the EOQ model by redefining total costs and solving for the optimum order quantity can handle all of the following assumptions except:
    a) constant ordering costs
    b) independent orders
    c) constant unit price
    d) constant carrying costs

    Answer: b Difficulty: 2

146. Inflation affects the EOQ model in all of the following ways except:
    a) changing the investment in accounts receivable
    b) encourages anticipatory buying
    c) increased carrying costs
    d) encourages buying early to avoid price increases

    Answer: a Difficulty: 2

ESSAY

147. Colonial Services has received a proposal from Tidewater Bankshares to establish a lock-box system to accelerate the receipt of $500 million annually on 1 million checks. By its own analysis Colonial believes such a system would decrease total float by 2.0 days. If Colonial can earn 12 percent before taxes on the released funds, what is the maximum that Colonial should be willing to pay the bank per check for the service? Use a 365-day year.

    Answer:

    $$P = (2.0) \frac{(\$500 \text{ million})(.12)}{(1 \text{ million})(365)} = \$0.329$$

    Difficulty: 2

148. Bonnie's Fashions is a national distributor of women's apparel. The company expects to receive 60,000 checks during the coming year totaling $48 million. A large bank has offered to install a lock-box system at a charge of $0.35 per processed check. If Bonnie's Fashions is able to earn 12 percent before tax on additional funds, what is the minimum amount of total float days that must be saved to make the system worthwhile? Use a 365-day year.

Answer:

$$0.35TF = 1.33 \text{ days} = TF \times \left[\frac{(\$48 \text{ million})(.12)}{(60,000 \ (365)} \right]$$

Difficulty: 2

149. Ruth's Cosmetics expects to have $30 million in credit sales during the coming year. In spite of a national distributing system, all remittances are sent to the home office. A proposed system can eliminate 3 days of float, releasing funds which, when invested, will earn 11 percent. What annual savings can Ruth's Cosmetics expect if the system is implemented? Use a 365-day year.

Answer:

$$\left[\frac{\$30,000,000}{365} \right] (3) \ (0.11) = \$27,123$$

Difficulty: 2

150. Elke's Pet Supplies earns 12 percent on its investment in marketable securities. A draft disbursing system has been proposed that will increase disbursement float by 2 days. Purchases next year are expected to total $6 million. Individual payments average $600. Use a 365-day year.

a. If the draft system is adopted, what amount of funds can the firm expect to release during the year?
b. If each issue draft costs the firm $0.10, should the draft system be adopted?
c. Should the firm consider any other factors?

Answer:

a. $\left[\dfrac{\$6,000,000}{365}\right] (2.0) = \$32,877$

b. $\dfrac{\$16,438}{600} = 27.4$ drafts issued daily

Total annual cost of drafts = (27.4) (365) ($0.10) = $1,000
Interest gained on released funds = $32,877 (0.12) = $3,945

Yes. The draft system should be accepted because the interest of $3,945 gained on the released fund is greater than the $1,000 cost of the system.

c. Those firms receiving payment by means of the draft may prefer another method of payment.

Difficulty: 3

151. Eskimo Mining expects to have credit sales of $5,000,000 this year. First National Bank is offering Eskimo Mining a lock-box system for $1,000 per month. Eskimo Mining estimates that the new lock-box system will reduce float by 5 days. What rate of return must Eskimo Mining earn on its marketable securities to make it worthwhile for the company to institute this lock-box system? Use a 365-day year.

Answer:
Rate of return earned on marketable securities

Income = $\left[\dfrac{\$5,000,000}{365}\right]$ x 5 days x rate = $1,000 x 12

Rate of Return = $\dfrac{\$12,000}{\left[\dfrac{\$5,000,000}{365} \times 5\right]} = \dfrac{\$12,000}{\$68,493} = .1752$

Difficulty: 3

152. Carrollton Plumbing Supplies expects total sales of $7,000,000 this year. Ten percent of the company's sales are paid in cash; credit sales are usually paid by check. The average check size is $1,000. Second National Bank is offering the company a lock-box system. The fees are $500 per month plus $.50 per check. Short-term marketable securities are currently earning 12 percent per year. What reduction in check collection time is necessary for Carrollton Plumbing Supplies to be neither better nor worse off from adopting the proposed system? Use a 365-day year.

Answer:
CTIME = reduction in check collection time

Credit sales = (.90)($7,000,000) = $6,300,000

Average number of checks received = $\dfrac{\$6,300,000}{\$1,000}$ = $6,300

$\dfrac{\$6,300,000}{365}$ x CTIME x .12 = $500 x 12 + ($.50)($6,300)

CTIME = $\dfrac{\$6,000 + \$3,150}{\left[\dfrac{\$6,300,000}{365}\text{ x }.12\right]}$ = $\dfrac{\$9,150}{\$2,071}$ = 4.418 days

Difficulty: 3

153. You have a choice between investing in a corporate bond or a municipal bond. The corporate bond has an annual yield of 14 percent, while the municipal bond has an annual yield of 11 percent. At what tax rate would you be indifferent between buying the corporate bond or the municipal bond?

Answer:

Before-tax equivalent yield on muncipal bond = $\dfrac{.110}{(1 - \text{tax rate})}$

Before-tax yield on corporate bond = .140

$140 = \dfrac{.110}{(1 - \text{tax rate})}$

$140)(1 - \text{tax rate}) = .110$

$(1 - \text{tax rate}) = \dfrac{.110}{.140}$ = .7857

tax rate = .2143

Difficulty: 3

154. Carraway Seed Sales, Inc. expects to generate sales of $18,000,000 in the coming year. All sales are done on a credit basis, net 30 days. Carraway has estimated that it takes an average of three days for payments to reach their central office and an additional day to process the payments. What is the opportunity cost of the funds tied up in the mail and processing? Carraway uses a 360-day year in all calculations and can invest free funds at 8%.

     Answer:

     Daily collections = $18,000,000/36 = $50,000
     Opportunity cost = (50,000)(4)(.08) = $16,000

     Difficulty: 3

155. The corporate treasurer of Sid's Flowers Inc. is considering the purchase of either a municipal obligation with a 6.6% coupon or an offering carrying a 10% coupon. Both bonds have a $1,000 par value. The company is currently in the 34% marginal tax bracket. Which security should the treasurer recommend?

     Answer:

     The after-tax yield to Sid's on the 10% offering is (1 - .34) (.10) = 6.6%. The after-tax yield on the municipal bond is the stated 6.6%. There is no difference in yield. If the risk is considered equal for both offerings, the treasurer would be indifferent.

     Difficulty: 3

156. Omega Art Supply expects to have $50 million in credit sales during the coming year. In spite of a national distributing system, all remittances are sent to the home office. A proposed system can eliminate two days of float, releasing funds which, when invested, will earn 9 percent. What annual savings can Omega expect if the system is implemented? Use a 365-day year.

     Answer:
     $$\frac{50,000,000}{365} \ (2) \ (.09) = \$24,658$$

     Difficulty: 3

157. You purchase $5,000 worth of supplies every 60 days and never take the trade discount of 2/10 net 60. How much could you save each (360-day) year if you took the discount?

Answer:

2% x $5,000 = $100
6-60 day periods per year
$100 x 6 = $600

Difficulty: 3

158. Fiesta Taco Company purchases 10,000 boxes of ground beef each year. It costs $10 to place each order and $5.00 per year for each box held as inventory.

a. What is the average inventory held during the year?
b. What is the economic order quantity for the ground beef?
c. How many orders will be made each year?

Answer:

a. Average inventory held $= \dfrac{Q}{2} = \dfrac{10,000}{2} = 5,000$ boxes.

b. $Q^* = \sqrt{\dfrac{2OS}{C}} = \sqrt{\dfrac{(2)(10)(10,000)}{5}} = 200$ boxes

c. No. of orders per year $= \dfrac{S}{Q^*} = \dfrac{10,000}{200} = 50$ orders.

Difficulty: 3

159. It costs a local appliance store $25 per unit annually -- storage, insurance, etc. -- to hold TV sets in their inventory. Sales this year are anticipated to be 750 units. Each order costs $15.

a. How many orders should be made during the year?
b. It takes approximately 2 weeks to receive an order after it has been placed. If the store insists on a 1-week safety stock (assume 50 weeks), what should the inventory level be when a new order is placed?

Answer:

a. $Q^* = \sqrt{\dfrac{2OS}{C}} = \sqrt{\dfrac{(2)(15)(750)}{25}} = 30$ sets.

No. of orders per year $= \dfrac{S}{Q^*} = \dfrac{750}{30} = 25$

b. 1 week safety stock = 15 sets
   2 week order lag = 30 sets
   Order Point = 45 sets

Difficulty: 3

160. Manfred Manufacturing is involved in the production of machine parts. The company uses 500,000 pounds of steel annually. The current purchasing cost for steel is $2.20 per pound. The carrying cost for inventory is 20 percent of the purchase price. The cost of ordering steel is $1,000 per order. The company has decided to maintain a safety stock of 20,000 pounds. The delivery time per order is 10 days. The company works 365 days a year.

a. Determine the optimal EOQ.
b. How many orders will be placed annually?
c. What is the average inventory?
d. What is the inventory order point? (That is, at what level of inventory should a new order be placed?)
e. What is the company's total inventory costs for the year?

Answer:

a. $Q^* = \sqrt{\dfrac{2(500,000)(\$1,000)}{(.20)(\$2.20)}} = 47,673$ lbs.

b. Number of orders placed annually $= \dfrac{500,000}{47,673} = 10.488$

c. Average inventory $= \dfrac{47,673}{2} + 20,000 = 43,836$ lbs.

d. 20,000 lbs. + 13,699 lbs. = 33,699 lbs.

e. Total inventory costs $=(43,836)(.20)(\$2.20) + 10.488(\$1,000) = \$29,776$

Difficulty: 3

161. A flower shop is trying to determine the optimal order quantity of the wicker baskets that it places many of its arrangements in. The store thinks it will sell 2000 of these baskets over the next year. The baskets cost the shop $2.00 each. The carrying costs of the baskets is $0.15 each per year. It costs the shop $8.00 to order.

a. What is the economic order quantity?
b. What is the total cost for ordering the baskets once a year? Four times a year?

Answer:

a. $Q^* = \sqrt{\dfrac{2SO}{C}} = \sqrt{\dfrac{2(2000)8}{.15}} = 462$ units

b. total cost: $(Q/2)C + (S/Q)O$
ordering once: $(2000/2)(.15)+(2000/2000)8=150+8=\$158$
ordering 4 times: $(500/2)(.15)+(2000/500)8=37.50+32 = \$69.50$

Difficulty: 3

162. The Bike Store orders $2000 worth of supplies every 30 days. If they take advantage of the 3/10 net 30 discount offered by their supplier, how much would they save over the year? Assume a 360-day year.

Answer:

3% x 2000 = $60 would be saved on each order
twelve 30-day periods in the year
12 x $60 = $720 would be saved over the year

Difficulty: 3

163. A local lamp store expects to sell 2000 lamps in the coming year. It costs the store $1.00 in carrying costs for each lamp and $10.00 for each order placed.

    a.   What is the economic order quantity for the lamps?
    b.   How many orders will be placed each year?
    c.   If the store wants a one-week safety stock and it takes one week to receive an order after it has been placed, what should the inventory level be when a new order is placed? Assume a 50-week year.

Answer:

a. $Q^* = \sqrt{\dfrac{2SO}{C}} = \sqrt{\dfrac{2(10)(2000)}{1}} = 200$

b.   # orders = S/Q^* = 2000/200 = 10 orders per year

c.   1-week supply = 2000/50 = 40 lamps
    order level = safety stock + 1-week order lag
    = 40 + 40
    = 80 lamps is the order point

Difficulty: 3

164. A textile manufacturer has cloth that has a $14 per yard carrying cost per year. This cloth is used at a rate of 25,000 yards per year, and ordering costs are $10 per order.

    a.   What is the economic order quantity for this cloth?
    b.   What are the annual inventory costs for this firm if it orders in this quantity?

Answer:

a. $Q^* = \sqrt{\dfrac{2SO}{C}} = \sqrt{\dfrac{2(25,000)10}{14}} = 189$ units

b.   Total costs $= (\dfrac{Q}{2}) C + (\dfrac{S}{Q}) 0$

$\qquad = (\dfrac{189}{2})\$14 + (\dfrac{25,000}{189}) \$10$

$\qquad = \$1,323 + \$1,322.75$

$\qquad = \$2,645.75$

Difficulty: 3

Chapter 16: International Business Finance

1. Compared with other developed countries, the U.S. is particularly reliant on foreign trade for self-subsistency.

   Answer: False Difficulty: 1

2. A minor reason for long term overseas investments of U.S. companies is the higher return from direct foreign investments.

   Answer: False Difficulty: 1

3. Revaluation occurs when a currency is made cheaper with respect to the dollar.

   Answer: False Difficulty: 1

4. Under a floating rate system, parity rates can fluctuate within a given range.

   Answer: False Difficulty: 1

5. Short-term daily fluctuations in exchange rates are caused by supply and demand conditions in the foreign exchange market.

   Answer: True Difficulty: 1

6. The foreign exchange market is similar in form to the New York Stock Exchange.

   Answer: False Difficulty: 2

7. An indirect quote indicates the number of units of foreign currency that can be bought for one unit of the home currency.

   Answer: True Difficulty: 2

8. Arbitrage is the process of buying and selling in one market in order to make a riskless profit.

   Answer: True Difficulty: 2

9. Spot exchange markets have the potential for arbitrage opportunities for a long period of time.

   Answer: True Difficulty: 2

10. The difference between the asked price and the bid price is known as the spread.

    Answer: True Difficulty: 1

11. A narrow spread indicates efficiency in the spot exchange market.

    Answer: True Difficulty: 2

12. Forward contracts are usually quoted for periods greater than 1 year.

    Answer: False Difficulty: 2

13. Forward rates, like spot rates, are quoted in both direct and indirect form.

    Answer: True Difficulty: 2

14. Forward contracts benefit only the customer due to a reduction in uncertainty.

    Answer: False Difficulty: 2

15. Exchange-rate risk arises from the fact that the spot exchange rate on a future date is unknown today.

    Answer: True Difficulty: 2

16. There is a minimal exchange risk if the international trade contract is written in terms of the domestic currency.

    Answer: False Difficulty: 2

17. If a foreign currency is expected to depreciate with respect to the home currency, the holder of a net liability in foreign currency will profit.

    Answer: True Difficulty: 2

18. The objective of a prudent financial manager is to eliminate all foreign exchange risk.

    Answer: False Difficulty: 2

19. Leading and lagging are financial techniques used to eliminate risk.

    Answer: True Difficulty: 1

20. The cost of debt used in the international investment decision is the lesser of the parent's or the subsidiary's cost of debt.

    Answer: False Difficulty: 2

21. Because a large part of a subsidiary's equity funds comes from the parent, the subsidiary should use the same cost of equity as the parent.

    Answer: False Difficulty: 2

22. "Millheim Electronics is an American firm operating in India, whose government refuses to allow Millheim to send its earnings out of the country" ...is an example of repatriation of profits.

    Answer: False Difficulty: 2

23. A major source of long-term capital overseas is in the Eurocurrency market.

    Answer: False Difficulty: 2

24. The efficiency of foreign current markets is insured, in large measure, by the process of arbitrageurs.

    Answer: True Difficulty: 2

25. A direct quote in Bombay tells one how many British pounds can buy one Indian rupee.

    Answer: False Difficulty: 2

26. The bid rate (also called the offer rate) is the number of units of home currency paid to a customer in exchange for their foreign currency.

    Answer: False Difficulty: 2

27. Foreign currency forward rates aid traders by reducing uncertainty regarding future market fluctuations.

    Answer: True Difficulty: 2

28. With international investing, unlike domestic investing, if the NPV of a project is negative, the project is not necessarily rejected.

    Answer: True Difficulty: 2

29. In an efficient foreign currency market, there are never situations where a profit can be made (after transactions costs) by exploiting pricing discrepancies in the market.

    Answer: True Difficulty: 1

30. In order to profit from an expected near-term increase in the relative value of the British pound versus the U.S. dollar, an investor would be wise to maintain a short position in pounds, then sell when the pound rises in relative value.

    Answer: False Difficulty: 2

31. Covered interest arbitrage can be taken advantage of when premiums in forward rates are not exactly equal to the interest rate differential between two countries.

    Answer: True Difficulty: 2

32. Purchasing power parity suggest that interest rates in different countries will adjust so that each currency will have the same purchasing power.

    Answer: False Difficulty: 2

33. It is often contended that in an efficient market, with rational expectations the forward rate would be an unbiased forecast of the same purchasing power.

    Answer: True Difficulty: 2

34. A multinational with a large number of receivables runs the risk of transaction exposure.

    Answer: True Difficulty: 2

35. The objective of hedging strategy is to have a <u>zero</u> net asset position in a foreign currency.

    Answer: True Difficulty: 2

MULTIPLE CHOICE

36. A wide bid/ask spread could indicate which of the following?
    a) the presence of arbitrageurs
    b) large volume transactions are taking place
    c) frequent trading of a currency
    d) none of the above

    Answer: d Difficulty: 1

37. The rate that a subsidiary or parent of the MNC charges other divisions of the firm for its products is called:
    a) a forward price
    b) an intrafirm transaction rate
    c) a transfer price
    d) an exchange price

    Answer: c Difficulty: 1

38. Some complexities of conducting international business include:
    a) multiple currencies
    b) differing legal requirements
    c) internal control problems
    d) all of the above

    Answer: d Difficulty: 1

39. Which of the following is a reason for international investment?
    a) to reduce portfolio risk
    b) to increase P/E ratio
    c) to gain an advantage in a foreign country
    d) all of the above

    Answer: a Difficulty: 1

40. A Spot transaction occurs when:
    a) one currency is deposited in a foreign bank
    b) one currency is immediately exchanged for another currency
    c) one currency is exchanged for another currency at a specified price
    d) none of the above

    Answer: b Difficulty: 2

41. Buying and selling in more than one market to make a riskless profit is called:
    a) profit-maximization
    b) arbitrage
    c) international trading
    d) cannot be determined from the above information

    Answer: b Difficulty: 2

42. Which of the following is true?
    a) the forward rate is the same as the spot rate that will prevail in the future
    b) only the forward rate is known
    c) the actual spot rate that will prevail in the future is not known today
    d) both b and c

    Answer: d Difficulty: 2

43. Forward rates are:
    a) quoted in both direct and indirect form
    b) quoted at a premium or discount
    c) beneficial to risk-reduction
    d) all of the above

    Answer: d Difficulty: 2

44. One theory that is useful states that the forward premium or discount should be equal and opposite in sign to the difference in the national interest rates for securities of the same maturity. This theory is known as:
    a) the forward rate theory
    b) the interest rate parity theory
    c) the exchange rate theory
    d) the covered interest arbitrage theory

    Answer: b Difficulty: 2

45. Which of the following is true regarding the correct price of the forward contract?
    a) if the quote is less than the computed price, the forward contract is undervalued
    b) if the quote is greater than the computed price, the forward contract is overvalued
    c) both a and b
    d) neither a nor b

    Answer: c Difficulty: 3

46. Exchange rate risk:
    a) arises from the fact that the spot exchange rate on a future date is a random variable
    b) applies only to certain types of international businesses
    c) has been phased out due to recent international legislation
    d) all of the above

    Answer: a Difficulty: 3

47. Exchange rate risk:
    a) exists when the contract is written in terms of the foreign currency
    b) exists also in direct foreign investments and foreign portfolio investments
    c) does not exist if the international trade contract is written in terms of the domestic currency
    d) all of the above

    Answer: d Difficulty: 3

48. Elimination of all foreign exchange risk:
    a) should be the objective of a prudent financial manager
    b) should be analyzed on a cost benefit basis
    c) both a and b
    d) neither a nor b

    Answer: b Difficulty: 2

49. Leading and lagging
    a) are important risk-reduction techniques
    b) are useful when hedging is not available
    c) can be successfully applied for an MNC
    d) all of the above

    Answer: d Difficulty: 2

50. Problems of multinationals include:
    a) cash management and positioning of funds
    b) managing receivables
    c) global control
    d) all of the above

    Answer: d Difficulty: 2

51. An important (additional) consideration for a direct foreign investment is:
    a) political risk
    b) maximizing the firm's profits
    c) attaining a high international P/E ratio
    d) all of the above

    Answer: a Difficulty: 2

52. If the NPV of a direct foreign investment is negative,
    a) the MNC should reject any proposals
    b) the MNC may consider establishing a sales office
    c) the MNC may consider licensing
    d) cannot be determined

    Answer: c Difficulty: 2

53. I. T. Canwait, Inc., a U.S.-based multinational, has just sold cans to a west German company, I.C. Spots, Inc. Spots will pay for the order in 60 days. I. T. Canwait is now exposed to which kind of risk:
    a) transaction
    b) translation
    c) operating
    d) financial

    Answer: a Difficulty: 3

54. Which type of exposure is generally considered just a paper gain or loss:
    a) transaction
    b) translation
    c) economic
    d) financial

    Answer: b Difficulty: 3

55. Firms generally do not hedge against which type of exposure:
    a) transaction
    b) translation
    c) economic

Answer: b Difficulty: 3

Chapter 17: Changes and Challenges in Finance

1. A convertible security is a preferred stock or debt issue that can be exchanged for a specified number of shares of common stock.

   Answer: True Difficulty: 1

2. Other things equal, the absence of conversion lowers the required rate of return on a bond.

   Answer: False Difficulty: 1

3. Once the convertible owner trades his convertibles in for common stock, he can retrade the stock back for the convertibles if he desires.

   Answer: False Difficulty: 1

4. A futures contract provides the holder with the option to buy or sell a stated contract involving a commodity or financial claim at a specified price over a stated time period.

   Answer: False Difficulty: 1

5. An option contract gives its owner the right to buy or sell a fixed number of shares at a specified price over a limited time period.

   Answer: True Difficulty: 1

6. If you expect a stock's price to rise it would be better to purchase a call on that stock than to purchase a put on it.

   Answer: True Difficulty: 1

7. If you expect a stock's price to drop it would be better to write a call on that stock than to write a put on it.

   Answer: True Difficulty: 1

8. The buyer of an option on a futures contract can achieve immunization against any unfavorable price movements, whereas the buyer of a futures contract can achieve immunization against any price movements regardless of whether they are favorable or unfavorable.

   Answer: True Difficulty: 2

9. When entering into a stock index futures contract, the investor agrees to buy or sell a stated number of shares of each stock on a certain index (like S&P 500) at a specified price at a specified time in the future.

   Answer: False Difficulty: 2

10. Stock index futures make it possible for portfolio managers to reduce or eliminate their portfolios' exposure to systematic risk.

    Answer: True Difficulty: 2

11. With futures contracts, the maximum loss is limited to the amount initially invested.

    Answer: False Difficulty: 1

12. More mergers occurred in the 1960s than at any other time.

    Answer: False Difficulty: 1

13. A primary problem in analyzing a potential merger involves placing a value on the acquired firm.

    Answer: True Difficulty: 1

MULTIPLE CHOICE

14. The popularity of options can be explained by:
    a) the degree of leverage afforded the investor
    b) the use of options as a type of financial insurance
    c) the use of options to expand the set of possible investment alternatives available
    d) all of the above

    Answer: d Difficulty: 1

15. _____ is a financial instrument that can be used to eliminate the effect of both favorable and unfavorable price movements.
    a) Convertible securities
    b) Warrants
    c) Options
    d) Futures

    Answer: d Difficulty: 2

16. A(n)_____ is a contract that requires the holder to buy or sell a stated commodity at a specified price at a specified time in the future.
    a) Warrant
    b) Option
    c) Future
    d) Convertible contract

    Answer: c Difficulty: 1

17. A(n) _____ gives the holder the right to buy a stated number of shares at a specified price for a limited time.
    a) Stock index futures contract
    b) Put option
    c) Call option
    d) Interest rate futures contract

    Answer: c   Difficulty: 1

18. An investor would buy a _____ if he/she believed that the price of the underlying stock or asset will fall in the near future.
    a) Call option
    b) Convertible bond
    c) Put option
    d) Future contracts to take delivery of an asset at a future date

    Answer: c   Difficulty: 1

19. A tender offer:
    a) must be approved by the board of directors of the target firm
    b) must be made at a price no higher than the current market price
    c) must be on a cash basis
    d) none of the above

    Answer: d   Difficulty: 2

20. When two firms combine into one firm that is the same as one of the initial firms, it is described as a:
    a) capital takeover
    b) stock repurchase
    c) merger
    d) conglomerate

    Answer: c   Difficulty: 1

21. A tender offer:
    a) may result in high costs of acquisition if the target firm's management attempts to block the purchase
    b) must be approved by the target firm's management
    c) has shares that are typically sold at a discount to the acquiring firm
    d) none of the above

    Answer: a   Difficulty: 2

22. The ultimate objective of the acquiring firm is to:
    a) maximize their own assets
    b) maximize their own earnings
    c) maximize their own shareholders' wealth
    d) maximize their dividends

    Answer: c   Difficulty: 2

23. The "synergistic effect" of a merger involves:
    a) the psychological impact of a merger upon the investment community
    b) the decision as to whether to let existing managers stay on after the merger
    c) the sudden increase in the stock price of the target firm during a tender offer
    d) the organizational compatability of the two firms involved in a merger

    Answer: d Difficulty: 2

24. A defense tactic which is used by management to counter tender offers is:
    a) a white knight
    b) greenmailing
    c) a rescuer
    d) all of the above

    Answer: a Difficulty: 2

25. If a firm is interested in avoiding a takeover, a "shark-repellant" technique is to reincorporate in which state:
    a) Nevada
    b) Rhode Island
    c) Pennsylvania
    d) Delaware

    Answer: d Difficulty: 2